CHILE SINCE INDEPENDENCE

The following titles drawn from
The Cambridge History of Latin America edited by Leslie Bethell
are available in hardcover and paperback:

Colonial Spanish America

Colonial Brazil

The Independence of Latin America

Spanish America after Independence, *c.* 1820 – *c.* 1870

Brazil: Empire and Republic, 1822–1930

Latin America: Economy and Society, 1870–1930

Mexico since Independence

Central America since Independence

Cuba: A Short History

Chile since Independence

Argentina since Independence

CHILE
SINCE
INDEPENDENCE

edited by

LESLIE BETHELL
Professor of Latin American History
University of London

CAMBRIDGE
UNIVERSITY PRESS

Published by the Press Syndicate of the University of Cambridge
The Pitt Building, Trumpington Street, Cambridge CB2 1RP
40 West 20th Street, New York, NY 10011–4211, USA
10 Stamford Road, Oakleigh, Victoria 3166, Australia

The contents of this book were previously published as parts of volumes III,
V and VIII of *The Cambridge History of Latin America*. copyright ©
Cambridge University Press, 1985, 1986, 1991.

First published 1993

Printed in the United States of America

Library of Congress Cataloging-in-Publication Data
Chile since independence / edited by Leslie Bethell.

p.   cm.

Contains parts of the previously published vols. 3, 5, and 8 of
The Cambridge history of Latin America.
Includes bibliographical references and index.
ISBN 0–521–43375–4. – ISBN 0–521–43987–6 (pbk.)
1. Chile – History – 1810   I. Bethell, Leslie.   II. Title:
Cambridge history of Latin America.
F3093.C546   1992
983'.06–dc20   92–17160

A catalog record for this book is available from the British Library.

ISBN 0–521–43375–4 hardback
ISBN 0–521–43987–6 paperback

CONTENTS

v

MAPS

PREFACE

The Cambridge History of Latin America is a large scale, collaborative, multi-volume history of Latin America during the five centuries from the first contacts between Europeans and the native peoples of the Americas in the late fifteenth and early sixteenth centuries to the present.

Chile since Independence brings together chapters from Volumes III, V and VIII of *The Cambridge History* to provide in a single volume an economic, social and political history of Chile since its independence. This, it is hoped, will be useful for both teachers and students of Latin American history and of contemporary Latin America. Each chapter is accompanied by a bibliographical essay.

1

FROM INDEPENDENCE TO THE WAR
OF THE PACIFIC

At a banquet in Valparaíso in 1852 the Argentine publicist Juan Bautista Alberdi proposed a toast to 'the honourable exception in South America'. In one very important respect, the story of nineteenth century Chile was, it is true, a striking exception to the normal Spanish American pattern. Within fifteen years of independence Chilean politicians were constructing a system of constitutional government which was to prove remarkable (by European as well as Latin American standards) for its durability and adaptability. This successful consolidation of an effective national state excited the envious admiration of less fortunate Spanish American republics, torn and plagued as so many of them were by recurrent strife and caudillo rule. A good part of the explanation of Chile's unusual record undoubtedly lies in what can best be called the 'manageability' of the country at the time of independence, not least in terms of the basic factors of territory and population. The effective national territory of Chile in the 1820s was much smaller than it is today. Its distinctive slenderness of width – 'a sword hanging from the west side of America' – was for obvious orographical reasons no different; but lengthways no more than 700 miles or so separated the mining districts in the desert around Copiapó, at the northern limit of settlement (27°S), from the green and fertile lands along the Bío-Bío river in the south (37°S) – the area traditionally referred to as the Frontier, beyond which the Araucanian Indians stubbornly preserved their independent way of life. The peripheral clusters of population which lay still further south, at Valdivia and on the densely-forested island of Chiloé (liberated from the Spaniards only in 1826), were remote, insignificant appendages of the republic; the same could also be said slightly later on of the struggling settlement on the Straits of Magellan established in 1843 and used as a penal colony. Leaving aside the Araucanians, who numbered perhaps

200,000, the population of Chile was still fairly small: it rose slowly from an estimated 1,000,000 at the time of independence to an official (and possibly conservative) figure of 2,076,000 in 1875. The overwhelming majority of Chileans lived and worked in the country's traditional heartland, in (or very close to) the central valley extending three hundred miles southwards from Santiago. By the standards of Argentina or Mexico, of Peru or New Granada, this was a very compact territory inhabited by a compact population.

It was in many ways a homogeneous population. Both ethnically and socially the colonial past had left indelible marks. North of the Bío-Bío, few if any Indians survived in separate communities. The tiny black and mulatto trace in the community seems to have vanished within two or three decades of the abolition of slavery (1823). Republican Chile was essentially a country in which a small creole upper class (with an aristocratic elite at its core) co-existed with the huge mass of the labouring poor, who were predominantly *mestizo* and predominantly rural. The ethnic and social divisions coincided. Politically, the struggles which followed independence reflected disagreements within the fold of the upper class rather than deeper conflicts in the body social more generally. The rural poor remained passive throughout the period and, in fact, well beyond it. This relatively simple social structure was not complicated by sharp cleavages of economic interest within the upper class or by anything very much in the way of serious regional tension. Santiago and its rich hinterland dominated the republic. The remoter northern or southern provinces, whether disaffected or not, were power-less to alter the balance in their own favour, as was shown very clearly in the civil wars of 1851 and 1859. Concepción and the south underwent a frustratingly slow recovery from the wars of independence; and although Concepción, by virtue of its role as a garrison town watching over the frontier, was able in the uncertain atmosphere of the 1820s to impose its will on the capital – as it did in 1823, with the overthrow of Bernardo O'Higgins, and again in 1829 – in normal times a determined central government in control of the army (or most of it) could not easily be dislodged.

The issues which divided the upper class Chilean politicians of the 1820s into the perhaps predictable camps of Liberal and Conservative were above all ideological and personal. The dominant figure of these years, General Ramón Freire, was a well-intentioned Liberal eager to avoid the authoritarian pattern set by his immediate predecessor, the liberator O'Higgins. The new republic drifted from one makeshift political experiment to the next. The complex and ingenious constitution devised by Juan Egaña at the end of 1823 broke down within six months, its moralistic conservatism rejected by the Liberals who surrounded Freire and who wished, as they put it, 'to build the Republic on the ruins of the Colony'. The vogue for federalist ideas which overwhelmed political circles soon afterwards owed less, perhaps, to regional aspirations than to the dogmatically radical convictions of the man of the moment, José Miguel Infante; it produced a draft constitution, numerous new laws, an atmosphere of growing uncertainty, mild disorders in several towns, and a propensity to mutiny on the part of the army. The 'anarchy' of the period has often been exaggerated by Chilean historians; it was very limited in comparison with the turmoil then occurring on the other side of the Andes. Another Liberal soldier, General Francisco Antonio Pinto, president from 1827 to 1829, briefly succeeded in organizing a government which showed signs of solidity, and a new constitution (1828), the fourth since independence, duly went into effect. It proved inadequate to stem the mounting reaction against Liberal reformism, coloured as this was by anti-aristocratic verbiage and a degree of anticlericalism. In September 1829, with the vital backing of the army in Concepción, a powerful tripartite coalition of Conservatives – the traditionalist and pro-clerical *pelucones* ('big wigs'), the followers of the exiled O'Higgins, and a tough-minded group known as the *estanqueros*[1] – launched a revolt against the Liberal regime. Freire, who sprang quixotically to its defence, was defeated in April 1830 at Lircay, the battle which ended the short civil war and ushered in more than a quarter of a century of Conservative rule.

The political settlement of the 1830s was, as has been suggested, one of the more remarkable creations of nineteenth-century Latin America. The credit for its success is usually assigned to Diego Portales, the Valparaiso trader who more than anyone was the organizing genius of the Conservative reaction. Certainly Portales's ruthless tenacity was a key factor in keeping the new regime together, though his tenure of office as chief minister was fairly brief. This in itself may have impeded the crystalliza-

---

[1] In 1824 the *estanco*, or state tobacco monopoly, was leased to the Valparaiso trading house of Portales, Cea and Co., which undertook to service the £1,000,000 loan raised in London by the O'Higgins government two years earlier. The enterprise failed, and in 1826 the contract was withdrawn, occasioning much ill-feeling. The *estanquero* group was composed of men associated with this ill-starred venture; their leader was Diego Portales.

tion of a caudillo tradition in Chilean politics, for while Portales's influence was all-important, his aversion to the trappings of power was genuine enough. 'If I took up a stick and gave tranquillity to the country', he wrote, 'it was only to get the bastards and whores of Santiago to leave me in peace.'[2] Nevertheless, his actions both in government and behind the scenes, his strict emphasis on orderly management, his, at times, harsh attitude towards the defeated Liberals and, not least, his insistence on national dignity – these fixed the tone of official policy for years to come.

The work of the Conservatives in the 1830s was later described by critics of the regime as in essence a 'colonial reaction'. That it was a reaction to the ill-starred Liberal reformism of the 1820s is clear enough. But it is perhaps more accurate to see the new political system as a pragmatic fusion of the tradition of colonial authoritarianism, still very strong in Chile, with the outward forms (and something of the spirit) of nineteenth-century constitutionalism. The Constitution of 1833, whose regular operations were not interrupted until 1891 and which survived in amended form until 1925, embodied many of the principal Conservative obsessions. It was discernibly more authoritarian than its ill-fated predecessor of 1828, and in particular very strongly presidentialist. Two consecutive five-year terms of office were permitted, a provision which led in practice to four successive 'decennial' administrations, the first being that of Portales's nominee General Joaquín Prieto (1831–41). The president's patronage, control of the judiciary and public administration, and powers over Congress were all extensive, though the legislature was left with an ultimate check on the executive through its technical right to deny assent to the budget, taxation and military establishment. The president's emergency powers, in the form of 'extraordinary faculties' or localized states of siege, were highly conspicuous: moreover, such powers were regularly used – in one variety or another they were in force for one-third of the entire period between 1833 and 1861. The centralist spirit of the constitution was equally notable. The feeble institutional relics of the federalism of the 1820s were now swept away completely. The Intendant of each province was now defined as the president's 'natural and immediate agent' – and so it was to prove in practice: the Intendants were in some way the key officials of the regime, each Intendancy becoming in a real sense the local nexus of government. The

[2] Ernesto de la Cruz and Guillermo Feliú Cruz (eds.), *Epistolario de don Diego Portales*, 3 vols. (Santiago, 1937), I, 352.

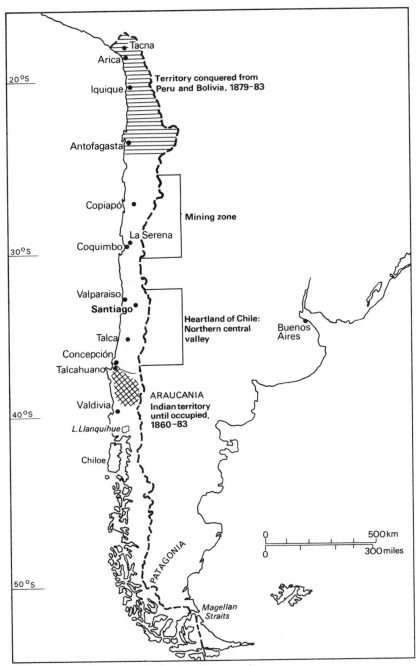

20°S

Tacna
Arica

Territory conquered from Peru and Bolivia, 1879–83

Iquique

Antofagasta

Copiapó

Mining zone

La Serena

30°S

Coquimbo

Valparaiso

Santiago

Heartland of Chile: Northern central valley

Buenos Aires

Talca

Concepción

Talcahuano

ARAUCANIA
Indian territory until occupied, 1860–83

Valdivia

40°S

L.Llanquihue

Chiloe

PATAGONIA

0   500 km
0   300 miles

50°S

Magellan Straits

Chile in the nineteenth century

hegemony of Santiago, already well entrenched, was thus reinforced at the expense of regional initiative.

No constitution, least of all in Spanish America, is efficacious on its own. The successful operation of the new political system depended on a number of well-tested techniques used with methodical persistence by the governments of the period. Some were more obvious than others. Repression was a recurrent tactic for three decades. By the standards of the twentieth century it did not amount to very much. The death sentence was far more often invoked than applied. The standard penalties for political dissent were incarceration, internal exile ('relegation'), or banishment abroad for a fixed period. Voluntary exile (sometimes under bond) was not uncommon, especially in the embattled decade of the 1850s. A less overt means of inculcating social discipline can be detected in the careful way in which the Conservatives restored clerical influence; until the 1850s the Church was a useful mainstay of the system. Likewise, the incipient militarism of the 1820s was curbed by a drastic purge of Liberal officers and by a comprehensive reorganization of the country's militias. By the middle of 1831 the National Guard numbered 25,000 men. It more than doubled in size later on and was a very credible counterweight to the regular army, whose peacetime establishment rarely went much above 3,000. Twice, in the mutinies of June 1837 and April 1851, the militias helped to save the regime from forcible overthrow. They also fitted very neatly into the government's control of the electoral process.

Electoral intervention runs like a constant theme through the entire period. It survived long after the repressive practices already mentioned. In fact it was a Liberal president who, when asked in 1871 by one of his ministers whether Chile would ever enjoy 'real' elections, curtly replied, 'Never!'[3] The electoral law of 1833 severely restricted the franchise, but spread the net just wide enough to include artisans and shopkeepers, many of whom formed the rank and file of the National Guard, which thus supplied a numerous voting contingent at every election. Quite apart from this invaluable support, the government resorted to any number of methods – intimidation, temporary arrest, personation, bribery – to prevent opposition voters from exercising their franchise and to secure comfortable majorities for its own candidates. The operation was co-ordinated by the Minister of the Interior, and his subaltern agents in the provinces, the Intendants, the departmental

[3] Abdón Cifuentes, *Memorias*, 2 vols. (Santiago, 1936), II, 69.

gobernadores and the *subdelegados*, were as adept as any modern Chicago ward boss (and possibly more so) in 'delivering' the vote. It is hardly surprising that seven out of the eleven congressional elections held between 1833 and 1864 (at regular three-year intervals) were either uncontested or virtually so. Even in the more tolerant political climate of the 1860s and 1870s, an opposition stood no chance whatever of electing a majority to Congress. Not until the 1890s did the executive cease to interfere directly in elections.

In its earliest years the new Conservative system both faced and survived the ultimate test of war. The relations between Chile and Peru deteriorated sharply in the early 1830s. Commercial rivalry, a brisk tariff war, and Peru's failure to repay a Chilean loan (itself part of the £1,000,000 loan raised by O'Higgins in London in 1822, on which Chile had long since defaulted) were not in themselves a sufficient cause for aggression. This was provided in 1836, when General Andrés Santa Cruz forcibly united Peru and Bolivia into a Confederation. Portales viewed the formation of this potentially powerful state as a threat to Chilean independence; it would not be an exaggeration to say that he pushed his country into war. He was himself one of its first victims. Discontent over the war brought renewed Liberal conspiracies, and the all-powerful minister was murdered by a mutinous army battalion in June 1837, an occurrence which seems to have greatly solidified support both for the war policy and for the regime in general. Portales's death delayed but did not deflect the course of events. The second of two Chilean expeditionary forces, under the command of General Manuel Bulnes, invaded Peru and defeated Santa Cruz's army at the battle of Yungay (January 1839). The Confederation dissolved. The war of 1836–9 was an example of national assertiveness which incurred strong disapproval from Great Britain and France, but it inevitably heightened the international prestige of Chile. At home, it enabled the Prieto government to adopt a more conciliatory attitude towards the opposition, while the victorious General Bulnes became the obvious successor to the presidency. Just before the election Bulnes was betrothed to a daughter of the former Liberal president, Francisco Antonio Pinto, thus confirming the apparent trend towards political relaxation.

General Bulnes's presidency (1841–51) has often been represented as an 'era of good feelings' and for much of the time this was true. In the early 1840s, indeed, Liberalism came close to being killed by kindness. But Bulnes, for all his generous bonhomie, did nothing to undermine the authoritarian framework; in certain respects (the stiff Press Law of 1846, for instance) he added to it. The revival of Liberalism as a political force towards the end of his second term owed much to the ambitions of his chief minister, Manuel Camilo Vial, whose following, well represented in Congress, went into active parliamentary opposition when Vial was dismissed (1849). The leading Liberal intellectual of the period, José Victorino Lastarria, attempted to give direction and coherence to this new opposition. Outside the congressional arena the young idealists Francisco Bilbao and Santiago Arcos, mesmerized by the French revolution of 1848, were active in trying to mobilize support among the artisans of the capital: their Sociedad de la Igualdad, with its meetings and marches, survived for much of the year 1850, until the inevitable imposition of emergency powers by the government. The main effect of this agitation, both Liberal and *igualitario*, was to frighten the Conservative party into accepting Manuel Montt as Bulnes's successor.

President Montt (1851–61) was the first civilian to govern Chile for more than a few weeks. His oddly opaque character has defied all attempts at precise historical portraiture. His talent was undeniable; so was his austere inflexibility. ('All head and no heart' was his bluff predecessor's private opinion.) Montt's election provoked three months of full-scale civil war, in which the challenge to the regime came not only from the Liberals but also, more seriously, from the southern provinces. The leader of the revolt, General José María de la Cruz, was in fact a Conservative and the cousin of ex-president Bulnes, who defeated him in a short but bloody campaign. For the moment the regime was safe. By the mid-1850s, however, Montt's authoritarian approach was inducing strains and tensions within the Conservative governing combination itself. These finally came into the open as the result of a noisy jurisdictional conflict between the government and the Church, which was now re-emerging as an independent factor in politics. In 1857 the bulk of the Conservative party defected and joined forces with what was left of the Liberal opposition. Those Conservatives who remained loyal to Montt founded a new National party, but it lacked the wider upper class support enjoyed by the nascent Liberal-Conservative Fusion. For a second time vigorous agitation led to renewed repression and so to a further armed challenge to the regime. The civil war of 1859 is chiefly remembered for the miracles of improvisation performed by the rebel army in the mining provinces of the north – the focus of the war – but once again the government won. This time, however, military victory was followed by political defeat. Montt found it impossible to impose his own choice for the succession. This would have been Antonio Varas, Montt's closest associate and a highly talented politician. An elderly, easygoing, benevolent patrician, José Joaquín Pérez, was selected in Varas's place. It was a decisive turning point.

Under President Pérez (1861–71), the last of the four 'decennial' presidents, the Chilean political system at last began to liberalize. Pérez himself, by virtue of what was called at the time 'a supreme tolerance born of an even more supreme indifference', did as much as anybody in nineteenth-century Chile to enhance the tradition of stable constitutionalism. Repression ended, even if electoral intervention did not – Pérez's ministers saw to that. The new president, though himself nominally a National, quickly summoned the Liberal-Conservative Fusion into office (1862). This alliance between former enemies proved a remarkably workable governing combination, though it naturally attracted the opposition not only of the displaced Nationals (whose loyalty to Montt and Varas won them the name of *monttvaristas*) but also of the strongly anti-clerical 'red' or 'radical' Liberals who presently became known as the Radical party. The 1860s thus saw an increasingly diversified ideological panorama, and (except electorally) the 'new politics' was allowed to grow and thrive, although as it happened, domestic rivalries were somewhat dampened down in 1865–6, when the aggressive actions of a Spanish naval squadron cruising in Pacific waters drove Chile and three of her sister republics into a short war with their former metropolis.[4] By the close of the 1860s Liberal notions of constitutional reform were occupying the forefront of the political stage. Such ideas, centred, above all, on limiting presidential power, increasingly formed common ground between the four main parties. The first amendment to the hitherto inviolate Constitution of 1833 was passed in 1871; significantly, it prohibited the immediate re-election of the president.

It was during the government of Federico Errázuriz Zañartu (1871–6) that the final transition to Liberal-dominated politics occurred. In the early 1870s 'theological questions' (as they were called) began to be taken up as political issues. They were less concerned with theology, in fact, than with the demarcation of ecclesiastical and secular functions in the national life; they generated a good deal of feeling, both pious and

---

[4] Such fighting as there was (and there was not much) took place at sea. Before withdrawing from the Pacific, however, the Spaniards subjected Valparaíso to devastating bombardment (March 1866).

impious. A dispute about private education in 1873, pitting anticlericals against the Conservatives, who were becoming more and more identifiable as the militantly Catholic party in politics, brought about the disintegration of the Fusion. The Conservatives went into opposition, and the way was thus laid open for a new dominant coalition with a Liberal focus. The clever Errázuriz conducted the necessary manoeuvres. The Liberal Alliance (1875) was the third of the great governing combinations of the period, but the least stable, since several factions of the powerful Liberal party were invariably to be found opposing as well as supporting the government. The Errázuriz presidency also saw further constitutional reforms, all tending to limit executive influence. Important changes in electoral procedure (1874) were designed to reduce official intervention, but in 1876 Errázuriz and the Alliance had no difficulty in imposing the next president in the usual manner. Their choice fell on Aníbal Pinto, the son of the Liberal president of the later 1820s.

If the outline of the Conservative settlement of the 1830s was still very much intact, its inner workings were nonetheless altering in significant ways. Party politics had developed apace since the Pérez decade; the parties themselves were acquiring rudimentary forms of organization. The Radicals, with their network of local *asambleas*, were perhaps the first group to devise a definite (if flexible) structure. The Conservatives were the first to hold a national party conference (1878). But voting on party lines in Congress was far from automatic. When in 1876 the Radical deputy Ramón Allende (grandfather of the future president) suggested that party considerations should outweigh private principle in congressional voting, the idea was greeted with several outraged reactions. Quite apart from this, it was becoming clear by the later 1870s that Congress as a whole aspired to a much greater degree of control over the executive than had been attempted or perhaps even contemplated previously. The constitution, as we have seen, was strongly presidentialist; but it was also possible, as politicians now proved, to give it a logical 'parliamentary' interpretation. Through constant use of the *interpelación* and vote of censure, congressmen made the lives of cabinet ministers increasingly tedious and arduous. This was particularly the case during Aníbal Pinto's presidency (1876–81), which coincided, as we shall see, with several parallel crises of a very acute kind. That Chilean institutions had survived the tempests of the 1850s, that they were growing noticeably more tolerant – these things were cause for pride, certainly, but there were some politicians, including Pinto, who regarded as sterile the political squabbles now often monopolizing congressional attention to the exclusion of more urgent national business, and others who wondered whether the tension between the executive and the militant legislature might not destroy the tradition of stability. 'Gentlemen of the majority, ministers', exclaimed a Conservative deputy in 1881, 'I tell you: Don't pull the string too hard, because the thing might explode!'[5]

The connection between political stability and economic progress is never entirely clear-cut. It nevertheless seems fair to argue that the considerable commercial expansion which Chile underwent between the 1820s and the 1870s owed something, at least, to the settled conditions to be found in the country, as well as to the international demand for what Chile could produce. Expansion was not, however, completely smooth. At the close of the 1850s, with the loss of certain overseas markets for wheat and flour, coupled with two poor harvests in a row and the exhaustion of some of the silver deposits in the north, there was a brief but serious recession. At other periods (notably from the end of the 1840s to the mid-1850s, and again from the end of the 1860s into the early 1870s) the growth of trade was very rapid indeed, and Chile enjoyed boom conditions. The total value of the country's external trade rose from $7,500,000 in 1825 to $74,000,000 in 1875. Government revenues increased somewhat more slowly, from $2,000,000 in 1835 to $16,400,000 in 1875; from the end of the 1830s they generally outran expenditure very comfortably.[6]

A highly cosmopolitan trading community established itself at Valparaíso in the years after independence, and the governments of the period saw trade with the maritime nations of the North Atlantic, especially Great Britain, as one of the main stimulants of progress. Indeed, the political settlement of the 1830s was accompanied by an 'economic settlement', largely carried through by the brilliant Manuel Rengifo, finance minister from 1830 to 1835 and again from 1841 to 1844. Rengifo blended liberalism with pragmatism in his economic measures, which included the simplification of the fiscal system and tariff laws, the consolidation of the public debt, and, not least, the establish-

---

[5] Cristián Zegers, *Aníbal Pinto. Historia política de su gobierno* (Santiago, 1969), 119. Ten years later, in the political crisis of 1891, the 'thing' did explode.

[6] The Chilean peso [$] maintained a more or less constant value throughout most of the period, being worth around 45*d.* in terms of sterling, or slightly less than an American dollar, except during the American civil war, when it was worth slightly more.

ment on a permanent basis of public warehouses (*almacenes fiscales*) at Valparaíso, where traders could store duty-free merchandise while awaiting favourable markets. That Valparaíso should be the dominant port on the Pacific coast was a cardinal maxim both for Rengifo and Portales.

Heavily dependent on customs duties for its revenues, the Chilean government had the strongest possible reason for wishing to augment the flow of trade, an aim which certainly reflected the view of the Chilean upper class as a whole. But broader considerations of national development were never entirely absent from the official mind. The state was active in many spheres, including the improvement of communications; and tariff policy did not ignore local interests other than those of exporters. The tariff reform of 1864, often presented by historians as a gadarene rush to free trade, was in many respects no more than a temporary aberration from the more standard nineteenth-century policy, which strove (rather ineffectively) to give at least a minimal degree of protection to certain domestic activities as well as to maximize trade. Nevertheless, it seems reasonably clear, given the extreme poverty of the new nation and the lack of a 'spirit of association' so frequently lamented by, *inter alia*, Manuel Montt, that even a much stronger dose of protectionism could hardly have done much to diversify economic activity or to develop an industrial base of any size. The country's options at this period were fairly narrow.

From the point of view of foreign trade, mining was by far the most important sector of the economy throughout the period. The miners of the north accumulated the largest individual and family fortunes of the time. The two thinly settled provinces of Atacama and Coquimbo, the area nowadays referred to by Chileans as the Norte Chico, constituted the most dynamic region of the country, with a population (about one-eighth of the nation's total in 1865) which rose much faster than was the case in the *hacienda*-dominated provinces of the central valley, thousands of whose people were lured to the ramshackle, rowdy and occasionally rebellious mining camps of the arid north; there were some 30,000 mine-workers there by the 1870s. Tough, enterprising, industrious, periodically volatile, fiercely proud − such was the distinctive culture of the mining zone. Its laboriously extracted riches had a vital impact on the rest of the nation, 'ennobling the central cities and fertilizing the fields of the south', as President Balmaceda was later to put it.[7] Of the three

[7] Roberto Hernández, *Juan Godoy o el descubrimiento de Chañarcillo*, 2 vols. (Valparaiso, 1932), II, 560.

principal metals mined in Chile in colonial times, gold did least well after independence, falling from an annual average production of 1,200 kg in the 1820s to a level of around 270 kg in the 1870s. Over the same period, by contrast, silver production rose from about 20,000 kg per annum to about 127,000 kg. (Given the persistence of smuggling, such figures are perhaps conservative). Copper, the most profitable of the three metals, was produced at an annual rate of 2,725 metric tons in the 1820s; this grew very steadily to 45,600 metric tons in the 1870s, by which time Chile regularly accounted for between one-third and one-half of the world's supply.

The allure of mineral wealth attracted numerous traders, speculators and prospectors to the northern deserts. The search for new veins of ore was incessant; the mining zone expanded slowly northwards into the Atacama desert and towards the long undefined border with Bolivia. The important early silver strikes at Agua Amarga (1811) and Arqueros (1825) were soon wholly eclipsed by the sensational discovery at Chañarcillo, south of Copiapó, in 1832. It was the single most productive mining district of the century, a veritable 'silver mountain' which yielded at least $12,000,000 in its first ten years and where by the mid-1840s there were over one hundred mines. The discovery of Tres Puntas (1848) was a further fillip to the boom, though less dramatic. The last silver rush of the period occurred in 1870, with the opening up of a major new mining district at Caracoles, across the border in Bolivia though worked almost entirely by Chileans. Copper mining depended less on new exploration than on the working of established veins of high-grade ore, but here too patient prospecting sometimes reaped a fabulous reward, as in the spectacular case of José Tomás Urmeneta, who searched for eighteen years in dire poverty before coming across, at Tamaya, his legendary deposit of copper. He was soon a millionaire, one of perhaps several dozen very rich men whose great fortunes came from the Norte Chico.

Chilean methods of mining changed only slowly and partially from the pattern established in later colonial times, which had been characterized by numerous small enterprises, individual or family entrepreneurship, simple technology and short-term marginal activity. By the 1860s, it is true, some of the larger mines – Urmeneta's at Tamaya, and José Ramón Ovalle's at Carrizal Alto, for instance – had gone in for extensive mechanization, and it is interesting that the two districts cited accounted for one-third of copper production in the 1870s. But the persistence of older practices – and a large number of small-scale operations which continued to rely, in preference to steampower, on the sturdy *barreteros* and *apires* who dug the ore and shifted it from the mine – is attested by many visitors to the north during this period. In the 1870s only some thirty-three mines in the Norte Chico used steam engines, leaving 755 which did not. Innovations in the smelting and refining of copper were a good deal more noticeable, with reverbatory furnaces (the 'English system') spreading from the 1830s onwards. Over the next two decades, in what amounted to a minor technological revolution, several large smelting plants were established on the coast, most notably at Guayacán and Tongoy in the Norte Chico and at Lirquén and Lota five hundred miles further south; these were Chile's first industrial enterprises of any size. They also processed Peruvian and Bolivian ores, and partially offset the producers' previous dependence on the smelting and refining industry of South Wales. The smelters' insatiable demand for fuel made deep inroads into the exiguous timber resources of the Norte Chico and contributed to the southward advance of the desert – that usually unremarked but basic ecological theme of Chilean history since colonial times. The main alternative to wood was coal, which was increasingly mined along the coast to the south of Concepción from the 1840s onwards. Here, domestic production was vulnerable to imports of higher-quality coal from Great Britain (or occasionally Australia), but held its own in the longer run, in part because a mixture of local and foreign coal was found to be ideal in smelting operations.

Chileans (sometimes first-generation Chileans) were outstanding among the mining entrepreneurs of this period. One or two of the copper concerns were British-owned, but these were exceptions, though foreign engineers were prominent throughout the mining zone. Men such as Urmeneta and a handful of others like him were naturally substantial capitalists in their own right, and they frequently turned their huge windfalls to good account, investing in transport and agriculture as well as in the mines, though not failing, either, to provide themselves with a suitably opulent style of life. Many of the lesser mining entrepreneurs were heavily dependent on a breed of middlemen known as *habilitadores*, who bought their ore in exchange for credit and supplies. This business was the foundation of several large fortunes, a famous example being the career of Agustín Edwards Ossandón, the son of an English doctor who settled in the Norte Chico just before independence. By the 1860s Edwards was one of the richest and most active capitalists in Chile. In 1871–2, in a well-known episode, he quietly accumulated and stockpiled vast amounts of copper, drove up the price by fifty per cent and realized a profit estimated at $1,500,000. By the time Edwards executed this audacious coup, Chile's nineteenth-century silver and copper cycle was reaching its climax. The silver mines were to maintain a high output for two more decades; but with production booming in the United States and Spain, 'Chili bars' became a decreasingly important component in the world supply of copper, no more than six per cent of which came from Chile by the 1890s. By then, of course, deserts further to the north were yielding a still greater source of wealth: nitrates.

Although mining dominated the export sector, it was agriculture which dominated most ordinary lives. Four out of five Chileans lived in the countryside in the 1860s. Here, as in so many other ways, the colonial legacy was overwhelming. Throughout the nineteenth century Chile remained a land of great estates, ownership of which conferred social status, political influence (if desired) and (less automatically before the 1850s) a comfortable income. This tradition of landownership is one of the keys to understanding Chilean history between colonial times and the mid-twentieth century. The precise number of haciendas in the mid-nineteenth century is hard to assess. The tax records of 1854 show that some 850 landowners received around two-thirds of all agricultural income in central Chile, and that of these 154 owned estates which earned in excess of $6,000 per year. (For purposes of comparison, it might be noted here that the president of the republic was paid a salary of $12,000, raised to $18,000 in 1861.) Haciendas occupied at least three-quarters of all agricultural land; most included large tracts of ground which went uncultivated from year to year. The estates were worked by a stable, resident class of *inquilinos*, or tenant-labourers, and, when necessary, by peons hired for seasonal work from outside. This type of rural labour system, as we know, was common (though with many variations) in many parts of Spanish America. When Charles Darwin rode through the Chilean countryside in the mid-1830s, he thought of it as 'feudal-like'. The Chilean *inquilino* was bound to the hacienda, allowed to cultivate his own small parcel of land in exchange for regular labour services to the landowner, by ties of custom and convenience rather than by those of law or debt. In the absence of traditional village communities of the European kind, the estate became the sole focus of his loyalty and formed his own little universe. 'Every hacienda in Chile', wrote an acute observer in 1861, 'forms a separate society, whose head is the landowner and whose subjects are the *inquilinos* . . . The landowner is an absolute monarch in his hacienda.'[8] For the tenant-labourers life was poor though not necessarily harsh; their farming methods were primitive, their diet monotonous and sometimes barely adequate and their opportunities to rise in the social scale very strictly limited. But the relative security of the hacienda could be contrasted with the plight of most of the peons outside – a destitute mass of people scraping a very precarious living by squatting on marginal land, by wandering the central valley in search of seasonal work, or in some cases by turning to cattle-rustling and banditry. From the viewpoint of the *hacendado*, there was plenty of surplus labour, as well as unused land, in the countryside. Neither was needed on a large scale before 1850 or so.

If agriculture was unproductive and unprofitable in the earlier part of this period, the reason is easy enough to identify. Local demand was quickly satisfied, while export markets were few and far between. The eighteenth-century grain trade with Peru, whose importance has probably been exaggerated by historians, was never quite re-established on the old scale following the wars of independence and the commercial rivalry of the 1830s. Between 1850 and 1880, however, the outlook for landowners improved quite radically, with haciendas responding immediately to the opening up of new markets overseas. As the only major cereal-growing country on the Pacific coast of America, Chile was well placed to take advantage of the sudden demand set up by the gold rushes in California and Australia. Exports of wheat and flour to California amounted to around 6,000 metric quintals (qqm) in 1848. Two years later no less than 277,000 qqm of wheat and 221,000 qqm of flour were shipped northwards. The boom was ephemeral – by 1855 California was self-sufficient – but it yielded high profits while it lasted, and it was responsible for consolidating a technically up-to-date milling industry in the Talca area and along Talcahuano Bay, as well as in Santiago itself slightly later on. By 1871 there were some 130 or so modern mills in Chile. (At the end of this period, further changes in the technology of milling were being pioneered in the middle west of the United States and in Europe, but these, by contrast, were slower to reach Chile.) Australia provided a second short-lived (and somewhat precarious) market for Chile in the 1850s, lucrative for a while. Landowners were well aware that geography and good luck were the causes of such windfalls, which were substantial enough: agricultural exports quintupled in value be-

[8] 'Atropos,' 'El inquilino en Chile', *Revista del Pacífico*, 5 (1861), 94.

tween 1844 and 1860. Nor was this by any means the end of the story. The experience gained in the Californian and Australian markets, combined with vital improvements in transport, enabled Chile in the 1860s to sell large quantities of grain (wheat and barley) to England: 2,000,000 qqm were exported in 1874, the peak year. Once again, however, Chile's competitive position in the international market place was more fragile than it appeared, and it was permanently undermined a few years later, when grain prices fell and new, more efficient cereal-growing countries were opened up.

The stimulus of these mid-century export booms brought some definite changes to the countryside. Most visible of these, perhaps, were the numerous irrigation canals now constructed, some of them remarkable feats of engineering. (The Canal de las Mercedes, sponsored by Manuel Montt and other *hacendados* in 1854, took thirty years to build and eventually extended seventy-five miles over very uneven terrain.) The quality of livestock was slowly improved, through the introduction of foreign breeds. With the growth of the towns, an expanding market for fruit and poultry greatly benefited nearby haciendas and the smaller (often specialist) farms known as *chacras*. Chileans had drunk their own wine since early colonial times; but the foundations of the great viticultural tradition which was later to produce the finest vintages in the western hemisphere were only laid in the 1850s, when pinot and cabernet grapes, brought from France, were grown locally for the first time. The government itself, as well as the Sociedad Nacional de Agricultura (in intermittent existence from 1838) tried to improve agricultural knowledge. Developments such as these, thus sketched, seem to convey an impression of vitality, but it is somewhat deceptive. Rural society and traditional farming methods were in no real way drastically disturbed, although it seems probable that monetary transactions in the countryside became more widespread than previously. There was relatively little in the way of high capital investment in agriculture (leaving aside irrigation works), and despite the enthusiasm of a number of progressive landowners, farm-machinery was never imported or employed on a large scale. (Oxen remained in universal use in Chile until the 1930s.) During the happy years of the export boom, landowners had ample reserves of both land and labour on which to draw. The acreage placed beneath the plough in these years may well have tripled or even quadrupled. New families from outside the haciendas were encouraged (and in many cases were no doubt eager) to swell the ranks of the *inquilinos*. The labour system itself was certainly tightened up, with greater demands being made on the tenant-labourers. Quite apart from *inquilinaje*, a variety of sharecropping practices, especially in the coastal range, were developed to help feed the export boom. The number of *minifundios* also seems to have risen. But in general it was the hacienda system itself, the basic underpinning of the nation's elite, which was most clearly consolidated by the changes of the mid-nineteenth century.

Such manufacturing as existed in Chile at the time of independence and for two or three decades thereafter was carried out by artisans and craftsmen in small workshops in the towns. In the countryside, the hacienda population largely clothed itself, though the growing import of British cottons probably had the effect over the years of reducing the extent of local weaving. The upper class was, on the whole, able to satisfy its demand for manufactured goods, including luxuries, from abroad, and was uninterested in promoting an industrial revolution. (Mining entrepreneurs were a partial exception here, and at the end of the period industrialism was viewed as a possible way forward for the country by a growing number of intellectuals and politicians.) There can be little doubt, however, that the expansion of national wealth after 1850 or so did provide certain opportunities for entrepreneurship in manufacturing, and such opportunities were sometimes seized – usually by foreigners, though these can better be regarded, perhaps, as first-generation Chileans. The first major industrial enterprises arose in connection with the export booms and were the copper smelters and flour mills mentioned already. In addition to these, the 1860s and 1870s saw the growth of small-scale factory production in such fields as textiles, food-processing, brick-making and glass-blowing. By the 1880s there were at least thirty breweries in the country. Furthermore, the needs of the new railways and of the mining industry itself stimulated the appearance of a number of small foundries and machine shops capable of repairing and in some instances even making equipment. In fact, what seems to have been a respectable metallurgical and engineering sector was developing with surprising speed by the early 1870s. There is growing evidence for supposing that the start of Chilean industrialization, often dated from the War of the Pacific, should be pushed back by about ten years.

It goes without saying that Chile's export-led economic expansion could hardly have taken place without improvements in transport and communications, which were also of obvious importance in consolidating the political coherence of the new nation. The number of ships calling at Chilean ports rose more or less constantly from the 1830s onwards, to over 4,000 per annum in the 1870s. Two 700-ton paddle steamers were brought to Chile from England in 1840 by a very enterprising American, William Wheelwright, the founder of the British-owned Pacific Steam Navigation Company. The outside world began to draw closer. From the mid-1840s it became possible, with suitable connections across the Panama isthmus, to travel to Europe in under forty days. (Sailing ships still took three or four months.) In 1868 the now well-established P.S.N.C. (whose initials later prompted several famous Chilean jokes) opened a direct service between Valparaíso and Liverpool by way of the Magellan Straits. Meanwhile, inland transport was slowly being revolutionized by the inevitable advent of the railway. The north of Chile, indeed, installed the first substantial length of track in Latin America. The line, built by Wheelwright and finished in 1851, linked Copiapó with the port of Caldera fifty miles away. It was financed by a group of wealthy miners, and it set the pattern for several later railways in the mining zone. The vital link between Santiago and Valparaíso had to wait somewhat longer. This was initially a mixed venture, the government subscribing about half the capital, but in 1858, following tiresome delays and difficulties, the state bought out most of the private shareholders; a swashbuckling American entrepreneur, Henry Meiggs, was entrusted with the completion of the line; and the last sections of the wide-gauge track were laid in 1863. Another mixed venture sponsored the third main railway, extending southwards through the central valley, a line of particular interest to cereal-growing *hacendados*. The Errázuriz government took this over in 1873, and only a few years later the line joined up with a further railway which by then had been built inland from Talcahuano and was pressing southwards into the romantic landscapes of Araucania. In 1882 there were nearly 1,200 miles of track in Chile, just over half state-owned. The state also subsidized and subsequently purchased the nascent telegraph network, construction of which began in 1852 – yet another enterprise of the indefatigable Wheelwright, to whom, in due course, a statue was raised in Valparaíso. Twenty years later the Chilean brothers Juan and Mateo Clark linked Santiago to Buenos Aires; with the laying of the Brazilian submarine cable in 1874 Chile was for the first time placed in direct touch with the Old World.

The increasing pace of economic activity during the third quarter of the nineteenth century left its mark on the country's financial and commercial institutions. Up to the 1850s the main sources of credit, for instance, had been private lenders or the trading houses. This now changed, with the appearance of the first proper banks – the Banco de Ossa and the Banco de Valparaíso, founded in the mid-1850s – and banking operations were sufficiently extensive to warrant regulation in the important law of 1860. The creation in 1856 of the notable Caja de Crédito Hipotecario funnelled credit to the countryside – in practice mainly to the big landowners. Joint-stock companies now became increasingly common, though supplementing rather than replacing the individual and family concerns and partnerships which had hitherto been the standard modes of business organization. The earliest were the railway companies; by the end of the 1870s well over 150 such enterprises had been formed at one time or another, predominantly in mining, banking and insurance, and railways. Chilean capitalism showed a markedly expansionist tendency in the 1860s and 1870s, with money flowing into the nitrate business in Bolivia and Peru as well as to the silver mines at Caracoles. Unregulated stock exchanges were operating in Valparaíso and Santiago from the early 1870s, at which point 'Caracoles fever' was driving investors into a speculative frenzy without precedent in Chilean history.

Foreign trade throughout this period was largely controlled by several dozen import-export houses centred on Valparaíso and the capital; these contributed much to the building up of the new money market, and remained influential thereafter in the developing corporate sector of the economy. Foreigners, whether as permanent residents or as transient agents of overseas trading houses with branches in Chile, were particularly prominent here, with the British leading the field. The British connection was fundamental to Chile. Investment in the country by Britons was mostly confined to government bonds – to the tune of around £7,000,000 by 1880 – but Great Britain was the destination for between one-third and two-thirds of all Chile's exports and the source of between one-third and one-half of all her imports in any given year. Imports from France also ran high, reflecting upper class tastes. As in colonial times, trade with Peru continued, but this was overshadowed by the links now being forged with the North Atlantic. The steamers, railways, telegraphs, banks and joint-stock companies all played their part in cementing Chile's solidifying association with the international economy now coming into being around the world. Politicians might occasionally denounce the British traders as the 'new Carthaginians' or even (in more popular vein) as 'infidels', but by and large their presence was welcomed as a vital element in what was confidently assumed to be the progress of the nation.

Sixty years after independence Chile was an altogether more prosperous land than would have seemed likely in 1810, as well as being more integrated economically than in colonial times. Her record in this respect contrasts forcibly with the stagnation evident in several of the other Spanish American republics. But the new prosperity was not distributed proportionately (still less evenly) to all sections of the people. The wealth of the upper class increased very strikingly, and the upper class had a fairly clear idea as to what to do with it. An American visitor in the mid-1850s observed that 'the great object of life' on acquiring wealth seemed to be to 'remove to the capital, to lavish it on costly furniture, equipage and splendid living.'[9] The gradual disappearance of older, more austere, supposedly more virtuous habits of life was lamented by writers of a moralistic cast of mind; and it is probably fair to say that the adoption of more sophisticated, European styles of living – fashions across a whole range from hats to horse-racing altered visibly between the 1820s and the 1870s – may well have deepened the psychological gulf between rich and poor; it may also be one of the keys to understanding the political liberalization which set in after 1861. The elite of Chilean society was never closed to newcomers. The new magnates of mining and finance were easily assimilated, as were the children or grandchildren of successful immigrants – though the much remarked contingent of non-Hispanic surnames in the Chilean upper class only became really conspicuous at the end of the century. (There was only one English surname in any of the cabinets before the 1880s.) The underlying coherence of this open, flexible elite was provided by a set of economic interests – in mines, land, banks and trade – which overlapped and often interlocked. The miners or traders who in different circumstances might have formed the vanguard of a *bourgeoisie conquérante* were from the start included at the highest levels of the social hierarchy, where fundamentally aristocratic outlooks and attitudes prevailed. The supreme upper class values were those concerned with family and landownership. The importance of family connections at this period cannot easily be exaggerated. It was something which often showed up in politics. President Bulnes was the son-in-law of one of his predecessors, the nephew of another and the

[9] [Mrs. C. B. Merwin], *Three Years in Chile* (New York, 1863), 95.

brother-in-law of one of his successors. In the century after 1830, the Errázuriz family gave the republic one archbishop, three presidents, and upwards of fifty congressmen. The attraction of rural property, likewise, integrated rather than divided the elite; landownership was the highly prized badge of aristocratic status. These powerful forces for coherence clearly encouraged continuity and stability rather than change and rearrangement in the social development of Chile.

Between the landowning upper class and the labouring poor, a small, miscellaneous 'middle band' of society grew perceptibly larger as the result of economic expansion. It consisted of the owners of the smaller businesses and farms, the growing number of clerical employees in trade, the subaltern members of the bureaucracy (which even in 1880 still numbered no more than 3,000), and the artisans and craftsmen of the towns. These last were what educated Chileans of the period meant when they used the term *clase obrera*. On the upper fringe of the middle band, frustrated would-be entrants into the best circles constituted a recognizable type, well described in some of the fiction of the time. From at least the later 1850s such people were known as *siúticos* and tradition attributes the neologism, still understood if no longer widely used, to Lastarria. Chilean artisans, for their part, were never well protected by commercial policy, but the growth of the towns (and upper class wealth) created a demand for services and products which could best be met locally, and many crafts and trades seem to have flourished, at least in a modest way. In their manners and aspirations such groups evidently took their tone from high society. Referring to the 'mechanics and retail shopkeepers' of the Santiago of 1850, a sharp-eyed visitor noted:

There is an inherent want of tidiness in their domestic life; but in public, fine dress is a passion with them, and a stranger would scarcely suspect that the man he meets in a fine broad-cloth cloak, escorting a woman arrayed in silks and jewelry, occupied no higher rank in the social scale than that of tinman, carpenter or shopman whose sole stock-in-trade might be packed in a box five feet square.[10]

The spread of mutualist associations in later years provided a greater degree of security for artisans and craftsmen. The first was founded in the printing trade in 1853 and did not last long; but by 1880, thanks to the efforts of the builder and architect Fermín Vivaceta and others, there were some thirty-nine societies of this kind enjoying legal status, foreshadowing the later emergence of trade unions.

[10] Lieut. J. M. Gilliss, U.S.N., *The United States Naval Astronomical Expedition to the southern hemisphere during the years 1849–50–51–52*, vol. I., *Chile* (Washington, 1855), 219.

A deep material and psychological chasm separated all the social groups so far mentioned from the great mass of the labouring poor in town and countryside, whose condition improved only marginally, if at all, over this period. Despite the higher number of families now being settled on the haciendas, the peons of the central valley were often obliged to look elsewhere for work. They migrated in their thousands to overcrowded and insalubrious districts in the main towns. Both *rotos* (urban labourers) and peons also flocked to the northern mining camps, and to the railway-building gangs, in Chile and overseas. When, at the end of the 1860s, the audacious Henry Meiggs (renowned for the remark that he would sooner employ five hundred Chilean *rotos* than a thousand Irishmen) embarked on grandiose railway-building schemes in Peru at least 25,000 Chileans answered his call. This outflow of labour provoked debates in Congress, with proposals to restrict emigration, while land-owners complained of a 'shortage of hands' in the countryside. In fact, there was no real shortage, and this was appreciated by those more acute Chileans who now began to subject the labouring poor to somewhat closer scrutiny than in the past.

If emigration was (briefly) a concern of Chilean legislators, the idea of immigration from Europe, as a means of 'civilizing' the lower classes, was suggested more frequently. Traces of xenophobia may have sur-vived among the poor, to be whipped up on occasion, as during the civil war of 1829–30, but in general foreigners were welcomed with open arms. ' "Foreigner" ', once said Antonio Varas, 'is an immoral word which should be expunged from the dictionary!' The census of 1875 counted 4,109 British, 4,033 German and 2,330 French residents in Chile, with people of other nationalities totalling nearly 15,000, a figure which included 7,000 Argentines. The role of the British in trade has already been noted; some prominent Chilean families came in due course from this quarter. The milling industry referred to earlier was largely estab-lished by Americans; Americans and British helped to build and then to operate the railway network; a high proportion of the industrial entre-preneurs of later years came from abroad. At a more modest level, foreigners also found a place in the expanding artisan class, notably in those trades which catered to the style of life favoured by the rich. European scholars and scientists such as the Frenchmen Claude Gay (author of a famous thirty-volume account of the country's natural and civil history) and Amado Pissis (who mapped the republic from 28°10'S to 41°58'S) did much to add to the store of Chilean knowledge; the government had a more or less systematic policy of employing such people. There was no mass immigration of the kind desired, but at the end of the 1840s the government encouraged the settlement of families from Germany in the thinly-populated southern territories around Valdivia and Lake Llanquihue. By 1860 there were more than 3,000 Germans in the south, hardy pioneers who cleared the forests and opened the land to cultivation.

This new official interest in the south spelled the beginning of the end for the independent Indian enclave of Araucania, which lay inconveniently between the new areas of settlement and the country's heartland north of the Bío-Bío. The suppression of the widespread banditry which followed independence in the southern provinces, complete by the mid-1830s, had placed the Araucanians in a somewhat more vulnerable position than previously; but for the next quarter of a century they were left largely undisturbed. As in colonial times, the army patrolled the frontier while the government in Santiago cultivated (and subsidized) a number of amiably disposed caciques. The agricultural expansion of the 1850s, however, drew settlers into the area south of the Bío-Bío, causing tension with the Araucanians. The Indian attacks on frontier settlements which followed (1859–60) raised the 'Araucanian question' as a political issue, much discussed over the next few years. The policy adopted by the Pérez government was, by establishing 'lines' of forts, to enclose the Araucanians within a diminishing belt of territory. The Indians resisted the encroaching Chilean army in a further series of assaults (1868–71), but by the end of the 1870s, with settlement spilling into the frontier, the 'lines' had drawn inexorably closer together. After the War of the Pacific, troops were sent in to 'pacify' and occupy the narrow fringe of Indian territory which remained. The long, proud history of Araucania drew to its pathetic close. The Indians themselves were given, on paper, a settlement deemed generous in the eyes of Santiago, but the pattern of land transactions on the frontier over the previous twenty years was hardly a good augury. The government strove in vain to regularize land transfers in the south, but failed to prevent the formation of new latifundia, often through chicanery and intimidation. Nor could the measures taken to protect the interests of the Araucanians against predatory landowners (great and small) be described as anything but inadequate.

The most vivid contrast, in the Chile of the 1870s, was between town and country. Civilization – that term so often used to justify the 'pacification' of Araucania – was perhaps most evident in its urban setting. Nineteenth-century Chilean urbanization (modest indeed by the standards of the twentieth century) was essentially a tale of two cities – Santiago, which grew from about 70,000 in the mid-1830s to 130,000 in 1875, and Valparaíso, which by the end of our period had reached close on 100,000. Other Chilean towns lagged far behind. During the mining booms, it is true, Copiapó enjoyed a prosperous heyday; Concepción, devastated by the earthquake of 1835, flourished again with the spread of wheat-growing and milling; and among the somnolent little towns of the central valley, Talca nurtured a well-developed sense of civic pride. But none of these places had populations of more than 20,000 in 1875. The predominance of the capital and the main port, underpinned by political and commercial hegemony, was unchallengeable. As contemporary drawings and prints show clearly, Santiago retained a definitely colonial appearance until around 1850, but the mid-century export boom quickly left its mark. By 1857 the normally sober Andrés Bello could write that 'the progress made in the last five years can be called fabulous. Magnificent buildings are rising everywhere . . .; to see the Alameda on certain days of the year makes one imagine one is in one of the great cities of Europe.'[11] The year 1857, in fact, saw the inauguration of the fine Teatro Municipal and the introduction of horse-drawn trams and gas-lamps in the streets. Architectural styles altered, French (or even English) models being preferred for the new aristocratic mansions now being built. The unusually active programme carried through by Benjamín Vicuña Mackenna, the almost legendary Intendant of the early 1870s, endowed the capital with avenues, parks, squares and the superb urban folly of the Cerro Santa Lucía, which delights *santiaguinos* to this day. Valparaíso, the first Chilean town to organize a proper fire-brigade (1851), underwent similar though less flamboyantly publicized improvements. Its business district took on a faintly British atmosphere. Both capital and port (and other towns later on) soon acquired a respectable newspaper press, which flourished with particular vigour in the more liberal political climate after 1861. The doyen of the Chilean press, *El Mercurio*, founded at Valparaíso in 1827 (and a daily from 1829), is today the oldest newspaper in the Spanish-language world.

Education in this period made slower progress than many Chileans would have wished, despite the best efforts of such presidents as Montt, whose obsessive interest in the matter was shared by his great Argentine friend Sarmiento. Illiteracy fell gradually, to around seventy-seven per

---

[11] Domingo Amunátegui Solar, *La democracia en Chile* (Santiago, 1946), 132.

cent in 1875, at which point seventeen per cent of the school-age population was undergoing some form of primary education. By 1879, too, there were some twenty-seven public *liceos* (two for girls) and a larger number of private schools providing instruction at the secondary level, along with the prestigious Instituto Nacional, where so many of the republic's leaders received their secondary (and for many years much of their higher) education. Higher studies (and especially professional training, to which women were admitted by the decree of 1877) were greatly stimulated by the formation in 1843 of the University of Chile. Modelled on the Institut de France, it was in its early years a deliberative and supervisory body rather than a teaching institution, but its standards were high. The distinct strengthening of intellectual and cultural life which now became noticeable owed much to the first rector of the university, the eminent Venezuelan scholar, Andrés Bello, who spent the last thirty-six years of a long life in Chile. Poet, grammarian, philosopher, educationist, jurist, historian, indefatigable public servant and senator – Bello had a patient and many-sided genius which inspired a host of devoted pupils and disciples. It is impossible in the space of this chapter to survey the cultural panorama of the period; but one rather singular aspect deserves to be noted. This was the primacy accorded to history, a primacy encouraged by the university and (in a small way) by the government itself. The result, between 1850 and 1900 or so, was the fine flowering of historical narrative represented, above all, in the works of Diego Barros Arana, Miguel Luis Amunátegui, Ramón Sotomayor Valdés and Benjamín Vicuña Mackenna. Of these four, Barros Arana was the most diligent and scholarly, Vicuña Mackenna the most lyrical and vivid. All can still be read with profit.

It is possible that this Chilean preference for history both reflected and reinforced the growth of national consciousness. Patriotism, to be sure, is never easy to assess. It may be doubted whether a clear sense of *chilenidad* really penetrated very far into the countryside before the 1870s. The people of the towns, by contrast, responded ardently to the victory celebrations in 1839; the *dieciocho*, the annual national holiday, though often a pretext for prolonged alcoholic indulgence, was an undeniably popular occasion; and private as well as public initiatives saw to it that statues were raised to the heroes of independence and other national figures, starting with General Freire in 1856. (Portales and O'Higgins got their monuments in 1860 and 1872 respectively). Educated Chileans were strongly inclined to see their country as superior to others in

Spanish America – and it is hard to resist the conclusion that in certain important respects they were right. 'We saved ourselves from the general shipwreck', wrote the rising Conservative politician Carlos Walker Martínez.[12] Chile as the *república modelo*, as an example to unruly, 'tropical' lands, was a recurrent theme in speeches and editorials. 'I have such a poor idea of the . . . sister republics', observed Antonio Varas in 1864, 'that . . . I regret we have to make common cause with them.'[13] Such opinions often coincided with foreign views of Chile, especially in Europe. (In April 1880 even *The Times* used the phrase 'model republic'.) European flattery was deeply pleasing to educated Chileans, many of whom believed that Great Britain and France (in particular) were leading the world up a highway of progress which in due course Chile herself was sure to follow: 'Europe's today is our tomorrow.'[14]

This mood of confidence and optimism was severely shaken by the multiple crisis of the mid-1870s. This can effectively be dated from the collapse in 1873 of the speculative bonanza induced by the Caracoles silver boom. The economic difficulties which mounted up thereafter stemmed in part from the serious international recession which began that year (the start of the 'Great Depression' which followed the long mid-Victorian boom), but they also reflected a more fundamental problem: with the appearance in the world economy of new and more efficient producers of both wheat and copper, Chile was now being displaced in her most important export markets. The springs of prosperity were running dry. Copper prices, briefly boosted by the Franco-Prussian war (as they had earlier been by the Crimean war), went into sharp decline. The value of silver exports halved within four years, though the cause often assigned to this – the shift to the gold standard by Germany and other nations – may have been exaggerated by historians. On top of all this, an alarming and untimely cycle of both flooding and drought in the central valley brought three disastrous harvests in a row. An abrupt rise in the cost of living plunged many thousands of poorer Chileans into destitution and near-starvation. There were disturbing symptoms of social unrest. The peso, stable for so long, began to depreciate, falling from 46*d*. in 1872 to 33*d*. by 1879. (It is faintly amusing to record that in this atmosphere of desperation, official hopes were briefly raised by a

12 C. W. Martínez, *Portales* (Paris, 1879), 452.
13 Antonio Varas, *Correspondencia*, 5 vols. (Santiago, 1918–29), V, 48.
14 Editorial, *El Mercurio*, 18 September 1844.

Franco-American confidence trickster who claimed to be able to convert copper into gold; he was lionized and had a polka named after him.) Fearing a catastrophic run on the now largely insolvent banks, the Pinto administration took the drastic step of declaring the inconvertibility of bank-notes (July 1878), which thus became obligatory legal tender; it was the start of a century of inflation. In its efforts to solve the acute fiscal dilemma (made still more acute by the need to service a national debt which had grown perilously fast over the previous few years), the government first resorted to cuts in public spending; the National Guard, for instance, was reduced to a mere 7,000 men. As the recession deepened, many intelligent Chileans, noting their country's heavy dependence on exports, advocated a stronger protectionist dose for the embryonic industrial sector (this was partly achieved in the tariff reform of 1878) and also the imposition of new taxes on the wealthy. This latter notion, according to the British consul-general, was well regarded 'by all but those whose pockets it would chiefly affect and who, for the misfortune of their Country, just now largely compose her Legislature'.[15] In fact, Congress in 1878–9 did agree, after much argument, to levy small taxes on inheritances and property. These had little effect on the crisis, from which Chile was saved not by fiscal improvization but by blood and iron.

The menacing international tensions of the 1870s derived from long standing border disputes with Argentina and Bolivia. Neither frontier had been precisely delineated in colonial times. The Chilean presence on the Magellan Straits after 1843 had raised the question of the ownership of Patagonia, which Argentines considered theirs. Chile, in effect, abandoned her claim to all but a fraction of this huge but desolate territory in the Fierro-Sarratea agreement of 1878, accepted by Congress despite the angry crowds outside the building and a strong speech from an irate former foreign minister, who lamented that Chile would now remain 'a poor republic' instead of becoming 'a great empire'. The agreement averted the danger of war with Argentina; there had been considerable sabre-rattling on both sides of the Andes. The problem with Bolivia was more intractable, for while few vital interests had been at stake in Patagonia this was emphatically not the case in the Atacama desert, one of the principal scenes of Chilean economic expansionism. Here in the 1860s, on the Bolivian littoral, the Chilean entrepreneurs José

---

[15] Consul-General Packenham to the Marquis of Salisbury, Santiago, 24 February 1879. Public Record Office, London: F.O.16/203.

Santos Ossa and Francisco Puelma had pioneered the extraction of nitrate, in growing demand abroad as a fertilizer. (Chilean capital was also prominent in the nitrate business in the Peruvian desert, further north; but the industry there was nationalized by the Peruvian government in 1875). In the Atacama, thanks to generous concessions by Bolivia, the powerful Compañía de Salitres y Ferrocarril de Antofagasta, a Chilean-British corporation in which a number of leading Chilean politicians held shares, was close to constituting a state within a state. Most of the population on the littoral was Chilean. Such a state of affairs is always potentially explosive. In 1874, in an attempt to settle the frontier once and for all, Chile agreed to fix it at 24°S in return for the Bolivian promise of a twenty-five-year moratorium on the further taxation of Chilean nitrate enterprises. The additional export tax of ten centavos per quintal suddenly imposed by the Bolivians in 1878 was clearly a breach of faith. (Whether the original Bolivian concessions were imprudent or not is another matter.) The refusal of the Compañía de Salitres to pay up brought threats of confiscation. In order to forestall this a small Chilean force occupied Antofagasta (February 1879) and went on to take control of the littoral. The conflict swiftly assumed graver proportions. Peru was drawn in by virtue of a secret treaty of alliance with Bolivia, concluded six years previously. Chile declared war on both countries in April 1879.

The War of the Pacific was seen at the time (by some) as a cynically premeditated exercise in plunder, with the aim of rescuing Chile from her economic plight by seizing the mineral wealth of the northern deserts. Others detected the invisible hand of more powerful nations and the foreign trading concerns so closely enmeshed with the nitrate business. The American secretary of state, the egregious James G. Blaine, even asserted later on that it was 'an English war on Peru, with Chile as the instrument', a verdict which it is difficult to sustain from the existing evidence.[16] It must, however, be said that Chilean politicians (not least those who held or had held shares in nitrate enterprises) were aware of the advantages which might accrue from control of the deserts and were equally aware of the country's dire economic position in 1879. Insofar as there had been a public 'willingness to war' over the previous months, this had mainly been directed against Argentina. Nonetheless it may well

---

[16] On these points, see V. G. Kiernan, 'Foreign interests in the War of the Pacific', *Hispanic American Historical Review*, 35 (1955), 14–36, and John Mayo, 'La Compañía de Salitres de Antofagasta y la Guerra del Pacífico', *Historia*, (Santiago) 14 (1979), 71–102.

be true that the eagerness with which the outbreak of hostilities was welcomed (generally, if not universally) was in some sense an outlet for the pent-up feelings of frustration which had accumulated during the years of recession. (Chile's action in February 1879 could plausibly be described as precipitate.) But neither Chile nor her enemies were prepared for war. Their armies were small and poorly equipped. Chile had cut back her military strength during the recession, while both the Peruvian and Bolivian armies were decidedly over-officered. At sea, Chile and Peru (Bolivia had no navy) were perhaps more evenly matched; and command of the sea was the key to the war. In the end, Chile's greater national coherence and traditions of settled government probably made the vital difference. At various points during this time of mortal danger, both Bolivia and Peru were afflicted by serious political upheavals. In Chile, by contrast, congressional and presidential elections were held as usual, cabinets changed without excessive drama and energetic politicking by no means ceased: neither the Conservatives nor the disaffected Liberal group led by Vicuña Mackenna (who had made an unsuccessful bid for the presidency in 1876) were invited into the cabinet, and they made up for this by mercilessly castigating the government's numerous hesitancies and failures in the conduct of the war.

The early months, taken up with a struggle for naval mastery, were a frustrating period of reverses for Chile, but also provided the single most memorable incident of the war. On 21 May 1879, off Iquique, the decrepit wooden corvette *Esmeralda* was attacked by the Peruvian ironclad *Huascar*. Although the corvette was outclassed and doomed from the outset, the Chilean commander, Captain Arturo Prat, refused to strike his colours. He himself died in an entirely hopeless boarding operation as the *Huascar* rammed his vessel, which, after further rammings, went down. Prat's heroic self-sacrifice turned him into a 'secular saint' without compare in the admiration of his countrymen. Five months later, off Cape Angamos, the Chilean fleet cornered the *Huascar* and forced her to surrender. This victory gave Chile command of the sea and enabled her to launch an offensive on land. Soon after the battle of Angamos, an expeditionary force invaded the Peruvian desert province of Tarapacá, forcing the enemy to fall back on Tacna and Arica to the north. Early in 1880 an army of 12,000 men, commanded by General Manuel Baquedano, undertook the conquest of these provinces too, in a desert campaign culminating in the ferocious battles of Campo de la Alianza and the Morro of Arica (May–June 1880). By this time, an intervention to halt the conflict had been mooted among the powers of

Europe, but the suggestion was effectively torpedoed by Bismarck. The United States, however, succeeded in arranging talks between the belligerents, aboard a cruiser off Arica, in October 1880. The conference broke down. The Chilean government, now in control of all the main nitrate-producing areas, would almost certainly have liked to make peace, but public opinion demanded the humiliation of Peru, in strident cries of 'On to Lima!' At the end of 1880 an army of more than 26,000 men, once again under Baquedano, disembarked on the central Peruvian coast. The extremely bloody battles of Chorrillos and Miraflores (January 1881) opened the gates of Lima. The war continued in the interior of Peru for two further years, with guerrilla forces resisting the army of occupation, but nothing could disguise the fact that Chile had won a total victory. A new Peruvian government eventually accepted, in the Treaty of Ancón (October 1883), most of the victor's stiff terms for peace. Tarapacá was ceded in perpetuity, and Chile was given temporary possession of Tacna and Arica – over which there developed a long diplomatic wrangle not finally resolved until 1929. The last Chilean soldiers left Peru in August 1884. A truce with Bolivia (April 1884) allowed Chile to remain in control of the Atacama until the negotiation of a full peace settlement, which only materialized in 1904.

Victory in the War of the Pacific gave Chile very substantial international prestige. For Chileans themselves there were the inevitable temptations to hubris, not entirely resisted. The optimism so seriously shattered by the crisis of the previous decade was swiftly recaptured, with the discovery that, as Vicuña Mackenna characteristically put it, 'in the Chilean soul, hidden beneath the soldier's rough tunic or coarse poncho of native weave, there throbs the sublime heroism of the age of antiquity'.[17] In every Chilean, it seemed, there was a soldier. With the conquest of the Bolivian littoral and the southern provinces of Peru, Chile enlarged her national territory by one-third. Possession of the nitrate fields meant that the country's wealth was enormously augmented overnight – and in the nick of time, given the apparent exhaustion of the sources of Chilean prosperity in the mid-1870s. As nitrate took over from copper and silver, the material progress undergone in the half-century or so before the war soon began to look modest in comparison with the boom of the 1880s. Such sudden national windfalls need to be carefully appraised and judiciously managed. For Chile, the model republic of Latin America, the victories of peace were, perhaps, to be less assured than those of war.

[17] Eugenio Orrego Vicuña, *Vicuña Mackenna, vida y trabajos*, 3rd edn (Santiago, 1951), 376.

.

2

FROM THE WAR OF
THE PACIFIC TO 1930

As Chile entered the 1870s the Republic could look back on 40 years of virtually uninterrupted constitutional stability – unique in Spanish America – and the evolution of a functioning multi-party system in politics. She could also look back on the growth of a modest but promising economy, based on the export of primary products from land and mine. Her population had doubled since Independence, from one to two million by 1875; her foreign trade, dominated from 1830 to 1870 by copper exports, had grown apace, providing adequate revenue for successive governments to initiate transport improvements, notably railways, develop educational programmes, provide urban amenities – and preserve law and order. In foreign affairs, Chile had not only maintained her independence but in the 1830s had also prevented the combined attempt of Peru and Bolivia to assert hegemony on the Pacific coast of South America.

The country's capacity to attain these objectives undoubtedly owed a good deal to the constitutional system created by Diego Portales (1793–1837), backed by a remarkably homogeneous landed aristocracy and based upon the authoritarian, centralizing constitution of 1833. That constitution, coldly realistic, recognized what Chile was rather than what it might aspire to be: it appreciated what Portales called 'the weight of the night', the sheer traditionalism of three hundred years of colonial control, during which the basic lineaments of society had been drawn, and accepted that independence from Spain was indeed a fundamental political act, but had virtually no economic or social content. For the society of Chile was essentially rural: a white aristocracy of land ruled the national life in all its branches while an illiterate peasantry, largely *mestizo*, obeyed. The great estates, virtually separate fiefdoms where the writ of the hacendado ignored the laws of the land, were still, as they had been for three hundred years, the basic social and economic characteristic of the new Republic.

This highly stratified society had evolved a political system much more sophisticated than that of her neighbours. All revolutions polarize opinions, and Chile was no exception. Politically, the Independence period produced conservatives and liberals, the former accepting separation from Spain but anxious to conserve the social *status quo*, the latter seeing in that upheaval the opportunity to extend freedom – from the church in intellectual and educational matters, and from arbitrary authority in politics. The conservatives triumphed in the 1830s but the liberal current still ran strong: from 1830 to 1880 it succeeded in modifying, though by no means destroying, the authoritarian structure of government through limited constitutional reform. And it began to assault the practices as well as the form of governmental authority, chief of which was the interference of the executive power, the president, in elections to the legislative, the Congress, thus generally assuring a pliant majority for its plans. Under the system, men and groups of different views formed embryonic parties which contested elections and, as Chile avoided both the excesses of *caudillismo* and the intervention of the military in the political process, by 1870 a political and constitutional system recognizable as functioning and viable by European or North American standards had evolved, giving Chile the accolade of being 'the England of South America'.

Chile also advanced economically, with exports of agricultural produce (notably wheat) and mining products (chiefly copper) expanding as the century proceeded. From the 1860s, the demands for improvements to the infrastructure, especially railways, forced government to turn increasingly to foreign borrowing as a supplement to trade revenues, but here too, through sound management and probity, Chile acquired an unparalleled reputation for promptly paying her debts, most unusual then in Latin America. By 1870, indeed, political maturity, financial responsibility and orderly evolution were internationally regarded as Chile's distinctive hallmarks in a somewhat disorderly continent. Only Brazil could compete with Chile in international esteem.

The 1870s, however, were a decade of disillusion. The onset of the world depression in international trade hit Chile hard as a primary producer, and internal political squabbling among the different parties threatened her vaunted tradition of governmental continuity. The mild-mannered president Aníbal Pinto (1876–81) sought accommodation with the political opposition rather than using his extensive powers under the constitution, only to find, in the midst of severe economic depression and much social distress, that conciliation was interpreted as weakness. His government, reeling from the effects of the world economic crisis, had been obliged in 1878 to take the currency off the gold standard and adopt a regime of inconvertible paper, a harsh shock to Chilean pride and to international opinion. For those who believed that the authoritarian constitution of 1833 and the presidential system were failing, the moment of confrontation seemed to have arrived.

Outside events then intervened. Since Independence Chile and her northern neighbours, Bolivia and Peru, had disputed the line of Chile's northern boundary in the Atacama desert, but the issue did not become acute until the resources of that barren land – chiefly guano and nitrates – became commercially exploitable, and foreign capital and entrepreneurship moved in to exploit them. A succession of treaties between the separate states regulated their relations, but in 1878 the unilateral abrogation by Bolivia of a treaty with Chile relating to foreign interests in Bolivian Antofagasta precipitated a diplomatic crisis. Peru, linked with Bolivia in a treaty of defensive and offensive alliance, desperately sought to avoid conflict; Chile, knowing of the treaty, sought to put pressure on both her neighbours and, when the Bolivian authorities refused to yield, declared war. The War of the Pacific (1879–83) ensued, at a time when Chile was quite unprepared for it both politically and economically. As it happened, however, her lack of preparation, economic weakness and political uncertainty – not to mention the deplorable state of her armed forces – looked like meticulous planning when compared with her adversaries, and the strong sense of nationalism – non-existent in Peru and Bolivia – was to prove a decisive asset. After an uncertain start, Chilean land and naval forces decisively defeated those of Bolivia and Peru, as they had in the 1830s, and from a country hovering on the brink of political disintegration and economic collapse in 1879, Chile emerged from the war in 1883 with her prospects transformed. Resisting strong Pan-American pressure for magnanimous treatment of defeated foes, Chile secured from the peace an extension of national territory no less than a third of the country's original extent and, in the nitrate regions of the Atacama – Peruvian Tarapacá and Bolivian Antofagasta – mineral wealth which would account for roughly half of ordinary government revenue for the next 40 years.

By the Treaty of Ancón (October 1883), concluded by Chile with a

Peruvian government which Chilean forces had helped to install, Peru ceded to Chile unconditionally and in perpetuity her province of Tarapacá. She also accepted Chilean possession of her provinces of Tacna and Arica for a decade, after which a plebiscite would determine their final ownership, the winner paying the loser ten million Chilean silver pesos. Other terms dealt with Peru's debtors, whose sorry investments had been partly mortgaged by Tarapacá's mineral deposits. A separate truce with Bolivia – the final peace treaty came only twenty years later – secured for Chile Bolivia's sole littoral territory of Antofagasta, with nitrate deposits only second in importance to those of Tarapacá.

The war itself had also given considerable impetus to Chilean industrialization in the provision of matériel, and to both agriculture and transport facilities through the necessity to provision from central Chile the army in the desert and the forces subsequently occupying Peru. This galvanization of the Chilean economy from its state of torpor in 1879 was to be sustained in the 1880s by the dynamic growth of the new nitrate industry. Chile's future seemed assured, and perhaps the most significant impact of her success in war was to enhance an already high reputation, imbuing her leaders with a sense of national self-confidence, in contrast to their feelings of almost universal pessimism a few short years before. No two Chilean statesmen of the nineteenth century better embodied this combination of national aspiration and patriotic pride than the two incumbents of the presidency during the 1880s, Domingo Santa María (1881–6) and José Manuel Balmaceda (1886–91). Both were profoundly liberal by conviction; both were no less autocratic in temperament, and possession of the presidency accentuated this trait: they were, in effect, to preside over the paradox of Chile's greatest material progress the century was to see, combined with the political and constitutional collapse of the system created after Independence by Diego Portales.

THE PRESIDENCY OF SANTA MARÍA, 1881–6

Domingo Santa María assumed the presidency of Chile on 18 September 1881, when the tide of war had already turned decisively in Chile's favour. Like most of his predecessors, he had been hand-picked by the previous president, and like them had been elected with massive intervention by government in the polls. Despite the war political passions ran high, inevitably so when the Congressional opposition, and notably the clerical Conservative party, was well aware of its impotence to ensure a free election. The preceding months had been marked by what the British Minister called 'many violent and indecorous scenes' in the legislature.[1] Nevertheless, Santa María had a clear field. But the manner of his election and the policies he was to unfold, particularly in religious affairs, were to embitter even further political life.

The incoming administration had inherited a religious situation of some delicacy. The death in 1878 of the ultramontane Rafael Valentín Valdivieso, Archbishop of Santiago for some 30 years, had re-opened with the Vatican the vexed question of the *patronato*, the government's claim as successor to the Spanish crown since independence to the right of nomination to high ecclesiastical office. With the death of Valdivieso, so long a thorn in Liberal flesh, President Pinto's government had named a man of more moderate temper, Francisco de Paula Taforo, but the Holy See had refused to accept the appointment. Santa María now sought to grasp this nettle and invited to Santiago an apostolic delegate, Celestino del Frate. But the mission was a total failure: del Frate advised the Pope to reject Taforo's nomination, and Santa María sent him his passports. The question of the *patronato* remained unresolved but, for Santa María, del Frate's mission provided the pretext for a direct confrontation with the church, and legislation was introduced to assault its still substantial prerogatives at three critical junctures of human life – birth, marriage and death.

In his presidential state of the nation message in 1883, having intervened decisively in the Congressional elections of 1882 to guarantee a majority for anti-clerical legislation, Santa María announced his programme – to remove from ecclesiastical jurisdiction the registry of births and deaths and transfer them to the state; to institute civil matrimony; to ensure liberty of conscience; and to permit the dead of whatever religious persuasion to be buried in cemeteries hitherto restricted to Catholics and controlled by the Catholic church. To José Manuel Balmaceda, minister of the interior, who had been educated in a seminary and originally destined for the priesthood, fell the difficult task of piloting these controversial measures into law. For although the government could count on its majority in Congress, it had to face the power of the church outside, and that power was still formidable. 'There is no doubt', wrote the correspondent of *The Times* in 1880, 'that the

---

[1] Pakenham to the Earl of Granville, Santiago, 6 July 1881. No. 38. Diplomatic. London, Public Record Office, Foreign Office archives, Chile (FO 16), vol. 213.

cowled or tonsured man is still the "lord of all" in this country; and with the women under his control, he may well afford to set the sneers of sceptic men and the enactments of the civil law at defiance.'[2]

It was a prophetic observation. The liberal laws were, indeed, forced through Congress, though in the teeth of acrimonious Catholic opposition, but outside Congress the effects were dramatic: for example, the vicar capitular of Santiago not only condemned the law on cemeteries but also refused to apply it, and in retaliation the government closed Catholic burial grounds and prohibited interments within churches, a long-standing but clearly unhygienic practice. Some lugubrious scenes resulted, such as clandestine burials of devout Catholics in defiance of government orders, the picketing of cemeteries by armed soldiers, the concealment of terminal illnesses and the subsequent smuggling of corpses out of houses in all kinds of coffins and by all means of conveyance.[3]

But the law was the law. Despite fierce Catholic resistance the legislation, once on the statute-book, was increasingly applied. The religious laws of the Santa María administration marked a decisive diminution of the power and influence of the church: they also marked the apogee of Chilean liberalism in the nineteenth century, and earned for Balmaceda the implacable hatred of the Conservative party. Much more than this, however, a paradox occurred which only time would reveal: with the passage of the laws the cement of anti-clericalism which had bound together many different men and groups of broadly liberal persuasion began to crumble, and there was no other ideological bond between them. The Radicals and the National party, not themselves benefiting from Santa María's electoral interventions, were nevertheless prepared to support his anti-clerical policies in Congress since they shared his passionate conviction that the powers of the church should be reduced. But that objective achieved, their natural objections to electoral intervention came to the surface. As for the president, with the new nitrate income he now had better opportunities to pursue ambitious programmes but far more political difficulties in doing so, and it would not suffice, in a country whose elite was as politically conscious as that of Chile, for the president simply to use his patronage to build up a personalist following. Santa María had succeeded Aníbal Pinto who, it was generally agreed, was not in the Portalian tradition. But both Santa

[2] *The Times*, 27 August 1880.
[3] Abdón Cifuentes, *Memorias* (2 vols., Santiago, 1936), I, 182–5.

María and Balmaceda were men of exceptionally strong will, absolutely determined to maintain presidential prerogatives according to the written constitution, and both saw the presidency as the dynamic motor of the whole machine. The very change in style from Pinto to Santa María, which Balmaceda was to underline when he came to power in 1886, seemed to the opposition parties not only a change of personality but also one of power, for where Pinto had yielded, Santa María and Balmaceda would fight. Thus the opposition came to confuse a well-founded theory of the limitations of presidential power with mere objections to its exercise by the strong men who wielded it. Furthermore, into an already complex constitutional and political equation there had been injected the unprecedented, unknown quantity of nitrate wealth, and the thorny question of how government should spend it.

THE NITRATE INDUSTRY AFTER THE WAR OF THE PACIFIC

With the end of the War of the Pacific and the accession to Chile of the nitrate regions of the north, the government was faced with a fundamental question of how to re-constitute the ownership of the industry and tap for Chile's benefit this unique natural resource. It was a complex question, first, because the tide of war sweeping across the nitrate regions had dislocated operations in an industry which, already in the late 1870s, had been plagued by uncertainty. That uncertainty had been created by the Peruvian government's abortive attempt in 1875 to assume a form of state control whereby the nitrate grounds and *oficinas* (refineries), hitherto in private hands, national and foreign, were placed under government ownership through the issue of interest-bearing bonds, made payable to bearer and redeemable eventually by the Peruvian government when it could raise sufficient funds. These bonds were, in effect, the title-deeds in 1879 to the then privately owned nitrate fields and factories (excluding hitherto unexploited fields which had not yet been alienated), easily transferable to third parties. But Peru's international credit had long been exhausted, and no loan to redeem the bonds was ever forthcoming. In consequence, their face value began to fluctuate, and when war came and Chilean successes made a Chilean victory most likely the price of bonds plummeted. That Chile would exact large territorial concessions from Peru and Bolivia was obvious to all involved, but no one knew what line her government would adopt towards nitrate interests in general and foreign interests in particular.

More than this, however, a large number of Peru's unsatisfied creditors abroad had long claimed that Peruvian government loans had been mortgaged on her nitrate province of Tarapacá, and had already sought the diplomatic support of their governments to underline the claim. If Chile, then, acquired Peruvian territory, would Chile also assume the debts allegedly secured on it? And if not, what price the future of an industry bedevilled by such imponderables? In such circumstances, many bondholders panicked and unloaded their holdings at ridiculously low prices to bolder speculators who were prepared to take risks against uncertainty. Pre-eminent among these was an English engineer, John Thomas North, who was already engaged in a number of enterprises in Peruvian Tarapacá, where he had lived and worked for over twenty years.

Already in 1880, the Chilean government had begun to debate the question, setting up a deliberative and advisory commission which was followed by another in 1881. Their reports, eschewing the Peruvian model of state intervention in nitrates, recommended the return of the industry to private hands and, to secure the stake of the Chilean government, export taxes on nitrate shipments. Since the nitrate certificates issued by the Peruvian government were the only legal titles to private ownership, those who then held them were in effect recognized as the legitimate claimants to the nitrate properties; thus it was that John Thomas North, 'the Nitrate King', and other non-Chileans secured a large share of the industry at comparatively small cost, realizing huge profits not only on the real value of the properties but also by their subsequent sale to joint stock companies which they floated on the London Stock Exchange in the 1880s.

Thus British interests, which in 1875 had held a minority position in the nitrate industry, came by 1890 to control 70 per cent (by value). The British takeover has been the subject of controversy ever since, largely because it was held that the Chilean government of the day lost a golden opportunity to acquire the industry for the state and thus permitted the major source of government income for the next 40 years to be subject to foreign control. Some historians, indeed, have gone much further than this, asserting that there was collusion between Chilean decision makers and the more efficient and more rapacious foreigners with their greater reserves of capital and higher technology, to whom they abandoned Chilean nitrate interests.[4] Recent research, however, has strongly

[4] Notably, Hernán Ramírez Necochea, *Balmaceda y la contrarrevolución de 1891* (2nd edn., Santiago, 1969).

modified such views. While there is no doubt of the free-enterprise philosophy of Chilean leaders of the day, it is now clear that other considerations of Chile's national interests predominated in their decisions. First, in returning the nitrate industry to private hands, the Chilean government effectively split foreign interests, and made it impossible for their governments to intervene without appearing to favour one set of nationals against another. Thus, whereas the nitrate entrepreneurs were delighted, the Peruvian bondholders were dismayed, and it took the latter twenty years to reach a satisfactory settlement. Secondly, by returning the responsibility for production, shipment, marketing and sale to private interests, while imposing taxes on the export of nitrate, the Chilean government acquired an immediate and major source of revenue without involving itself in such matters. Finally, on the subject of the antebellum Chilean stake in Peruvian Tarapacá, it is now clear that this had already been totally undermined by Peruvian policy in the 1870s, and that while Chilean interests may well have held a more substantial holding than British in 1875, it was more between 1875 and 1879 rather than in the 1880s that this holding was drastically reduced.

For the Chilean government nitrate revenues were a bonanza, and the rapid expansion of the industry and trade in the 1880s provided it with an income which enabled it both to pursue ambitious programmes of public expenditure and also to avoid the need to modernize the internal system of taxation, a path which, had it wished to pursue it, would have brought government into confrontation with the vested interests which dominated Chile's political, economic and social life. As it was, from a contribution of 5.52 per cent of ordinary government revenue in 1880, export taxes on nitrate and iodine (a by-product) rose to 33.77 per cent in 1885 and to 52.06 per cent in 1890.[5] But such windfall wealth was a mixed blessing. The international nitrate market was highly unstable owing to the primary use of the product as a fertilizer and thus subject to the vagaries of climate and agriculture, often of sudden impact and unpredictable behaviour. Overproduction of nitrate, saturating the world market, meant falling prices for producers and distributors alike. Consequently, they looked to restore the balance between supply and demand, and the usual device was a producers' combination to limit output on a quata system until that occurred; moreover, by the late 1880s the majority of those producers and traders were foreigners, less

5 R. Hernández Cornejo, *El salitre* (Valparaiso, 1930), 177.

sensitive to Chile's national needs than to the interests of their stockholders and their own fortunes. For the Chilean government, increasingly dependent on nitrate revenues as a major proportion of its budget, the unpredictability of the market meant uncertainty of income and planning alike, and producers' combinations the surest way to reduce revenue at a stroke. The fact that control of the industry seemed in the 1880s to be passing increasingly into fewer, and dubious, hands was also worrying. North and his partners, for example, purchased the bonds of the Pampa Lagunas *oficina* during the War of the Pacific for £110,000 and provided a further £140,000 for installations, later floating two London companies at a total capitalization of £2,122,000 to exploit the property. The comparable expansion of his enterprises – and his ambitions – in Tarapacá in the 1880s excited not only the admiration of often misguided investors in London but also the apprehension of native Chileans, not least those whose policies were predicated on a sure and steady income from nitrates. The conflict inherent in this situation came to a head in the presidency of Balmaceda, precisely at the moment when internal Chilean issues, political and constitutional, which had been long in gestation, came to a head to create a national crisis as severe as any in the Republic's history.

THE PRESIDENCY OF BALMACEDA, 1886–91

Though few Chilean presidents can have assumed office under more auspicious circumstances than José Manuel Balmaceda, the political environment of his accession was one of acrimony and conflict. To the out-going president, Santa María, he was the natural successor, and the full weight of the governmental machine was thrown behind his election as the official Liberal candidate, not only to the disgust of the clerical conservative opposition – to whom Balmaceda's name was anathema – but also to the chagrin of some broadly liberal groups for whom, by now, the practice of electoral intervention had become odious. Though such groups recognized Balmaceda's outstanding record as a public servant – member of Congress since 1870, minister to Argentina in the critical year of 1879, foreign minister in 1881, and minister of the interior from 1882 to 1885 – and admired his powers of oratory and persuasion, they objected to the system which would put him in power, and joined moderate conservatives and a small group of opposition Radicals to support a former minister, José F. Vergara. These liberals, the *sueltos* or 'free-lance' party, led by a well-known intellectual, historian and educationalist, Miguel Luís Amunátegui, provided the first evidence that the formerly united Liberal party, the party of government, was now losing its cohesion. But the juggernaut of electoral intervention rolled on unimpeded; Vergara withdrew his candidacy before the final votes were counted, and Balmaceda assumed office on 18 September 1886.

In the five years since Balmaceda first entered government Chile had changed considerably. Not only had the northern frontier been pushed forward some 600 miles by the War of the Pacific, but the process of bringing under more effective central control the still-independent Indian lands south of the river Bío-Bío and the even more remote territory of Magallanes had also begun to gather momentum. Military force and colonization had been the twin arms of successive Chilean governments in this process in the 30 years since the 1850s, but the movement was intermittent and halting, for between the Bío-Bío and the river Toltén further south lay Araucania, inhabited by the fiercely independent Mapuche Indians whose sporadic revolts and more frequent depredations inhibited the progress of settlement. The last general rising of the Mapuche took place in 1880–2: its suppression, largely by Chilean forces transferred from the victorious desert campaigns in the north, was the final nail in the coffin of Indian independence, stubbornly maintained since the beginnings of the Spanish conquest. The building of forts at Temuco and Villarica in 1881 and 1883 respectively in the heart of Indian territory was the physical expression of that fact, and the establishment in 1882 of a General Colonization Agency in Europe to recruit immigrants to southern Chile was, in effect, the deliberate resumption of policies initiated three decades before, but not since then effectively pursued. In 1883 the first German colonists arrived in Talcahuano, to be followed in succeeding years by an influx of European immigrants to Chile averaging over 1,000 a year throughout the 1880s.

Similarly, in Magallanes and Tierra del Fuego, the decade 1875–85 was a period of considerable geographical exploration followed by economic exploitation, particularly in sheep-farming. When in 1876 the governor of the territory, Diego Dublé Almeida, visited the Falkland Islands and brought back sheep (although failing to persuade islanders to accompany them), thus laying the foundations of the region's major activity, Magallanes and Tierra del Fuego ceased to be merely remote appendages of the Chilean Republic, claimed largely for their strategic significance, but became regions of distinctive character and economic importance. Again, European immigration played a decisive part. Though numbers were small – the total population of southern Chile in 1885 was little over 2,000 – quality was more important than quantity alone, and English and Scottish sheep farmers in particular played a major role.

As for the chief prize of the War of the Pacific, the nitrate regions, Balmaceda became president precisely when the nitrate industry was entering its most dynamic phase of expansion. Between 1884 and 1886, at a time when the world market was saturated, the first producers' combination to restrict output had been set up, but this had collapsed, and rising world demand again saw the *oficinas* of Tarapacá in full activity. At the same time, John Thomas North and his associates were launching a large number of new companies on the London Stock Exchange. Tarapacá and to a lesser extent Antofagasta began to boom: ports such as Iquique and Pisagua experienced a growth not only in exports of nitrate but also in imports of foodstuffs, machinery and equipment to sustain the highly artificial mining communities in the Atacama desert, dependent for almost every commodity on the outside world. The short-lived postwar boom in nitrates had already drawn into the regional economy a sizeable migrating population – labourers from central Chile, Bolivia and Peru, engineers and mechanics from Europe, notably Great Britain, and traders, bankers and businessmen; the population of Antofagasta rose from 5,384 in 1875 to 21,213 ten years later, that of Tarapacá as a whole from 38,255 to 45,086 in the same period, and Iquique, the chief nitrate port of Tarapacá, saw an increase from about 9,200 to almost 16,000.

The regional manifestations of economic change in Chile during the 1880s were part of a national process of growth and development which also had social and cultural implications. Its principal motors were the linked factors of population growth and increasing urbanization. Between 1875 and 1885, the total population of Chile increased from 2,075,971 to 2,497,797, but much more striking was the structure of the population. Whereas in 1875 the rural population was almost double the urban – 1,350,426 to 725,545 – by 1885 the proportions had changed dramatically: rural population had increased slowly to 1,456,032, but urban population had risen by one quarter to 1,041,765.[6] The most

---

[6] Population figures in Latin America are notoriously unreliable. Those for Chile, however, are more reliable than most, owing to the existence of a competent, if not entirely perfect, National Statistical Office from 1843, and the work of Markos J. Mamalakis, 'Historical statistics of Chile', (4 vols., Yale University, mimeo), later published in four volumes (Westport, Conn., 1978–83). The figures cited here are from vol. II of the mimeographed version, Table IIA1fl.

striking increases of urban over rural population occurred precisely in the nitrate regions, where population was concentrated more and more in ports of shipment and importation, the nitrate *oficinas* being scattered throughout Antofagasta and Tarapacá, and in those provinces where incipient industrialization had proceeded furthest – Santiago, Valparaíso and Concepción. In Santiago province, while the urban population rose in 1875–85 from about 186,000 to 228,000, the rural population fell strikingly, from 180,000 to 102,000.

The migration of sizeable numbers of rural labourers, who were not attached to specific plots of land as *inquilinos* were, for example, had long been a characteristic feature of Chilean history, not least because of the country's peculiar shape: migrants moved north and south with the seasons of the agricultural year and the production cycle of crops. But, from mid-century, population was increasingly drawn out of the countryside into urban environments and occupations with the development of northern mining, the extraction of coal around Arauco, Coronel and Lebú, the building of railways, and the development of the larger towns with their food and drink processing factories, tanneries, furniture stores, textiles and other basic consumer industries. The years spanning the War of the Pacific saw an accentuation of this movement as industrialization spread, and before the war itself many believed that Chile ought to industrialize more rather than be totally dependent in her export trade on primary products of the land and the mine. Attempts in the 1870s to organize manufacturers as pressure groups, however, came to little. But in 1883, significantly after the spurt in industrialization which the War of the Pacific stimulated, the Sociedad de Fomento Fabril (SFF) was founded, with government encouragement and subventions precisely for this purpose. The SFF has been described by a historian of Chilean industrialization as 'in part pressure group, regulator of internal industrial conflicts, technical service organization and social club'; it represented 'the institutionalization of Chile's industrial sector into a cohesive nucleus that was large enough to effectively maintain industrial objectives before public opinion and to serve as a direct link with the government'.[7] Nothing symbolized better than the SFF the process of change in the Chilean economy which, however slow and imperceptible at first, gathered momentum, entailing in the process social diversification and the emergence of new political forces. But, while the Chile

---

[7] Henry Kirsch, *Industrial development in a traditional society: the conflict of entrepreneurship and modernization in Chile* (Gainesville, 1977), 42.

which Balmaceda inherited was indeed a Chile in transition, the crisis which was shortly to shake the old constitutional order to its foundations came not from outside the traditional power structure but from within.

Balmaceda assumed office intending to reconcile the diverse liberal groups and, at the same time, to placate the conservatives. Among his first acts was the resumption of relations with the Holy See and the appointment of an agreed candidate as Archbishop of Santiago: Mariano Casanova, a distinguished theologian and a personal friend of the president. It was Casanova who was to take the lead in the establishment in 1888 of the Catholic University of Chile, the country's first private university. Balmaceda's first ministry, composed of representatives of the Liberal and National parties, was a conciliatory one, and Balmaceda quickly gave proof of his aim to avoid the bitter political struggles of the past: municipal elections in Santiago towards the close of 1886 were entirely free of governmental interference, and the defeat of government candidates was offset by the gain of goodwill which resulted from its neutrality.

Such olive branches to calm the political scene were intended to create broad support for Balmaceda's basic internal policy, in fact a continuation of Santa María's programme but one which, with massive revenue flowing in from nitrate duties, could now be greatly enlarged. There was to be heavy public spending on major construction projects such as railways and docks, and in social investment, particularly education, colonization and municipal buildings. Additional expenditure was also allocated to the strengthening of Chile's military capabilities, both defensive and offensive, through port fortifications, new ships of the line, and adequate barracks and military schools – understandable proposals from a Chilean statesman who had been so long at the centre of the conduct of foreign policy, and now, as president and commander-in-chief of the armed forces, was responsible for national security.

Balmaceda's was an ambitious programme, and it was pursued energetically. A new ministry of industry and public works was created in 1887, and within a year was assigned more than one-fifth of the national budget, while the ministry of education took one-seventh. By 1890, in budgetary estimates for an expenditure of $67,069,808, over $21,000,000 was allocated to the ministry of public works and some $6,628,000 to education. Government intentions which these figures represented were translated into action: from a school enrolment of some 79,000 in 1886, the number rose to 150,000 by 1890; railway construction was pushed ahead, assisted in the south by the bridging of the Bío-Bío, Chile's widest river; the great dry dock at Talcahuano was completed and a canal was built along Santiago's own river, the Mapocho. Foreign immigration was encouraged with government assistance: between 1886 and 1890 almost 24,000 Europeans settled in Chile, not only as farmers on the forest frontier but also as skilled artisans in the growing cities. New hospitals, prisons, government offices and town halls were erected.

Such a programme had many implications, however. First, it was predicated on continuing high government income from nitrate exports, and these could not be guaranteed with an unstable world market. Secondly, it created in the hands of government an immense tool of patronage in the shape of governmental posts and the award of contracts, as well as labour forces dependent on them. Thirdly, while it satisfied some, it also disappointed many, whose aspirations, personal or public, had been aroused by the programme itself. A new town hall or school in one community might be an object of pride for its citizens, but it would be one of envy for less favoured neighbours. And there were wider issues surrounding that key question of politics and government: the allocation of resources. Since Chile's adoption of paper money in the crisis of 1878, a growing body of opinion regarded the return to a metallic currency standard as the major national economic objective, though this was still a minority view among politicians, many of whom as wealthy landowners benefited appreciably from the regime of inconvertible paper. To the *oreros*, however, increasingly apprehensive about the quantity of paper in circulation, the liberal rights of emission under loose banking laws, fluctuating exchange rates and high public expenditure, the new nitrate wealth represented quite literally a golden opportunity to retire paper money and return to what they regarded as financial respectability, and the postponement of reform a national disaster. For Balmaceda, however, his programme was paramount, and he so identified himself with what he saw as the national interest that opposition to any part of it came to appear as factious and selfish, if not unpatriotic.

The honeymoon period in national politics which followed Balmaceda's accession lasted little more than a year. By 1888 the various liberal groups which formed the government were already competing with one another for office. In March the former policy of conciliation collapsed. Under pressure from his strongest supporters, the Liberales de Gobierno, Balmaceda allowed intervention in the Congressional elections and, inevitably triumphant, it was they, and they alone, who came to occupy ministerial posts. The National party – small in numbers but strong in talent, and controlling a large part of the Chilean press – were particularly incensed: henceforth, their loyalty to the strong executive, a characteristic feature of the party since the days of Manuel Montt (president from 1851 to 1861), could no longer be taken for granted. As for Balmaceda, increasingly obsessed with his own programme, the problem of allocating favours grew commensurately with the growth of revenue. The public works programme enhanced the value of techno-crats and administrators, but people naturally talented in this direction were not necessarily to be found amongst the traditional oligarchy. Hence there came into being 'new men', such as José Miguel Valdés Carrera, minister of industry and public works, or Hermógenes Pérez de Arce, superintendent of railways, technocrats to their fingertips, who believed strongly in what they were doing and in the work their chief had given them. It was not difficult in such circumstances for an opposition already convinced of Balmaceda's obsessive egotism to believe that the president of the republic was building a personal following which would blindly follow his every whim.

Opposition suspicions of Balmaceda's intentions hardened in 1889, when speculation was already rife about likely successors to the presidency in 1891. Among his intimates, Enrique Salvador Sanfuentes, a wealthy hacendado but not prominent politically, was widely tipped as Balmaceda's candidate, since he had risen to favour quite rapidly in 1888, becoming minister of hacienda in April and minister of public works in October. In March 1889, as the key minister in Balmaceda's Cabinet – since he was responsible for the central part of the president's programme – Sanfuentes accompanied Balmaceda to the nitrate regions, the first visit by a Chilean head of state to those recently incorporated parts of the Republic. Balmaceda's well-publicized tour of the northern provinces was for a variety of motives. Apart from its propaganda value for a president politically harassed in Santiago and seeking provincial support, there was a basic economic reason why a visit to the nitrate regions was then opportune. By 1889, the activities of John Thomas North in Tarapacá had grown apace; apart from his nitrate companies, his new Bank of Tarapacá and London, his control of Iquique's water supply through the Tarapacá Waterworks Company, his Nitrates Provisions Supply Company and, above all, his Nitrate Railways Company, owning the line which linked most important *oficinas* to the ports, all betokened an attempt at monopoly which in the eyes of many represented a threat to all other interests in the province, and not least those of the government, whose revenues now turned so precariously on nitrate taxes.

In one respect confrontation had already arrived. In 1886, Santa María's government had cancelled the privileges of the Nitrate Railways Company on the grounds of non-fulfilment of contract, and Balmaceda had inherited a complex legal question as the Company challenged the government in the courts, alleging constitutional impropriety in the annulment of its privileges. Moreover, its lawyers included a number of prominent Chilean politicians opposed to Balmaceda, notably Julio Zegers, North's chief lawyer in Chile and hitherto a life-long liberal associate of Balmaceda's, but by 1889 leader of a liberal group, the *convencionalistas*, whose primary purpose was to eliminate personalism in the choice of future presidents by having an agreed candidate selected at a convention of all liberal groups. Zegers's position as North's lawyer coupled with his political stance, however, led Balmaceda and his coadjutors to see him as a traitor to the national interest which they felt they represented.

Balmaceda's speeches on his northern tour were well-tailored to local pride and expectations but he also took the opportunity to make major pronouncements on the nitrate industry, particularly at Iquique, the capital of Tarapacá. Here he referred to the dangers of a foreign monopoly of the industry, suggested that his government would look more closely at the possibility of encouraging greater Chilean participation in it, and generally persuaded a number of commentators that he intended to pursue a more nationalistic line with regard to foreign interests. Yet he also went out of his way to reassure existing interests that Chile needed their capital and enterprise. It was, in fact, a speech which could mean all things to all men but, with a new nitrate combination possibly in the offing, it was a shrewd tactic to induce hesitancy among the predominantly foreign producers, the chief of whom, John Thomas North, was himself paying a visit to Chile at that time. On Balmaceda's return south the two men met on three separate occasions, but nothing dramatic emerged from the encounters. The Chilean government pursued its attack on North's railway monopoly in Tarapacá, skilfully exploiting other British interests which were equally opposed to it, but it did little to undermine the predominant foreign interest in the nitrate industry as a whole.

It is possible that political preoccupations, which grew in intensity in

1889 and 1890, caused Balmaceda to shelve any plans he might have had: it is equally possible, and on the existing evidence far more likely, that such plans were limited in scope and vague in intention, and Balmaceda's posthumous reputation as an economic nationalist was greatly exaggerated. His primary concern with regard to nitrates had nothing to do with foreign predominance but everything to do with monopolistic control, a danger he thought North represented. That apprehension was shared by other foreign (notably British) producers. At the same time, with falling prices of nitrate in an over-stocked world market, *all* producers, foreign and Chilean alike, had little option in 1890 but to form a common front to restore equilibrium, and hence profitability, through a combination to restrict output and equalize supply and demand. Here Balmaceda had no allies in the nitrate industry and little power to affect events.

As it was, however, the political/constitutional crisis predominated. Balmaceda's return from the north in March 1889 was followed immediately by a cabinet crisis, arising from the resignation of Sanfuentes as a gesture to refute the notion that he was Balmaceda's choice for president in 1891, and the delay in choosing a successor from the various liberal groups. Within less than two months, an adverse vote in the Senate overthrew the ministry, and Balmaceda had to try again. This time he approached the National party but could not accept their terms. Balmaceda's reaction was to form a ministry of those noted for antipathy to the Nationals, who moved into clear opposition. Thus Balmaceda lost his automatic majority in the Senate and his majority in the Chamber of Deputies fell to ten. A further crisis in October made matters worse: Balmaceda apparently agreed not to influence the forthcoming presidential election in return for opposition support in Congress, and appointed a 'neutral' ministry, but within a month that ministry also resigned since, it said, it could not trust the president.

Whilst the parties jostled for ministerial office in 1889, crucial constitutional issues had crystallized, and the opposition increasingly took its stand on them. Whereas, when Balmaceda assumed office, the one significant professed aim of opposition was freedom of elections, by 1890 that had been enlarged to include the independence of the parties from the president and the subordination of the executive to the legislature. The latter demand was best expressed in a constitutional system, like true parliamentary government, where no ministry or cabinet survives without majority support in Congress or Parliament. In Chile, under the constitution of 1833, and despite subsequent modifications reducing the powers of the executive, ministers were only accountable to the president, who made and unmade them himself. On this issue, the constitution was unequivocal. On the other hand, no president, however persuasive or preponderant, could ignore the fact that to Congress was entrusted by that same constitution the right to accept or reject essential legislation, and particularly approval of the budget and the size of the armed forces: these legislative powers were the principal leverage which Congress had over unco-operative presidents, though they had been weakened (in fact but not in law) by executive interference in elections and the establishment thereby of pliant legislatures. Now, however, the progressive alienation of former supporters by Balmaceda's character and policies had effectively nullified that strength, unless the president were prepared to confront Congressional opinion, insist that ministers were accountable to him and to him alone, and demonstrate that the insistence by Congress on its rights could be blunted by buying off or forcing out, by whatever means, what Balmaceda regarded as factious opposition.

Balmaceda seemed prepared to do this. In his next ministry, he appointed as minister of industry and public works José Miguel Valdés Carrera, the best-known protagonist of the claims of Sanfuentes, the alleged 'official' candidate for the presidency in 1891. It was this act which led Julio Zegers and the *convencionalistas* to withdraw their support from government, thus finally depriving Balmaceda of his majority in Congress. Balmaceda then closed Congress and chose a new ministry, including Valdés Carrera, and the first six months of 1890 were marked by opposition attacks on Balmaceda, through the press they controlled and at public meetings, and by government reactions, including the founding of two new newspapers to put its case. Quite contrary to precedent, Balmaceda called no extraordinary session of Congress in this period, and the battle there could not be resumed until the ordinary session was convoked on 1 June, as the constitution insisted. Congress opened with a dignified speech from Balmaceda, proposing constitutional reforms, but opposition motions of censure on the new ministry were carried by large majorities in both Houses. This was followed on 12 June by a motion from Julio Zegers in the Chamber of Deputies to postpone all discussion of the law authorizing the collection of taxes until the president appointed a ministry enjoying the confidence of Congress, a motion which also secured large support. Since Balmaceda stood firm on his prerogatives, and Congress was adamant about its rights, complete impasse obtained, and no business beyond recrimination was transacted. To one foreign observer, indeed, the president was 'losing his hold on the country' and, he thought, 'it is doubtful how far His Excellency could command the services of the troops against Congress'.[8] The troops, however, were shortly to be employed elsewhere.

With government apparently paralysed at the centre, dramatic events took place at the periphery of Chilean territory. Early in July, the longshoremen of Iquique in Tarapacá went on strike, demanding among other things payment in national currency rather than in *fichas*, the employing companies' wage tokens which could only be exchanged in company stores. They were joined by mule-cart drivers, casual labourers and, soon, by nitrate workers themselves, and indiscriminate looting of warehouses and shops began. Despite immediate calls from the harassed employers for government assistance to put down the disturbances, Balmaceda took no action beyond urging employers to come to terms with the strikers. The stony refusal of the employers even to discuss terms turned some miners into saboteurs, and machinery was wrecked at a number of *oficinas*, that of San Donato – owned by prominent partners of John Thomas North – being totally destroyed. At this juncture the government intervened: troops were sent north to engage in bloody battles with the strikers, and wholesale repression of their unions took place. But the strike wave had spread throughout the nitrate provinces and it was almost a month before order was finally restored. It cost Balmaceda dear. His initial inactivity enraged property owners and alarmed the oligarchy, while his final decision to send in troops completely alienated the miners who, in less than a year, were themselves to be troops in the battles against him. Yet the strikes of 1890, the first major social conflict in Chilean history, were also a portent. They had their origins in harsh working and living conditions on the nitrate *pampa* and in the exploitation of labour, unrepresented in the political system of Chile. It is true that, in the late 1880s, new but still insignificant political forces emerged in Santiago, primarily the Democratic party formed in 1887 as an offshoot of the Radicals, and composed of politicians such as Malaquías Concha who believed that more attention should be paid to working-class interests. But it was in the north, in the nitrate deserts, that the real origins of working-class militancy were found, where future

[8] Kennedy, the British Minister, to Salisbury, Santiago, 21 June 1890, no. 47, Diplomatic. FO 16/259.

labour conflicts had their sharpest expression, and where, in time, pioneer organizers emerged to fashion genuine political movements to represent working-class demands.

Though the origins of the labour unrest of mid 1890 were inherent in local conditions, the disturbances were not unrelated to the general political situation and the tension growing throughout Chile as the constitutional crisis remained unresolved. Throughout the winter of 1890 neither president nor Congress would yield: Balmaceda refused to change the ministry to meet Congressional wishes, and Congress continued to refuse to discuss presidential bills, while promoting a number of its own. Personal attacks on both sides appeared in the press; a public meeting of some 8,000 in Santiago in July called on the president to give way, but Balmaceda replied that he would fight to the bitter end. On 24 July, Zegers called in Congress for the impeachment of the ministry and a declaration of Balmaceda's unfitness to continue in office, as a result of which Balmaceda, according to his strict constitutional right, declared Congress closed. Further mediation between government and opposition proved fruitless; from then to the end of the year, the situation deteriorated. Congress not only refused to pass essential legislation, notably the estimates for 1891 and the law governing the size of the armed forces, but also spent its time discussing and censuring the crimes and follies – as it saw them – of the Balmaceda administration. For his part, Balmaceda, by now persuaded that accommodation was impossible, had begun to purge the army of elements whose loyalty might be suspect. The crucial date was 1 January 1891, the deadline in the constitution for the passage of the bills governing the budget and the armed forces. If they were not passed by that date, Balmaceda would have to act unconstitutionally or yield to Congressional demands for a ministry it could trust. The majority in Congress now had little doubt that Balmaceda would fight, and set up a *junta* to resist him, seeking the support of senior officers in the army and navy towards the end of December. While the idol of the army, General Manuel Baquedano, declined to give his support, the navy chief, Admiral Jorge Montt, agreed to support Congress. On 1 January 1891, when Balmaceda declared in a justificatory manifesto the essential laws to be still in force, he set in motion the wheels of Congressional revolt. A week later in defiance of Balmaceda's orders almost the entire Chilean fleet, with a large number of congressmen on board, left Valparaíso for the north of

Chile, to begin a civil war which would last eight months, take over 10,000 lives, and destroy in the process the Portalian system of authoritarian, presidential government.

The war itself was a very strange affair. Assisted by previous purges and immediate wage increases for the army, Balmaceda largely retained its loyalty. The fleet, however, supported Congress and, in February, seized the northern nitrate province of Tarapacá, setting up a rival government at Iquique. Since Balmaceda lacked the means to transport troops north and tackle the congressional forces there, and since Congress lacked an army to attack Balmaceda in central Chile, both sides were obliged to stand off from critical combat until one had secured decisive superiority in arms. The Atacama desert lay between them. In effect, the war was transferred abroad as both sides sought in America and Europe the armaments each required – Balmaceda warships, Congress ground munitions – diplomatic support and the sympathy of international opinion. In all three, the Congressionalists proved more successful. Meanwhile, however, though largely passive, the combatants were not idle in Chile itself. In the north, the Congressionalists recruited and trained an army from the nitrate workers; a crucial factor was the presence of a Prussian military adviser, Emil Körner, recruited by Balmaceda's government in 1886 to modernize and professionalize Chile's army; he quarrelled with the president over service priorities and threw his considerable expertise behind Congressional efforts to create an army. Balmaceda's government, controlling the central valley, was faced with a sullen populace and sporadic sabotage, and did not hesitate to use repressive measures, alienating in the process a good part of neutral opinion in the constitutional conflict. Balmaceda was in a difficult position: deprived of nitrate revenues which, from February 1891, flowed into Congressional coffers; lacking the means to prosecute the war and, indeed, apply a blockade of Congressional ports except on paper by decrees which foreign governments refused to accept; and progressively losing the propaganda war abroad, he could only wait hopefully for the arrival at Valparaíso of two ironclads, then being built in France, and trust that his agents could frustrate Congressional efforts to secure weapons for its new army. That race he lost: at the end of August, the Congressional fleet, loaded with well-drilled, well-armed men, landed near Valparaíso, and in the bloody battles of Concón and Placilla overwhelmed the Balmacedist army, equipped with antiquated weapons and quite inadequately led. The triumph of Congress was complete. Balmaceda took refuge in the Argentine Embassy in Santiago, to write his reflections on the tragedy which had overwhelmed him, to take farewell of his family and friends in a number of poignant letters and, on 19 September, almost exactly five years after his assumption of the presidency, to take his own life with a pistol shot to the head. His adherents, high and low, suffered for their association with exile, loss of property, exclusion from public office and, in some few cases, death. The civil war, like the political struggle which preceded it, had been long and bitter, and its results were to have far-reaching effects on subsequent Chilean history.

One controversy surrounding it concerns the significance of the role played by foreign nitrate interests in the genesis and development of the prewar crisis and in the eventual triumph of the revolution against Balmaceda. According to one view, Balmaceda had a concrete national policy for the nitrate industry, entailing less foreign interest and indeed control, as part of his general programme of enlarging the role of the state in the national economy. It is argued, however, that the threat to foreign interests, personified by North, was paralleled by a threat to the dominant internal oligarchy through the growth of the power of the state, and so both combined to overthrow Balmaceda. Circumstantially, there seems a strong *prima facie* case for this view, and a number of contemporary observers shared it. More recent research, however, has strongly modified and even completely undermined this interpretation. First, it reveals that Balmaceda had nothing like the clearly constructed policy on state intervention in the economy – including nitrates – ascribed to him; secondly, it demonstrates that the principal agents used by Balmaceda to challenge North's attempts at monopoly control were other foreign interests, with which the president was prepared to deal; and, thirdly, it shows that the nitrate policy pursued by Balmaceda's successors, far from being favourable to foreign interests as was previously argued, was in fact much more positively against them than that of the martyr-president. These revisionist views have also restored – for the time being at least, and until fresh evidence is available – more traditional interpretations of the struggle between Balmaceda and his Congress as primarily constitutional and political, rather than economic, with the personal factor also playing a major part. Events succeeding the civil war of 1891 in the internal history of Chile indirectly support the primacy of politics as the determinants of action, as Balmaceda himself testified.

THE 'PARLIAMENTARY REPUBLIC', 1891–1920

In the 'political testament' which Balmaceda wrote shortly before he committed suicide, he prophesied that:

although parliamentary government now exists in Chile . . . there will be neither electoral liberty, nor clearly defined parties, nor peace among the circles of Congress. Victory and the submission of the vanquished will produce a temporary calm; but soon the old divisions will be re-born, with the same bitter situations and moral difficulties for the Chief of State . . . The parliamentary regimen has triumphed on the battle-field, but this victory will not endure . . .[9]

He was to be proved right, though partly for the wrong reasons.

The Congressional victory in 1891 marked a significant divide in Chilean political and constitutional history. Having rebelled in order to assert the predominance of the legislative power over the executive, the triumphant but heterogeneous parties in Congress now controlled Chile. Whereas previously the strong powers of the president and, above all, his capacity to intervene in elections to secure a pliant Congress had, to some extent at least, acted as a barrier to factionalism, those restraints were now removed completely, though the process of dismantling them had begun long before. Temporary unity had been forged in Congress through a common object of aversion – Balmaceda and the system of which he was the last representative – but, that removed, unity went with it, as Balmaceda had foreseen. The legislature now not only predominated over the executive; it controlled it, for the latter lacked the ultimate weapon it must possess in a parliamentary system when faced with obstruction or defeat in the legislature, namely the power to dissolve it and to seek, through new elections, a fresh mandate. A bogus form of parliamentary government was thus imposed on Chile, and personal factors played their part in this transformation. Admiral Jorge Montt had personified the revolution in uniform as commander-in-chief of a rebellious and ultimately successful naval and military force. Not a politician, he was the perfect compromise candidate of the victorious parties for the presidency from 1891 to 1896: conciliatory, mild-mannered, not forceful, and very conscious of the principles of anti-authoritarianism for which the revolution had been fought.

His intention [he told the British Minister] was to allow the Ministers great independence of action in their several Departments of State; to abstain from

---

[9] Translated from J. Bañados Espinosa, *Balmaceda, su gobierno y la revolución de 1891* (2 vols., Paris, 1894), II, 653–4.

interference with the legislative bodies, and to confine the Intendentes and Governors of provinces to their administrative duties, forbidding interference in political matters and especially on elections.[10]

This respect for a parliamentary system eliminated the need to rewrite the existing constitution, and Montt's acceptance of the president's new role – very far removed from the conceptions of most of his predecessors – meant that modifications in practice became far more significant than changes in form. Chief among these was the elimination of direct government interference in elections, the major aim of opposition to Balmaceda: the surrender of that executive weapon after 1891 meant that presidents henceforth had to rely on alliances and coalitions in a multi-party Congress. Thus, automatic majorities for government initiatives no longer existed, and government was the prey of shifting allegiances and temporary alliances. Indecisive rule and hesitant compromise were the inevitable results.

Two other factors compounded this situation. First was a new law of Communal Autonomy approved by Congress in 1892. Long championed by conservatives in particular, and notably by M. J. Irarrázaval, seduced by the example of Switzerland, and also by some liberal groups, who saw in wider powers for local authorities a further barrier to executive influence, this measure sought to free municipalities from central control. But the effective use of more local autonomy depended on adequate financial resources, and for these the legislature did not provide. Hence, central control was replaced by the equally dubious power of the locally powerful, and government agents in elections gave way to the power of the local purse as hacendados and other men of means substituted bribery and corruption for central interference, so that by the end of the century seats in Congress had come to be quoted at a fixed price.

Secondly, and a total paradox, were the character and policies of Balmaceda's heirs, those politicians who had supported him during his life and sought to vindicate his views when he was dead. The persecution of Balmacedists, rigorous while it lasted in 1891 and 1892, abated with the passage of a selective amnesty in 1893, to be followed in 1894 by a more comprehensive measure. Thus by 1894 the prominent supporters of Balmaceda such as Enrique Sanfuentes and Julio Bañados Espinosa had fully returned to public life. The *convivencia chilena*, in this period the

[10] Kennedy to Salisbury, Santiago, 7 November 1891. No. 121. Diplomatic. FO 16/266.

social solidarity of the Chilean upper class, had clearly reasserted itself, and the Balmacedists, or Liberal Democrats as they called themselves, returned to politics as if it were business as usual. But not quite: the Balmacedists were, after all, the legatees of Balmaceda's political testament, which had forecast factional politics in the absence of a firm executive. Their task was to make the martyr's words come true. Thus, in order to expose the weakness of a febrile executive, they, more than others, combined with other groups for purely factional advantage, and left them for the same reason: their role in making the parliamentary republic unworkable was a salient feature of the period.

The political panorama at the end of Montt's presidency in 1896 was a mosaic: at one extreme stood the clerical Conservatives, led by the patriarchal Manuel José Irrarázaval, still the party of the church and determined to defend its remaining prerogatives, notably in Catholic education; at the other, the Radical party, distinguished above all by its virulent anti-clericalism and determination to make the state the universal provider of education, but schizophrenic in its attitude to class, undetermined as to whether it was exclusively the mouthpiece of the middle and professional classes or whether it should embrace the lower orders as well. Between these two genuinely ideological groupings lay the amorphous mass of liberals – the Liberal party which had broken with Balmaceda over electoral intervention but now had no ideology to bind it together beyond vague beliefs in electoral liberty, freedom of the press and of association, broad anti-clericalism and the supremacy of the Legislature over the Executive; the National party, increasingly minuscule, and distinguished chiefly by its adherence to impersonal government and, paradoxically, by its loyalty to the tradition and name of the family of Montt; and, finally, the Balmacedists or Liberal Democrats, with a common veneration for the defunct president and a loose attachment to what they believed he had stood for, but united primarily as a disruptive force, determined to extract from the new system the maximum advantage as a large minority party with the power to prevent any other grouping from governing effectively. Chile's multi-party system, antedating the revolution of 1891, but exacerbated by it, was thus distinguished by lack of ideological cohesion making for a genuine party system on the one hand, and by social solidarity across party lines on the other. Opportunism was the creed of most, and only the Conservatives and Radicals had a distinctive ideology, revolving around clerical issues, apart from the still tiny Democratic party, which, alone, actively sought artisan as well as middle-class support. That party, however, only appeared in the Chamber of Deputies in 1894 and in the Senate in 1912, so paramount was the control of the traditional oligarchy and so narrowly restricted the franchise. Chile's political and constitutional form allowed the oligarchy to play a political game, in which different groups jostled for power and influence against a national background of economic and social change which went unreflected in political representation. The 30 years between 1890 and 1920 were thus characterized by increasing social tension as economic changes increased the working class and the urban population, and pressures for social reform – in housing, education, health and working conditions – could not be expressed through political channels. The alternative outlet – sporadic violent protest – was generally met with repression, and the undoubted merits of Chile's parliamentary system, a civilized method of conducting political business on strictly constitutional lines for the small minority which took part in it, were found increasingly incongruent for a national society in a state of rapid transition.

Between 1895 and 1920, Chile's population increased from some 2,688,000 to 3,715,000; in the same period, the growth of urban and rural population more or less kept pace with one another, at around 500,000 each nationally. But the larger cities – Santiago, Valparaíso and Concepción – grew disproportionately faster than the rural population of their respective provinces. Thus Santiago's population increased from some 300,000 to 547,000, while the rural population of the province only rose from 116,000 to 139,000; the corresponding figures for Valparaíso show an urban increase from 173,000 to 266,000, and a rural rise from 48,000 to only 55,000, while those of Concepción are no less striking, with a rise in urban population from 95,000 to 142,000, and in rural, from 94,000 to 105,000.

The growth of the major cities reflected, in part, a national development in which nitrate income acted as a motor to the whole economy. Long before nitrate revenues made their impact, Chile was well on the way to becoming an integrated national economic unit as, from the mid nineteenth century, improvements in communications, and not least railways, knit the country together, enabling the government's writ to run in regions (such as the Norte Chico and the southern forest zone) hitherto largely peripheral to central government concerns. The expansion of wheat cultivation in the south, of viticulture in the central valley, of industrial enterprises in low-technology consumer goods such

as textiles, ceramics and building materials – all well under way by the
War of the Pacific – reflected that fact, and a degree of industrial
concentration had already occurred. These processes, however, were
much accelerated by the rise of nitrates in the national economy. The
consumer demands of the northern *oficinas* and ports galvanized other
parts of the structure, and the ripple effect of nitrate's growth on
southern agriculture, for example, was noteworthy: 'Beans, maize,
lentils, peas, dried fruit & c.', wrote the British Consul-General in 1887,
'are seldom exported; the Chilean producer finding for these, as for his
flour and barley, a better market in the northern desert region . . . In the
same way, the large and increasing wine and beer production of the south
finds a market in the north . . .'[11] Moreover, the growth of government
revenue derived from nitrate also had its impact. Despite cyclical falls in
government income caused by the erratic nature of the nitrate trade, the
overall trend of rising income from nitrate export taxes between 1891
and 1920 enabled successive governments to push ahead with
infrastructural projects which employed sizeable labour forces and
created consumer demands, as well as enlarging a government bureaucracy based on Santiago which itself expanded rapidly. Railways are a
classic example. By 1893, the great strategic central line built by the
government had reached Temuco, 690 kilometres away to the south,
and by 1913 Puerto Montt, a further 400 kilometres, while to the north,
by 1914 the central line reached Pintados at the southern end of the
province of Tarapacá, linking there with the privately owned nitrate
railways system. Also in 1914 the Arica–La Paz (Bolivia) line, 438
kilometres long, built by Chile in part-fulfilment of her treaty with
Bolivia of 1904, was opened to traffic, to join the existing British-owned
line from Antofagasta to La Paz. The Transandine line linking Santiago
with Buenos Aires, which was under construction from the 1880s and a
major feat of highland engineering, was also open by 1910, while the
growth of transverse feeder lines from the central trunk along the length
of Chile's heartland – many of them privately owned – proceeded apace
in these years. By 1914, Chile possessed 8,638 kilometres of railways,
5,584 kilometres (over 60 per cent) of which were state-owned,
compared with less than 50 per cent of the entire national network only
seven years before.

The employment such construction created, and the rising permanent

[11] Newman to Salisbury, Valparaiso, August 1887. Report on the Trade and Commerce of Chile for
the Year 1886 (London, 1888), *Parliamentary Papers*, c, 3.

railway labour force whose absolute number is difficult to quantify, were probably considerable, and they were a factor in rural migration. So was increasing industrialization. The parliamentary period saw a sizeable expansion of Chilean industry in terms of both the growth of establishments and their variety, and of the labour force to operate them. The food and drink processing industry, cement works, ceramics, sugar refining, clothing; leather products, wood and paper, chemicals, foundries, machine-shops and metalworking establishments all expanded considerably in the period, and largely in private hands. Much of the technology was imported; many of the entrepreneurs were foreign-born, and a good deal of capital came from outside Chile. Nevertheless, by 1914 Chile possessed an increasingly important manufacturing industry, catering primarily for national needs but with some of the larger firms holding export markets in neighbouring countries.

Government stimulation of economic activity in the parliamentary period was not, of course, fuelled entirely by revenues from taxes on nitrate exports, nor income derived from imposts on imports and exports in general, nor from taxation. A sizeable proportion of necessary funds came from foreign loans. Between 1885 and 1914, indeed, over £50 million was borrowed abroad, of which more than 60 per cent was spent on public works, including railways. But Chile's possession of nitrates, coupled with her distinguished reputation as a prompt payer of debts – even during 1891 that record was maintained – gave her high standing in international finance, and loans were easy enough to float on reasonable terms. The modernization of her major cities – Santiago and Valparaíso particularly – through the growth of transport facilities, improved lighting, sanitary improvements and impressive public buildings, owed much to this source. So did educational improvement. For, despite the instability of cabinets, government and administration went on, providing a continuing stimulus to the expansion of public services, of which education was one. Educational development is reflected in growing literacy: in 1885, it was estimated that 28.9 per cent of Chile's population was literate, but by 1910 the proportion was over 50 per cent, though heavily concentrated in the growing cities.

The parliamentary period in Chilean history, 1891 to 1920, was thus a paradox. It was a period of rapid social and economic change, but one of political impasse. It saw considerable urban improvement combined with rural stagnation, so far as the lives of its peasantry were concerned. Socially and occupationally, it was an era of transformation; while the traditional oligarchy, drawing to itself by the social magnet of acceptability 'new men' in banking, commerce, industry and the professions, and from all parts of the Republic, continued its dominance of public life, new groups had emerged – managers, bureaucrats and teachers – and new classes of urban workers, nitrate miners, the lower ranks of the public service, and the petty functionaries of all kinds of enterprises. Moreover, while the economy developed and some social services improved, others did not. The rapid expansion of the cities was marked by a disparity of housing between the urban opulence of the rich and the squalid slum settlements of the poor. A North American visitor to Santiago in 1900 wrote, 'I have been in Santiago houses which have upwards of fifty rooms, and which are furnished as expensively as some of the palaces of Europe',[12] but the *conventillos* in the working-class suburbs presented a different picture. These were one or two storey buildings, housing whole families in a single room; 'beds were often used around the clock, warmed during the day by night shift workers, then left for those returning in the evenings'. But if the cheek-by-jowl contrasts of housing in the great cities between rich and poor was great, that between urban and rural environments was even greater. 'The homes of the rotos [workers] are little better than our pig-pens', wrote our North American visitor of peasant houses in the central valley.[13] Health disparities were even greater: while the Santiago aristocrat might consult physicians in Paris or London for persistent ailments, the poor of Chile died. The overall infant mortality rate (deaths per 1,000 of live births) between 1890 and 1915 was 293,[14] but it fell disproportionately on the poor. And in education, while the overall advance was not insignificant, again the urban areas profited, the rural not at all.

It was these immense differences which created the social question in Chile during the parliamentary period, and which eventually raised the question of the capacity of the constitutional and political mechanism to cope with it. The nitrate riots of 1890 had been a portent of things to come. The first two decades of the twentieth century saw a worsening of social conflict, deriving from particular causes but occasioned by a general situation. Affecting all classes, but the poor more than most, was the steady depreciation of the Chilean peso and the incidence of inflation.

[12] Frank G. Carpenter, *South America, social, industrial and political* (New York, 1900), 218.
[13] *Ibid.*, 239.
[14] Markos J. Mamalakis, *Historical statistics of Chile*, vol. II, *Demography and labor force* (Westport, Conn., 1980), 40. This figure has been calculated from Professor Mamalakis's basic data.

The average annual increase in the cost of living was 5 per cent between 1890 and 1900, 8 per cent between 1900 and 1910, and 6 per cent between 1910 and 1920, modest rates by today's standards, but exacerbated in their effects in the Chile of the period by the impact of inconvertibility of paper money, which enabled producers and exporters to make their profits in international currencies whose values fluctuated little, while paying their labourers in paper which continually depreciated in real value. Price stability in Chile had been elusive since 1878, and was destined to remain so for another hundred years. An attempt to restore it between 1895 and 1898 when Chile temporarily returned to the gold standard failed, largely because the circumstances for conversion were most unpropitious – 1895–8 was the trough of the downturn in world commodity prices which had begun in the 1870s, and also a war scare arose with Argentina which caused the government to divert expenditure to emergency arms purchases. The defeat in 1898 of the *oreros* confirmed the monetary system as one of inconvertible paper, the internal value of which consistently fell. Not surprisingly, therefore, the workers reacted.

In 1903, the port workers of Valparaíso went on strike for higher wages and shorter hours; blacklegging led to riots, and when troops sent from Santiago restored order it was at the cost of 32 killed and 84 wounded. In 1905, when the imposition of import duties on cattle from Argentina in the interests of domestic breeders drove prices up, disturbances in Santiago went on for a week until suppressed at the cost of 60 dead and 300 wounded. This *semana roja* ('red week') was followed in 1906 by a serious strike in Antofagasta, when the British-owned nitrate and railway company refused an increase in wages and an extended midday meal break, and a year later a massive strike was bloodily suppressed at the nitrate port of Iquique, the dead being counted in hundreds. The violent expression of social protest had its counterparts in organizational resistance to labour exploitation and intellectual questioning of 'the system'.

The key figure in the growth of the organized labour movement was Luis Emilio Recabarren (1876–1924), born into a modest family in Valparaíso and a printer by trade. An early and prominent member of the Democratic party, which he joined in 1894, he found his true vocation in 1903 when invited to found and operate a newspaper for the workers' mutual benefit association (*mancomunal*) of the northern nitrate port of Tocopilla. *El Trabajo* was only the first of many workers' organs he was to create and edit. He was elected deputy for Antofagasta in 1906, but Congress refused to let him take his seat. After a period of exile in Argentina and Europe – where unproven statements say he met Lenin – he returned to Chile in 1908, broke with the Democratic party in 1911 and founded the Partido Obrero Socialista in 1912. The POS, which by 1915 had a number of branches in the nitrate north, Santiago and Punta Arenas, was held together by Recabarren's personality and energy. From his nitrate base in Tarapacá, this by now national figure created party newspapers, often of ephemeral existence but of permanent impact, and thereby recruited a small but dedicated band of followers and an imperceptibly growing force for radical social change in Chile. In 1915, the POS held its first national Congress and began to elaborate its institutional structure and to radicalize the existing trade union organizations.

Those organizations had diverse origins and a chequered history. As the Chilean working class grew, and notably the non-agrarian sector, they were faced with a lack of understanding of their living and working conditions by either those who employed them or those who, in theory at least, represented them in Congress. Lacking a true constitutional or political channel to express their grievances, workers in particular localities and specific occupations began to form a variety of self-help organizations from the late nineteenth century. Indeed, the first embryonic unions in Chile had appeared by 1870: mutualist societies among urban artisans, co-operative bodies set up to provide elementary social security for their members and some educational opportunity through self-help classes and publications, but emphasizing co-operation, not confrontation, with employers and government. For these reasons, their lack of interest in changing the social order dramatically, seeking instead a respectable place in it, was quite acceptable to governments and to the Catholic church which, following the papal encyclical *De Rerum Novarum* of 1891 (the first *ex-cathedra* pronouncement to touch seriously on social and economic questions), had patronized a philanthropic approach to the lower orders in Chile. Radically different in outlook and purpose were the so-called 'resistance societies', formed under the influence of anarchist and socialist ideas imported – sometimes by migrant workers and union leaders – from Argentina. Generally industry-based, their immediate objectives were practical, related to working conditions, and their members were united in working together, as port workers, for example, transport operatives, printers, and so on. They were forerunners of later forms of Chilean trade unionism, not least in their political outlook, but their importance declined as anarchism lost its appeal with the passage of time. Finally, and most importantly, there were the 'brotherhoods' or *mancomunales*, most strikingly emergent in the nitrate north where the mining population was ever increasing until 1914, due essentially to internal migration from the south. Socially, the *mancomunales* were highly homogeneous and, though the nitrate population was scattered – each *oficina* was virtually an independent state – there was high mobility of labour as miners moved in search of better conditions from place to place. Hence their organizations were territorial rather than occupational by nature and their concerns were living and working conditions, as well as social improvements such as education. But the *mancomunales* were distinguished above all by their class nature, and it was the *mancomunales* which, though always repressed, mounted the series of increasingly large and more serious strikes in the nitrate regions during the parliamentary period.

Yet the first proper unions arose among crafts and trades in the major cities under anarchist influence in the first decade of the twentieth century. Such were the Carpenters' and Shoemakers' Federations and, most significant of all, the Railway Workers who, a year after a wage cut by the State Railways in 1908, founded their first federation. Though essentially a mutualist body in origin, this organization named itself in 1911 the Grand Workers' Federation of Chile, and in 1917, now named the Chilean Workers' Federation (Federación Obrera Chilena, FOCH), it opened its ranks to all workers. It attracted considerable support, particularly in the north and south of Chile, less so in Santiago and Valparaíso where anarchist influence was still strong. As time went by, as social tensions increased and economic circumstances deteriorated, particularly in the period immediately after the first world war, so the FOCH became more militant. Indeed, the incidence of strikes in Chile and the number of workers involved increased dramatically in those years, rising from 16 strikes involving some 18,000 workers in 1916, to 105 strikes involving 50,000 workers in 1920.[15]

In these developments, Recabarren played a leading role, though he sought to keep his POS and the FOCH as distinct, though co-ordinated, entities. In 1919, FOCH was re-organized: thereafter, its grass-roots expression was the union which affiliated all workers in a particular area,

---

[15] Brian Loveman, *Chile: the legacy of Hispanic capitalism* (New York, 1979), 227.

irrespective of their jobs, and its expressed aims – like those of the POS – included the abolition of the capitalist system. The progressive radicalization of the FOCH, the impact of the Russian Revolution of 1917 and the growth of an international Communist movement deepened the division in Chilean labour between those, like the Democratic party, who, having played no small part in the organization of the working class, sought to operate within the existing political system, and those, like Recabarren, who had come by the 1920s to reject it. In 1921, the split came: the FOCH decided to affiliate itself to the Moscow-led Red International of Labour Unions and, a year later, the POS became the Chilean Communist party, but both lost members in consequence. It has been estimated that the membership of FOCH alone fell by 50 per cent, from some 60,000 to 30,000 between 1921 and 1922. By then, the parliamentary republic had reached a point of crisis.

Throughout the period of the parliamentary republic political parties and personalities, apart from the Democratic party (which never obtained the support of more than a small minority of what was, in any event, a very limited electorate), jockeyed for power, usually brief in a system of politics characterized by shifting alliances and coalitions. Indeed, for much of the period, opposing groupings were usually referred to as the Alliance and the Coalition, the distinguishing feature being the presence of the Radical party in the former and the Conservative party in the latter. Both were strong minority parties, with deep roots in antagonistic ideologies on questions of state and church, and they provided the only ideological cohesion – not always all that strong – within the two bodies. The rest – Liberals, Liberal Democrats, Nationals, and so on – oscillated in their support of different presidential candidates and their subsequent support of their ministries. The aristocratic game they played, a kind of political 'musical chairs', was obsessive as a way of conducting national business, but not even the most conservative politician was unaware that Chile was changing and that the growth of extra-Congressional forces was gathering momentum. Responses, however, varied. Throughout the period, a number of intellectuals as well as novelists like Luis Orrego Luco and Baldomero Lillo critically dissected the ills affecting the Republic, and in particular the 'social question', that widening division between rich and poor which the political system was apparently unable to resist. Essayists, such as Alejandro Venegas writing as J. Valdés Canje, and Francisco Encina in *Nuestra inferioridad económica* (1912), attacked the country's inability to develop a useful and wider educational system and to establish a truly national economy rather than one subject to the vagaries of international commodity markets or foreign entrepreneurs. While some progress was made in the field of labour and social welfare legislation – a law for workers' housing in 1906, obligatory Sunday rest for workers in 1907, laws for insurance against industrial accidents in 1917 – these were mere palliatives, so rapidly had the working class grown and so limited had been the attempt to tackle fundamental social questions. And rural labour still remained unorganized, depressed, with deplorably low living standards.

Chile's rulers in the period had some achievements to their credit. They presided over a growing economy; they had vastly improved the amenities in major cities and, not least, they had kept the country at peace. War scares over boundary disputes in the south with Argentina had erupted frequently in the 1890s, and arms races had resulted, to the detriment of both countries. But common sense prevailed: in 1902, under British arbitration, Chile and Argentina resolved their conflicting territorial claims in the far south, and signed a general treaty of arbitration for future possible disputes. Two years later a definitive treaty of peace with Bolivia ended the uncertain armistice of the War of the Pacific. No progress was made, however, on the resolution of the Tacna–Arica dispute with Peru, a legacy of that same war, despite frequent attempts to resuscitate the provisions of the Treaty of Ancón to settle it. Chile continued to control both territories and, according to persistent and bitter Peruvian complaint, to harass Peruvian residents, import Chilean settlers and thus swing the balance of the population in Chile's favour for such time as a plebiscite might be held. (At the same time, Chilean governments did put a good deal of money into Tacna and Arica, not least in education.) Yet this issue remained a war of words, protracted and bitter though it was throughout the period.

Where the parliamentary leaders stand condemned is in their apparent inability not so much to recognize a society in transition, for most were aware of changes taking place, but to reform their institutions so as to cater for them. Stronger governments in the period – and notably that of Pedro Montt (1906–10) – presided over rapid infrastructural progress, such as extensive railway building; Montt had also to cope with a devastating earthquake in 1906 which all but destroyed Valparaíso, and an economic crisis in 1907–8, fuelled by stock exchange speculation of the most irresponsible kind, yet the leadership he gave the Republic in his short period in office (he died prematurely) was largely stultified by the system he had to operate, resulting in nine ministries in four years, an average life of four months and twenty-one days. His successor, Ramón Barros Luco, aged 75 when he assumed the presidency, had fifteen ministries in five years, four of which lasted less than three weeks. Between 1891 and 1915, no fewer than 60 ministries were formed, with an average life of a little over four months. Ministerial rotation was, of course, highly democratic in form, and strictly parliamentary in practice, as the many parties jostled for power and position. Chile experienced in these years neither dictatorial government nor military intervention in politics, and these were part of a valuable historical tradition which the parliamentary period underlined. But the price was stultification of ministerial initiative, lack of long-term planning and, above all, a certain discontinuity of government business which led presidents to concentrate on immediate and necessary objectives, such as the passage of the budget or the acquisition of arms, but obliged them to neglect more lengthy measures such as social reform. It is not surprising that the strains in the social fabric of Chile were acute by the end of the period. More remarkable, perhaps, was their containment by the system to that date, despite fierce, sporadic and generally bloody confrontations of workers with the forces at the disposal of government. In this respect, continuity of administration contrasted strongly with instability of politics and government, but it was a national asset which was also eroded. As civil servants and officers in the armed forces themselves began to suffer from deteriorating social and economic conditions, their obedience to a system of government long recognized as effete could no longer be taken for granted.

ALESSANDRI, MILITARY INTERVENTION AND IBÁÑEZ

The 'social question' came to a head during and after the first world war. Though never a belligerent, Chile was an immediate casualty of that conflict, so closely integrated was her export economy in a world trading system now dramatically disrupted. Britain and Germany were Chile's two leading trading partners – indeed the former had been so for most of her independent existence; now the two major maritime powers were at war, and their ships were required elsewhere. Within two months of the outbreak, Chilean nitrate exports had fallen by more than half, and the population of the nitrate region fell dramatically as *oficinas* closed and workers returned south. Since nitrates were the motor of the Chilean economy, the dramatic fall in production – of 134 *oficinas* working in July 1914, only 43 remained active by January 1915 – had a negative effect on almost the entire structure. Yet the crisis, though severe, was also short lived. In 1915, nitrate quickly recovered, first because its use in explosives became of great importance to Britain and her allies, and secondly because the closure, through blockade, of traditional major markets such as Germany and Belgium led to neutrals, notably the United States, increasingly a supplier of munitions to the Western allies, taking larger supplies. This was a portent: one major effect of the war was to enable the United States to become Chile's chief trading partner, as Germany was largely eliminated and British interests – particularly in Chile's import trade – were inevitably curtailed. This process was accentuated after the United States entered the war in 1917, and the boom in Chilean export commodities fuelled a resurgence of general economic activity and industrial expansion, part of which – textiles, for example – grew to compensate for the lack of imports from such traditional suppliers as Britain. But, like the depression which preceded it, the boom was comparatively short-lived. The postwar depression was world-wide, but exacerbated in Chile's case by other factors: the fall in demand of nitrate as hostilities ceased, the fact that large stocks had been accumulated in consuming countries, and the impetus in Germany during the war, when natural nitrate could not be obtained, given to synthetic production. That cloud, then no bigger than a man's hand, would grow inexorably as the process spread to other countries, and would eventually destroy the market in natural nitrate. By the beginning of 1919, a large number of *oficinas* had again ceased working, with much of the labour force, as in the past, migrating south in search of work. In a deepening economic crisis, labour agitation grew markedly in 1918 and 1919 with strikes, massive demonstrations (one in Santiago in November was reported to involve 50,000 workers) and inevitably, given the near-panic reaction of the upper classes, confrontations with the police. These were often bloody affairs: in February 1919 a strike in Puerto Natales in Magallanes of virtually all workers involved in sheep-processing industries was viciously put down at a cost of 15 dead, 4 of them soldiers, and 28 seriously injured. In September, the FOCH, whose provincial branch in Magallanes had called the strike at Puerto Natales, staged a general strike in Santiago, while for part of the year the nitrate provinces of Antofagasta and Tarapacá were under virtual martial law, labour leaders being forcibly sent south.

Such was the background of the rise to national prominence of one of the more significant and controversial figures in modern Chilean history, Arturo Alessandri Palma, twice president of the Republic (1920–5, 1932–8). Of nineteenth-century immigrant Italian stock, Alessandri, born in 1868 on a farm in the agricultural province of Linares, had opposed Balmaceda when a student in 1891, had entered Congress in 1897, and had his first, short, ministerial experience a year later. A typical product of the parliamentary period, Alessandri, a Liberal, had spent almost twenty years in Congress before events in 1915 thrust him to the forefront of national life. Adopted as Liberal candidate for a Senate seat for the nitrate province of Tarapacá in elections that year, Alessandri conducted a demagogic campaign in which the passions of his supporters – many of them working class – and of his opponents spilled over into violence, culminating in March in the assassination of a police inspector. Alessandri's candidature was a direct challenge to traditional political bosses who had run the province as though it were a private fief, and he secured 70 per cent of the very limited vote in an election characterized by much corruption on both sides. More significantly for the future, he aroused national attention through his energy and eloquence, and for his vitriolic attacks on the opposition side of an establishment to which, of course, he had himself belonged for two decades. But the 'lion of Tarapacá', as he was called thereafter, had also established himself as a possible future presidential candidate.

The Congressional elections of March 1915 resulted in a majority in the Senate for the Alianza Liberal – Liberals, Radicals and Democrats – and in the Deputies for the Coalición – Conservatives, Liberal Democrats or Balmacedists, and Nationals. Presidential elections followed in June. Juan Luis Sanfuentes, younger brother of Enrique Salvador Sanfuentes whose alleged candidature as the president's nominee in 1890 had been a fundamental factor in the latter's fall, stood for the Coalición; Javier Angel Figueroa Larraín for the Alianza. Sanfuentes won narrowly, partly through his own personality but no less through his command of ready money. Supported by an unstable coalition of heterogeneous parties and opposed in the Senate by an equally fractious alliance, Sanfuentes could only deploy his not inconsiderable talents for political manoeuvre to resolve the impasse of presidential impotence, a time-wasting task and, as it turned out, a fruitless one. The next Congressional elections, in March 1918, gave the Alianza a bigger majority in the Senate and command of the lower chamber as well. But, within the Alianza itself, which did not so much represent as reflect ill-defined aspirations of the middle and working classes, a deep division existed between those such as Alessandri, who had sensed a new national mood, and those whose political horizons were still limited by the narrower struggle for power and patronage within the existing system, from which, of course, they benefited.

The Sanfuentes administration did at least maintain Chilean neutrality during the first world war, despite considerable pressure from the United States after 1917, and there is no doubt that this was in the national interest. But it created complications. Both Peru and Bolivia, where *revanchist* sentiment against Chile was very strong, had followed Washington's advice and broken relations with the Central European powers, largely in the hope of securing support for their respectives cases against Chile after the war. But little came of this: though the war of words, especially over Tacna and Arica, became more vituperative until in 1918 both Chile and Peru withdrew their respective consuls from the other's territory, actual war scares never became reality. The issue remained on ice, though it proved useful to certain Chilean political interests in 1920.

By that time, national attention – in a period of acute postwar economic depression – was increasingly focused on the presidential elections of 1920. Alessandri, having headed the ministry for a mere six months in 1918 only to see his reform programme rejected, had now clearly emerged as the candidate of those forces in the Alianza Liberal believing in change, and he had been working hard to secure that position. Within the alliance, the Radical party was achieving predominance: it had now declared its official condemnation of both the ruling oligarchy and of the capitalist system, but its rise was resented by the Liberal politicians, many of whom, no less alarmed by Alessandri's emergence, withdrew their support. These dissidents joined the Liberal Democrats and the National party, and proclaimed Luis Barros Borgoño as their candidate, Alessandri's official nomination by the other grouping following in April 1920. The Conservatives, recognizing in Alessandri the major threat to their interests and having no suitable candidate of their own, threw in their lot with the lesser evil and supported Barros Borgoño.

The campaign was marked by great personal energy and scathing denunciation of the oligarchy by Alessandri, coupled with promises of a sweeping programme of reform: 'I wish', he said, on his nomination, 'to be a menace to all reactionary spirits, to those who resist all just and necessary reform, for they are the propagandists of confusion and disturbance.'[16] The result was very close. On 25 June, amid unprecedented scenes of public clamour, it was announced that in the electoral college (elections were then indirect on the model of the United States) Alessandri had obtained 179 votes to his opponent's 174. Both sides challenged the result: finally a full Congress passed the issue to a Tribunal of Honour, which on 30 September declared Alessandri elected, by 177 votes to 176. Congress ratified the result by a vote of 87 to 29 early in October, and Alessandri assumed the presidency on 23 December 1920.

In the period between the election and Alessandri's finally assuming the presidency, a peculiar incident had occurred. At a time of great national uncertainty over the election, and with labour agitation reaching a peak in the nitrate regions, the government, through its minister of war, Ladislao Errázuriz, suddenly mobilized the armed forces, alleging that Peruvian and Bolivian troops were massing on the northern frontier for an invasion of Chile. This was complete fabrication, yet throughout July and August a large Chilean army, posted to the north, waited in vain in the desert region for action. While it did so, many of its members were made acutely aware of their lack of material and provisions; of harsh and unhygienic living conditions; of divided commands and inadequate direction. True or not, the notion grew that the army was being used for purely political ends, and Alessandri himself – who in 1919 had had contacts with restive army personnel desirous of reform – did not discourage that view. What became known as 'the war of Don Ladislao' reinforced those opinions strongly critical of Chilean politics and government which had been growing among service officers for some time. As early as 1907, a military league (Liga Militar) had been set up as a secret organization of army officers, discontented with the parliamentary system's inefficiencies and notably those which affected service effectiveness. Five years later, a similar body for the navy was set up, equally clandestine, but no less concerned about professional shortcomings and the system which permitted them. Though these bodies never really surfaced and were, in effect, disbanded, what they represented persisted in the minds of certain service personnel, who

---

[16] *El Presidente Alessandri y su gobierno* (Santiago, 1926), 32. No author or compiler is indicated.

increasingly saw in their own underpaid, ill-provisioned and, so far as promotion was concerned, rigidly hierarchical and immobile chains of command, nothing more than a mirror image of the Republic itself.

Alessandri's presidential programme in 1920 was an elaboration of his ministerial programme of 1918. His first minister of the interior, Pedro Aguirre Cerda (who became president in 1938) was in charge of a programme of social reform and economic measures designed to alleviate the worst effects of the worldwide depression now engulfing Chile. Though Congressional obstruction was soon apparent, the parliamentary battle was overshadowed early in 1921 by a tragic event in the nitrate regions. At the *oficina* of San Gregorio, closed at the end of January by the depression in the nitrate market, a dispute between workers and the police erupted into violence in which 41 died and 80 were injured, of whom 32 subsequently died from their injuries. To conservative opinion, Alessandri bore much of the responsibility for inflaming the masses during his campaign; for the opposite camp, he was equally responsible as head of state, ultimately in charge of law and order. In Santiago, Congressional obstruction of his programme persisted, and the opposition retained control of the Senate in the elections of March 1921, although the Chamber of Deputies fell to the Alianza, the Radicals alone gaining a third of the seats. For the next four years, little was achieved, against a background of mounting economic distress and social unrest.

In 1920 the first national census for 25 years showed that the national population had risen by a million, from 2,695,000 to 3,730,000. Santiago had doubled its population and now had half a million inhabitants. Other cities, although their growth was less dramatic, still grew at a rate quite incommensurate with the capacity of the regional economies to absorb the additional numbers in productive employment. Sixteen cabinets in rapid succession had attempted to govern over a period of four years, during which time the value of the peso had fallen by half and government revenue had slumped. By 1924, the treasury was so exhausted that civil service and armed forces' pay was six months in arrears, as one subsequently important military figure recalled many years later:

We had no certainty of getting bread, meat or vegetables for the troops, nor fodder for the horses. One day, the regiment's accountant informed me that our meat purveyor had not provided supplies because six months had passed since he was last paid . . . We could only dig into our own pockets . . . and managed to raise 100 pesos. Can you imagine that? . . . with 100 pesos to buy meat, we had to feed a regiment of 250.[17]

Public demonstrations in the face of distress increased, and a large number of protest organizations sprang up, mostly in support of Alessandri and in opposition to the obstructionism of the Senate, where the National Union, as the former Coalición was now called, had a majority.

Amid talk of civil war, Alessandri and the opposition looked for compromise, and late in January 1924 reached a short-term accord. In return for Alessandri's promise not to use executive pressure in the Congressional elections due in March, the opposition agreed to a number of procedural changes in Congressional business to speed things up. They also agreed – and the decision was fraught with unexpected consequences – to support a proposal to pay members of Congress a salary, contrary to previous practice. But as in 1890, neither side trusted the other. Alessandri, therefore, decided not only on massive intervention in the Congressional election, but also on the use of the army in that process. 'There is', he said shortly before the election, 'a majority in the Senate which . . . has sought to frustrate the movement which I represent and which, at this moment, is embodied in me . . . I have taken it upon myself to purify the parliamentary benches.'[18] Shortly afterwards, instructions about the election were telegraphed to provincial government officials, and the army was used to 'maintain order', a euphemism to cover its often blatant harassment of the opposition. But the latter was by no means inert, and intimidation and bribery were used freely by both sides. In the event, given the greater power of the governmental machine, the Liberal Alliance underlined its majority in the Deputies and won control of the Senate. It was, however, a pyrrhic victory for Alessandri. For what followed was months of sterile debate in Congress on unimportant issues, in which his own fractious following showed itself no more responsible on national issues than the opposition. The one accord they reached was on the bill for Congressional salaries, which passed from the Deputies to the Senate in June. By that time, however, the impatience of the armed forces had reached its limit, though the expression of their exasperation was by no means uniform.

In the higher echelons of the army, a conspiracy was hatched with

[17] Retired General Bartolomé Blanche, as interviewed by Wilfredo Mayorga, *Ercilla*, 7 July 1965, p. 5.   [18] Alberto Cabrero, *Chile y los chilenos* (Santiago, 1926), 258.

Unionist politicians to overthrow Alessandri through an organization called TEA (Tenacity, Enthusiasm and Abnegation), in which General Luis Altamirano, Inspector-General of the army, was involved. Lower down, a number of middle-ranking officers had been meeting at the Santiago Military Club to discuss their professional grievances and the national situation: prominent among them were Major Marmaduke Grove Vallejo and Major Carlos Ibáñez del Campo. As it happened, it was this group which pre-empted the plans of TEA by direct action, though of a moderate kind, early in September.

As the Congressional salaries bill was being debated in the Senate on 2 September, some 50 junior army officers in the public gallery punctuated the debate with loud applause for those who opposed it, and they repeated this action a day later. When the minister of war, a civilian, asked Captain Luis Pinochet for a list of those present, the latter declared that he was no clerk, but the officers agreed to leave the building if Minister Mora would meet them later, and so they departed, their sabres rattling as they left. 'The rattling of the sabres', as this episode was called, began a process of consultation between government and army which resulted in a request from Alessandri for a list of projects they thought essential, for presentation to Congress: if Congress refused them, the president declared, he would close it down and, with the army, 'make a new Chile'. The list was drawn up by Ibáñez, now emerging as the leader of the junior officers, and his aide, Lieutenant Alejandro Lazo, approved by their colleagues, and presented to Alessandri on 5 September. It was a considerable list of demands: veto of the Congressional salary bill; action on the budget (the subject of interminable wrangling in Congress); legislation on the income tax; new laws on promotion, salaries and pensions for the services; stabilization of the erratic peso; immediate payment of back salaries to all government employees; a labour code and other social laws; and, in addition to the dismissal of three ministers specifically named, the future exclusion of the armed forces from the supervision of elections. Prior to its presentation, Ibáñez had persuaded his colleagues to set up a *junta* as their executive body (the Junta Militar y Naval), and it was this body which met the president. It was not a smooth meeting, Alessandri rejecting the demand for the dismissal of ministers as insubordination, but saying that he would do his best on other matters. Lazo declared: 'we have not come to request, but to demand', and only conciliatory words from the senior officer present persuaded Alessandri not to terminate the meeting. Aguirre Cerda, as chief minister, was sent for and the list re-read; his attempts to discuss it were brusquely interrupted, and the meeting ended with the resignation of war minister Mora – one of the *junta*'s demands – and the latter's agreement to communicate through General Altamirano of the high command.

There is no doubt that Alessandri believed he could use the officers for his own purposes; it is equally clear that, whatever sympathies they had with him about ·Congressional behaviour, they did not trust him, and that they were determined to play not just an active role in the regeneration of Chile but the predominant one. That same afternoon, the cabinet resigned and Alessandri appointed General Altamirano as minister of the interior: Altamirano designated another General, Juan Pablo Bennet, as minister of war and Admiral Francisco Neff as finance minister, thus giving the services strong control of the administration. While some members of the *junta* distrusted Altamirano, an alliance of convenience between the military wings was formed. On 8 September, a day after Alessandri's veto of the salary bill, Congress passed all the *junta*-sponsored legislation in one afternoon, but the *junta* insisted on remaining intact until totally assured that its objectives had really been attained. Alessandri then played his last card: he proffered his resignation as president, but this the *junta* refused, suggesting instead six months' leave of absence abroad which was also approved by Altamirano. Later that same night Alessandri and his family sought refuge in the embassy of the United States, and two days later departed for Argentina, quietly and with no reaction from the people who, four years before, had clamorously installed him in the presidential palace.

Congress was then closed; the civilian members of the ministry resigned, and a governmental *junta* of Altamirano, Bennet and Neff assumed power, with the avowed intention of handing it back to civilians as soon as possible. The other *junta*, however, had other ideas: it rejected above all the notion of restored civilian rule without, first, major constitutional reform to prevent a repetition of what had led to intervention in the first place. And, unlike the new military government, whose representatives were high-ranking officers of considerable social status, the junior officers led by Ibáñez and Grove were acutely aware of Chile's social tensions and they sought social and economic, as well as political, change. The next three months saw a widening of the difference between the two wings of the military movement, against a background of widespread support for the intervention itself. The rift widened progressively from October 1924 to January 1925, as it became increasingly apparent to the *junta militar* that the government was hand-in-glove with right-wing politicians, and quite uninterested in major reforms.

Finally, in January 1925 the critical point arrived. Many prominent *junta* officers were transferred in their commands to areas where they would have little power, and were replaced by men sympathetic to the government. On 16 January, Ladislao Errázuriz, the archetypal conservative to the *junta*'s way of thinking, announced his candidature for the presidency with government support. On 23 January, after careful preparation Grove and Ibáñez sprang a coup, seized the presidential palace, forced the resignation of its incumbent, and installed a new provisional *junta*, headed by the inspector-general of the army. Four days later, he was replaced by a respected civilian, Emilio Bello Codecido, son-in-law of Balmaceda, whose assumption of office was part of the price negotiated with the navy high command, at first ill-disposed towards the coup. A general and an admiral joined Bello Codecido in the ruling *junta*, but its ministry consisted largely of Alessandri supporters, reformists to a man. A telegram to Alessandri in Rome invited his return to resume his presidency, and in March return he did to scenes of massive acclaim.

Throughout these turbulent days and, indeed, since the initial military intervention of September 1924, the key role in the activities of the *junta militar* had been played by Carlos Ibáñez, and it was he who was eventually to emerge as the major force in Chilean government for the next seven years, and, like Alessandri himself, to remain a dominant figure in national life almost until his death in 1960. Despite his long public career, his tenure of the presidency twice (1927–31, and 1952–8), his controversial governments, and the vast volume of literature which has been written about him, Carlos Ibáñez del Campo remains a most enigmatic figure in Chilean history. Nothing in his previous career suggested the role he was to play from 1924. Born in 1877, like Alessandri in the province of Linares, he entered the Military School in Santiago in 1896. He was known to fellow-students as a taciturn, methodical, hardworking cadet, but one who had few intimates. In 1900, after graduation and promotion to first lieutenant, he went with a Chilean military training mission to El Salvador, married a native of the country and, above all, distinguished himself in a conflict with Guatemalan forces in 1906. Thereafter his career was that of a Chilean military man of the middle rank. A consummate horseman, he became commandant of the Santiago Cavalry School in 1921, and was holding that post when the political crisis of 1924 occurred. By then his experience as a soldier had been varied and wide, but it had been a professional career, and he had shown no political ambition. From 1924, however, in circumstances which, in his view, called for patriotism, discipline, order and a clear sense of direction, Ibáñez found his true vocation on the national stage. His characteristics in 1927 were admirably summarized by the British Minister:

He is a man of few words, very reserved, and a keeper of his own counsels; he is poor . . . his house is a model of Spartan simplicity; he is one of the very few men in public life in Chile against whom I have never heard a charge of corruption or venality. I believe that he himself is inspired merely with his desire to serve his country to the best of his ability and his lights . . .[19]

His time, however, had not quite yet arrived.

During his involuntary exile, Alessandri had not been idle. He had spent much time thinking about the constitutional system in Chile. On his triumphant return, with six months to serve before his presidential term expired, he set about the task of its reform in a political climate which the interim government of Bello Codecido had done much to improve. The idea of a constituent assembly to thrash out a new constitution foundered, though Alessandri set up a very large Consultative Commission to deliberate the matter in April. The effective work was done, however, in a subcommittee under his own aegis, which drafted the new constitution to be submitted to a national plebiscite. Yet contrary to all appearances in Santiago, the country was not calm. In May and June, discontent in the nitrate regions erupted in violence, and Alessandri called on the army to quell it. After bloody confrontation the miners surrendered but a massacre took place at the *oficina* of La Coruña, and over 600 lost their lives. The new constitution was submitted to plebiscite on 30 August. It offered voters, who numbered a mere 302,000 out of a total population of more than three million, a choice of total approval, total rejection, or acceptance if it were amended to allow parliamentary government to continue. Only 134,000 voted, of whom 127,000 marked their papers for total acceptance; the Conservatives abstained because they objected to the separation of church and state in the new constitution; the Radicals – the largest and most significant

[19] Hohler to Chamberlain, Santiago, 25 January 1928. Annual Report on Chile for 1927. FO/A 1630/9.

political party – did the same, since they wished the old parliamentary system to continue.

The constitution of 1925 restored strong presidential government to Chile. It provided for direct presidential elections instead of the former indirect system, it allowed the incumbent to serve six years instead of five, although he was not immediately re-eligible, and it created a permanent qualifying tribunal to oversee elections. It separated church and state, with the Archbishop of Santiago, Crescente Errázuriz, acting as a moderating influence on extreme Catholics who opposed it. It limited the delaying powers of Congress on money bills, and included a whole series of important social provisions, including one giving the state the power to limit property ownership if the common good required it. It reversed the practices of the parliamentary period by making ministers accountable to the president rather than Congress, and they could not be members of Congress themselves. Yet it also contained provisions which, as time revealed, weakened its major intentions. Thus, by separating the dates of presidential, Congressional and municipal elections, it subjected the political system to permanent electioneering which thus became the main preoccupation of government to the detriment of business. It allowed for the final selection of the president by an overall majority vote in Congress should no candidate gain a plurality at the polls and, in a multi-party system where this was always likely to occur, this implied bargaining and compromise to validate the popularly successful candidate's election, another weakening factor for a possibly strong executive. Yet it was a reaction – in form at least – to the indecisive years 1891–1925, and it marked the definite expansion of state intervention in national economic affairs. But it still had to be applied.

Alessandri himself had little chance to use his new instrument, for the president was preoccupied in his last months with his minister of war, Carlos Ibáñez. The latter looked with apprehension on the return of civilian rule, and Alessandri, who on his return had surrounded himself with his old sycophantic supporters, made no secret of his animosity towards Ibáñez, the incarnation of the military intervention of 1924. He had been obliged to keep the powerful Ibáñez at the war ministry, but he hoped to ensure that presidential elections late in 1925 would lead to the elimination of the military from politics. Ibáñez, however, had other ideas. Increasingly convinced – and with some reason – that the oligarchy and the politicians had learned little from recent events, he now put himself forward for the presidency, but refused – as precedent demanded – to resign from the war ministry, his lever of power. Fearful of the consequences of a head-on clash, Alessandri resigned in October, handing over power *ad interim* to his opponent of 1920, Luis Barros Borgoño. But at this point, for reasons still obscure, Ibáñez wavered, and agreed to withdraw his candidacy if *all* the political parties could agree on a sole candidate, and this they did, choosing an elderly, amiable but not particularly astute public figure, Emiliano Figueroa Larraín. Only one other candidate stood, a former army doctor and minister of health in the government which preceded Alessandri's return, José Santos Salas, who, with a campaign starting from scratch, without political party backing and without funds, secured 80,000 votes to Figueroa's 184,000. Santos Salas represented the lower classes in that election: he did not win but his candidacy was a sign that the old political parties did not go unchallenged.

For a year and a half, the unhappy Figueroa struggled with a recalcitrant Congress, where the parties reverted to their old political games, and also with his minister of war, Ibáñez, who quietly, efficiently and ruthlessly built up his personal position to the point where in February 1927 he secured the resignation of the minister of the interior and his own appointment to the post. Two months later, President Figueroa resigned; the immediate cause was the demand of Ibáñez for the dismissal of Figueroa's brother as head of the Supreme Court, part of a general clean up he had initiated of the public services which had resulted in widespread arrest and exile. When Figueroa went, Ibáñez took over as president until elections could be held. At the same time, he declared his intention of standing himself, and he had widespread support. Only the now-struggling Communist party – for that body too had suffered from Ibáñez who was a staunch anti-communist – put up a competing candidate, Elías Lafferte, then in exile on the Pacific island of Más Afuera. At the election in May, Lafferte got 4,000 votes; Ibáñez, 127,000 of the 137,000 cast. Thus, elected constitutionally if not exactly properly, Ibáñez assumed the presidency of Chile, with the mission he had been refining since 1924, that of regenerating the Republic in his way.

Ibáñez gave Chile four years of autocratic – some would say repressive – efficient, honest and prosperous government. His ministers were not appointed with any regard to the parties in Congress but were chosen as individuals of technical competence and administrative ability. Indeed, his deliberate intention was to ignore Congress except in so far as it was necessary, under the new constitution, to collaborate in the passage of legislation. And he would brook no opposition there: as the British Minister reported in 1928, Congress had

received Cromwellian treatment at the hands of the President, who has made it clear that the flowers of oratory which grew so luxuriantly in its atmosphere are not to his liking; that they, the two Chambers, are there to give an air of constitutionality to the measures of his government, and that though a little constructive criticism will be accepted, obstruction or opposition . . . will not be tolerated.[20]

Nor was it: left-wing agitators (as Ibáñez saw communists and socialists), professional politicians (whom in the mass he profoundly despised), aristocratic leaders of society – all who opposed his government were treated alike, and faced imprisonment or exile for persistent and troublesome opposition. He restricted freedoms to which Chileans had grown accustomed, such as that of the press which, though not rigorously censored, was certainly watched. He effectively curtailed the privileges of Congress which had degenerated into licence under the previous system; he sought to bring trade unions under central control, and he was tough on their leaders. But such curtailment of rights previously enjoyed, and no less often abused, Ibáñez justified on the grounds of national necessity, as he embarked on an ambitious administrative, economic and social programme.

Credit institutions were set up to encourage both agriculture and industry, and a large programme of public works was inaugurated. A whole stream of educational reforms was initiated – the educational budget doubled between 1925 and 1930 – and they included specific provisions for the growth of technical education, the lack of which had been so lamented by social critics of the parliamentary era. The 'social legislation' of 1924–5 was codified and elaborated; the modern police force of Chile, the *carabineros*, was created through re-organization and better training facilities, and the armed services were professionalized further and well equipped. Many of these reforms had their unattractive side: the new labour laws, for example, were highly paternalistic, but they did recognize for the first time workers' rights to organize, to bargain for improvements with employers, and also, though in a limited way, to strike. There seems little doubt that, with employment rising and the visible signs of economic recovery all around in new works – ports, roads, schools, docks, irrigation projects in the countryside, impressive

[20] *Ibid.*

public buildings in the cities – the Ibáñez era brought the Chilean population as a whole a higher standard of living than ever before, and it is a moot point how many were tacitly prepared to pay the price of losing some freedoms for that result. The politicians, of course, were not: throughout his presidency Ibáñez was plagued by plots and rumours of plots, inspired and often organized by former friends who had now become enemies. But as long as the economy continued to grow, as long as the mass of the people remained content, and as long as the armed forces remained loyal and the political dissidents under control, all would be well.

For three years all did go well. Indices of output volume by sectors – gross domestic product, agricultural production, mining, industrial output and construction – for the period 1914–30 reached their highest peak in 1927–30.[21] Construction advanced spectacularly, as did mining, the latter because of the recovery of nitrates from the depression of the mid 1920s and the rapid growth of large-scale copper mining, exemplified by Chuquicamata in the north and El Teniente in the central valley. Chilean exports, by value in pounds sterling, rose from about £22 million in 1926 to over £34 million in 1929; imports from almost £18 million to £24 million, thus giving Chile a highly favourable balance of trade. At the same time, there was a massive growth in foreign investment: though Ibáñez enacted protective legislation for certain nascent industries, his attitude towards foreign capital for major projects, as in copper mining and public works, was one of liberality, and foreign (notably North American) money poured into Chile during his presidency. United States investment in Chile rose from only $5 million in 1900 to $625 million by 1929, much of it made during the Ibáñez years. Indeed, the predominant position of US interests in large-scale copper mining really derive from this period. The Ibáñez government also contracted large loans abroad to finance the public works programme, and had, in these euphoric years, little difficulty in doing so. Yet budget surpluses were the rule, despite heavy outlays on the new credit institutions, partly because Ibáñez's minister of the treasury for much of the time, Pablo Ramírez, reformed the internal tax structure, producing almost 33 per cent of state revenue from internal taxes in 1929, compared with 24 per cent in 1927.

Ibáñez also had another major achievement to his credit – the

[21] Gabriel Palma, 'Chile, 1914–35: de economía exportadora a sustitutiva de importaciones', *Nueva Historia*, 7 (1982).

definitive solution of the vexatious and long-standing boundary dispute with Peru over the territories of Tacna and Arica. Alessandri had himself, as president, re-opened the issue with Peru, and in 1922 both countries had agreed to submit the question to the arbitration of President Harding of the United States, though what question was to be submitted was not clear. When the parties met in Washington it was only after much tergiversation and legal wrangling that terms were agreed, but in 1925 President Coolidge, Harding's successor, handed down his award: it ordered the plebiscite to be held, and thus broadly upheld the Chilean position, while giving Peru definitive title to a small portion of still-disputed territory, not clearly in Tacna. A commission was established to oversee the plebiscite, and detailed arrangements made to hold it. The political turbulence in Chile in 1925 and further legal wrangles, charges of violence and violence itself punctuated the history of the North American commission until June 1926, when, complete impasse having been reached, it returned home. Before this, however, the United States government had offered both Chile and Peru its good offices as mediator to try to reach an accord by direct negotiations which both sides accepted, though not until July 1928 did the two countries actually resume diplomatic relations, broken off long before. It was Ibáñez who grasped the nettle and, ironically, it was Emiliano Figueroa who went to Peru as ambassador with his proposals in 1928. After much detailed negotiation, but now in an atmosphere of ever-growing cordiality, agreement was reached in 1929; Tacna was returned to Peru; Chile retained Arica. Peru was also to receive US$6 million in compensation for the definitive cession of Arica, and other clauses regulated future border relations and commercial traffic across them. It was a major diplomatic and international initiative, but it did not please all Chileans, and it gave Ibáñez's enemies further ammunition to accuse him not only of internal repression but also of betraying the country.

If economic well-being was the main pillar of Ibáñez's efficient but tough government, the erosion that set in with the advent of the Wall Street crash of 1929 was to undermine it and bring it down. So dependent was Chile in the late 1920s on its primary commodity exports, nitrates and copper, and on foreign loans and investment continuing to fuel public works and development in general, that the dramatic interruption of both exports of commodities and imports of capital, beginning in late 1929 but reaching the peak of its impact in 1930–2, made Chile a primary victim of the world depression which then set in. In 1929, Chilean exports were valued at 2,293 million gold pesos, imports at 1,617 million; she had a favourable balance of trade valued at 676 million gold pesos. By 1930, exports had fallen to 1,326 million gold pesos, and imports to 1,400 million, leaving a deficit of 74 million. By 1932, exports had fallen to 282 million gold pesos by value, and imports to 214 million in the depths of the world depression – Chile's foreign trade, in fact, suffered more than that of any other country in the world. Investment stopped, and by 1932, Chile had to suspend payments on its foreign debt for the first time in over a hundred years.

The social consequences of the dramatic economic downturn appeared first in mining. At the end of December 1929, 91,000 men had been employed in the industry; two years later only 31,000 were in work and, as in previous similar situations, the ripple effects of falling demand for minerals appeared in other sectors of the economy, not least agriculture as markets for foodstuffs declined. As 1930 proceeded, the Santiago newspapers were full of reports of growing unemployment, the abrupt cessation of public works, ministerial studies of economies in administration, cuts in the salaries of government servants, and similar indications of a deepening crisis.

Retrenchment was the government's only possible response, but government revenue fell faster than its capacity to cut expenditure. And, since the economic benefits brought to Chile by the Ibáñez regime were the main justification for acceptance of its political limitations, the disappearance of those gains revived political criticism and censure. The government became increasingly unpopular: press attacks on its handling of the crisis increased and demonstrations began. Ibáñez, struggling against a situation he could not have foreseen, reacted by attempting to silence the critics, and the authoritarian nature of the government was underlined in stricter control of the press, more imprisonments of opposition leaders and physical suppression of demonstrations. By the early months of 1931 the situation had become critical and the central structure of power was beginning to break up.

On 9 July 1931 the finance minister resigned 'for reasons of health', and the whole Cabinet followed, to give Ibáñez a free hand, but it took several days to form a new ministry. The new minister of the interior was Juan Estéban Montero, a Liberal, who, with the finance minister, frankly admitted recent errors, political and economic. Encouraged by such openness, opposition groups took heart: on 19 July, for example, at a meeting of the National Association of Catholic Students, one participant attacked military involvement in government and praised the new ministry. His hopes were premature, as two days later, unable to get its way with Ibáñez, the Cabinet resigned, and another was appointed whose members were closer to the president's way of thinking. Massive street demonstrations began to form in the late afternoon, and grew more boisterous as night came. Amid scenes of mounting tension, the civilian members of the new ministry then resigned, but the next one, formed on 23 July, was faced with street demonstrations in which large numbers were injured and which culminated on 25 July with large-scale violence in different quarters. The medical profession then declared a strike, as did the lawyers, banks closed at midday and commercial activity stopped. The news was then released that the previous day a young medical student, Jaime Pinto Riesco, reading a newspaper with a group of friends, had been shot in cold blood by a policeman who had tried to snatch the paper from him. It was this incident which acted as the final catalyst of resistance to the government: a large number of professional associations (*gremios*) – lawyers, doctors, engineers, dentists, teachers and bank employees – all demanded the restoration of full public liberties, and while public agitation mounted a teacher was also killed by the police. By 26 July it was only too clear that Santiago was on the brink of chaos and, bowing to the inevitable, Ibáñez resigned. The news was met with wild scenes of rejoicing and public demonstrations. As a leading Santiago daily newspaper expressed it: 'What overthrew the dictatorship was not a revolution, but quite the opposite. It was the irresistible force of public opinion which sought to put an end to a revolutionary situation and return to constitutional and legal normality.'[22] The writer might have been less sanguine had he been able to foresee that in the eighteen months after the fall of Ibáñez, Chile would experience no fewer than nine governments in office, ranging from moderate conservative to avowedly socialist, two general strikes, a mutiny in the fleet, and several coups, as the country plunged deeper into economic depression. All that lay in the future as Ibáñez, isolated now more by circumstances than by temperament, went into exile in Argentina. But, like Arturo Alessandri's in 1925, his eclipse in 1931 was temporary. Both would cast long shadows across future Chilean history.

[22] *El Diario Ilustrado*, 24 August 1931.

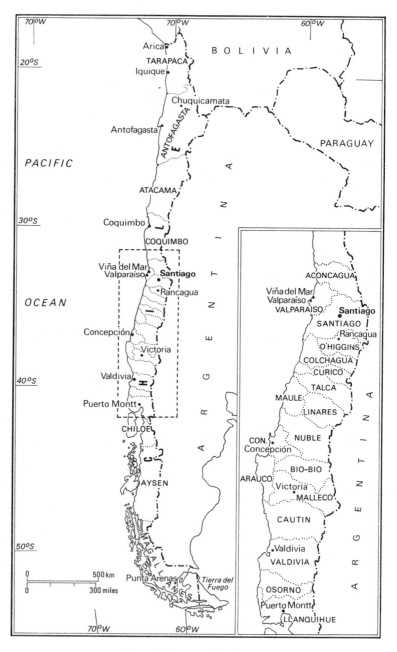

Twentieth-century Chile

3

CHILE, 1930–1958

During the three decades after 1930 – and indeed until the coup which brought down the government of Salvador Allende in 1973 – Chilean politics were unique in Latin America. Only Chile sustained in this period an electoral democracy including major Marxist parties. And for almost fifteen years, between 1938 and 1952, Radical presidents held power through the support, erratic but persistent, of both the Socialists and the Communists, with lasting consequences for the nation's political development. These multi-party governments based on multi-class alliances simultaneously pursued industrial growth and social reform. They failed, however, to attack the roots of Chilean underdevelopment in either the latifundia-dominated rural sector or the United States-dominated external sector.

From the 1930s Chilean reformers criticized the excessive national dependence on the foreign sector that had been highlighted by the world depression. After that crisis, Chile gradually achieved greater self-sufficiency: between the 1920s and the 1940s the estimated share of gross domestic product (GDP) being sold abroad declined from approximately 40 to 20 per cent, as did foreign capital as a proportion of the total capital in Chile.[1] By contrast, direct U.S. investments grew by 80 per cent from 1940 to 1960, the vast majority of this foreign capital going to the mining sector. Overwhelmingly controlled by U.S. companies from the 1920s to the 1960s, copper came to account for some 50 per cent of Chilean exports, copper and nitrates nearly 80 per cent. Not only was the United States the leading foreign investor in Chile; it also regained its position as Chile's premier trading partner after a spurt of German competition in the 1930s. Chile consistently relied on the United States for

[1] Aníbal Pinto Santa Cruz (ed.), *Antecedentes sobre el desarrollo de la economía chilena, 1925–1952* (Santiago, 1954), pp. 78–82.

manufactured consumer goods and, increasingly after the Second World War, for food and capital goods.

The foreign sector contracted as a proportion of GDP as domestic industry expanded. The proportion of the economically active population working in industry climbed from 15 per cent in 1930 to 20 per cent by 1952, while the proportion in agriculture and fishing, which together constituted the largest single employment sector, fell from 39 to 31 per cent. Between 1940 and 1954 industrial production increased 246 per cent and agriculture only 35 per cent. This trend continued into the early 1960s, when urban industry, construction and services came to account for 78 per cent of GDP, compared with 12 per cent for agriculture, fishing and forestry. As a result, manufactured goods shrank from 50 per cent of the value of Chilean imports in 1925 to 16 per cent by 1969. Most of this import-substitution industrialization took the form of consumer items, which accounted for 95 per cent of Chilean manufacturing output at the end of the 1940s. Yet although manufactured consumer products declined as a percentage of imports, Chilean industry remained heavily dependent on foreign raw materials, semi-processed goods, parts, capital and technology; more than one-fourth of the primary products used by domestic industry came from abroad.

The service sector expanded more than any other area of the economy: from 36 per cent of the active population in 1940 to 41 per cent by 1960, mainly thanks to an increase in those engaged in government services from 5 to 8 per cent. The growth of the bureaucracy slowed in the 1950s, but that of public investment did not. Indeed, the public sector already accounted for more than half of domestic investment capital in the 1940s. Measured in 1950 pesos, total government expenditure nearly doubled from 1940 to 1954 and continued to spiral upwards thereafter. Allocations for economic development climbed from less than one-fourth of the total government budget in 1940 to more than one-third by 1954. Although foreshadowed in the 1920s, it was during and after the depression that Chileans began increasingly to look to the state for solutions to the problems of underdevelopment.

Increasing population growth as well as the expansion in manufacturing and services swelled the urban areas (which, among other consequences, enlarged the potential constituency for the Left). The total population rose from 4.3 million in 1930 to 5.9 million in 1950 and 7.4 million in 1960. Low by Latin American standards, Chile's average annual population growth rate of 1.5 per cent (1925–52) did not generate unmanageable pressures for expanded governmental services. However, the rate increased from 1.3 per cent in the 1930s to nearly 1.8 per cent in the 1940s, while per capita income grew at an annual average of only 2 per cent. Thanks to declining mortality, Chile's population growth rate had by the 1960s reached 2.5 per cent – close to the Latin American average. From 1940 to 1952, the urban population increased 42 per cent, the rural barely 3 per cent. According to national censuses, the total population shifted from 49 per cent urban in 1930 to 53 per cent in 1940, 60 per cent in 1952, 68 per cent in 1960 (and more than 70 per cent by the 1970s).

Urbanization accentuated the traditional dominance of central Chile over the peripheral regions. Santiago Province's share of the national population grew from 16 per cent in 1930 to 30 per cent in 1952, after which it continued to account for about one-third. In the same years, its proportion of national industry rose from 37 to 65 per cent. The outlying regions complained about internal colonialism, under which their mining and agricultural reports paid for the growth of manufacturing, bureaucracy and wealth in and around the capital city. While the North and South produced more than 80 per cent of all exports, Santiago and its port of Valparaíso consumed more than 50 per cent of all imports. Benefiting from popular resentment of exploitation by the urban and rural elites of the central region, the Left's presidential candidates – Pedro Aguirre Cerda in 1938, Gabriel González Videla in 1946 and Salvador Allende de Gossens in 1958 – registered their highest percentages of the ballots in the distant northern and southern provinces. In office, however, they tended to ignore regional grievances and, by expanding industry and the state apparatus in the cities of the Centre, further compacted power and prosperity in the country's historic nucleus.

Chile's interlocking upper class, which owned the great estates (*fundos*), factories, mines and banks, probably accounted for less than 10 per cent of the population. Middle-class white-collar employees, small proprietors and merchants, intellectuals and professionals probably accounted for some 15 per cent and the lower class, increasingly urban, comprised around 75 per cent. Most of the population classified as illiterate – nearly 25 per cent – belonged, of course, to the lower strata.

The rural and urban upper class – often interconnected through families and portfolios – dominated oligopolistic means of production in all economic sectors. According to the 1930 census, 7 per cent of all farms surveyed accounted for 81 per cent of the value of rural property. Fewer than six hundred families owned 1 percent of all farms but 62 per cent of all agricultural land, while 82 per cent of owners possessed only 5 per cent of all farm-land. The Radical governments, usually backed by the two Marxist parties, ignored this inequitable distribution of rural property so as not to antagonize *latifundistas* and inflate food prices. An estimate for the 1950s revealed that 10 per cent of landowners still held 86 per cent of the arable land, while 75 per cent of the country's farmers claimed only 5 per cent of the soil. While retaining their control over land and labour, the rural elite endured a shift in government favouritism to the urban sectors as national trade, credit, currency and price policies all encouraged industry and construction.

These rural and urban elites excercised political influence through such institutions as the Sociedad Nacional de Agricultura (SNA) and the Sociedad de Fomento Fabrie (SFF), the latter being the less antagonistic of the two towards the Popular Front. They also exerted influence through the Roman Catholic Church and the armed forces. They operated politically mainly through the Conservative and Liberal parties, whose leaders came from equally aristocratic, landowning backgrounds and therefore set aside their nineteenth-century squabbles over the role of the Church to unite against the threats of populism and socialism; both parties relied heavily on the support of intimidated peasants, especially in the central provinces.

The Chilean upper class and the Right were frequently intractable and repressive, but they distinguished themselves in this era by coping with new contenders for power principally through minimal concessions and co-optation. At least compared with their counterparts in most other Latin American countries, they seldom resorted to overt violence as a means of social control. Gradually and reluctantly they surrendered direct political domination to challengers representing the middle and lower classes. However, the upper class retained significant veto power, imposed firm limits on reform and continued to hold economic privileges and social status. In the 1930s and 1940s, their accommodation of Popular Front politics did not cost them dearly; on the contrary, many elements among the elite made substantial economic gains. By the end of the 1950s, 9 per cent of the active population still received at least 43 per cent of national income.

Serving as brokers between the upper and lower strata, the middle groups were politically strengthened in the inter-war years. Never a tightly knit social sector, the urban middle class asserted itself through professional organizations, student associations, intellectual societies, the secretive Masonic order, the military, the bureaucracy, unions and, above all, reformist parties. It identified most closely with the Radical Party, which enrolled professionals, merchants, teachers, white-collar employees, bureaucrats, small-mine owners and even dissident members of the elite, especially in the outlying provinces. Although numerous Radical leaders issued from the same exclusive social circles as the Conservatives and Liberals, their commitment to industrialization and state interventionism in order to dilute middle- and working-class discontent established tenuous links with the Left. At the same time, the middle sectors played a prominent role in new parties, notably the Partido Socialista (PS) and the Falange. During the 1930s and 1940s, these middle groups, simultaneously seeking support from beneath and acceptance from above, usually rallied the workers as allies in order to gain ground within the system. Through Popular Front politics, the *capas medias* benefited more than the lower classes. As in other regional populist movements, they became increasingly defensive about their gains through the growth of the state, education and industry and decreasingly enthusiastic about coalitions with labour. Always divided – normally between the upper middle class more in tune with the Right and the lower middle class more sympathetic to the Left – some middle-sector Chileans, especially professionals and small businessmen, applauded the Radical government's switch to conservative policies in alignment with the United States at the end of the 1940s.

The majority of workers toiled in the countryside. The term peasants, or *campesinos,* consisted loosely of three main groups of agricultural labourers: *inquilinos,* about half the rural work-force, who were tied to the great estates; *afuerinos,* migratory labourers who suffered even worse poverty than the *inquilinos;* and *minifundistas,* small-property owners. Rural workers, who became more independent of conservative landowners during these years and sometimes protested against their squalid living conditions, still lagged far behind urban labourers as an electoral force for the Left. The Radical governments of the 1940s neglected their plight and impeded their unionization; miners received roughly four times and industrial labourers three times the income of farm workers, who saw their real wages decline by nearly 20 per cent. Similar to patterns elsewhere in the hemisphere, this bargain between urban reformers and rural oligarchs traded peasant poverty and subordination for upper-class toleration of populist participation in national politics.

During the Popular Front years, the minority of politically active workers lived mainly in the cities and mining towns, venting their grievances primarily through trade unions and the Socialist and Communist parties. One reason for their unusually vigorous record of mobilization and militancy was that a relatively slow rate of population growth created a smaller labour surplus than in much of Latin America. Moreover, the strongest proletarian concentrations emerged in the under-populated and isolated mining zones, where labour's struggles against foreign companies controlling a crucial enclave acquired exceptional strategic and national importance. The political dedication and skill of the Marxist parties channelled those protests into the most dynamic radical electoral movement in the hemisphere.

Despite impressive gains, labour remained weak, partly because of the small size of the industrial proletariat. The artisan sector – those in enterprises of four or fewer workers – still accounted for approximately 60 per cent of the industrial labour force in the 1930s, at least 50 per cent in the 1940s and 46 per cent in 1960. The labour code permitted industrial unions only in factories with at least twenty-five workers and prohibited national labour federations, which therefore arose outside the legal framework. Moreover, agricultural unions remained virtually outlawed until the 1960s. Given such restrictions on labour activities, workers had to rely on the interventionist state and thus on political parties for assistance with job security, wages, working conditions and welfare benefits. At the same time, the Popular Front coalitions encouraged unionization. The number of legal unions more than quadrupled between the early 1930s and the early 1940s, but they still represented only a tiny fraction of the workforce, rising from 8 per cent in 1932 to nearly 13 per cent by 1952, and then falling back to 10 per cent in 1959 under less favourable administrations and economic conditions. This slow growth of unionization – and of the electorate – kept stable political institutionalization well ahead of disruptive mobilization.

From 1932 to 1958 Chile's political system remained adaptable and resilient despite fundamental conflicts between traditional parties and avowedly revolutionary groups. Like their adversaries, the Left accepted the inherited rules of the game whereby all political forces joined heterogeneous coalitions in order to win elections and function effectively in Congress. Among and within the parties of the Left – the Socialists and the Communists – battles raged over tactical issues of leadership, coalition partners and details of programmes, but until the Cuban Revolution of 1959 these groups rarely questioned the strategic necessity and desirability of immersion in the multi-party, polyclass electoral and bargaining system. In particular, both Marxist parties muffled their ideological objectives to facilitate alliances with the moderate Radical Party.

The narrow scope of the electorate also reduced the impact of workers and their parties, since only literate males of at least twenty-one years of age could vote in most elections in this period. Women received the franchise first in the municipal elections of 1935, then in the 1949 congressional elections and finally in the 1952 presidential election. Despite leftist support for their suffrage rights, women voted disproportionately against Marxists; together with factionalism and repression, this contributed to the decline of the Left in the late 1940s and early 1950s. The exclusion of women and illiterate men from most elections until the 1950s reduced potential voters to some 20 per cent of the population. Among those eligible to vote, fewer than half usually registered. Out of those inscribed on the electoral rolls, close to 80 per cent normally cast ballots in presidential contests. In other words, between 7 and 9 per cent of the total population voted for presidential candidates from 1932 until the beginning of the rapid expansion of the electorate in 1952. For example, less than 5 per cent of the national population gave Aguirre Cerda's Popular Front its victory in 1938. Until the 1950s populist politics in Chile, in contrast to some other Latin American countries, did not involve any major expansion in electoral participation. Despite the under-representation of workers at the ballot box, the Left, realizing the limits of rightist toleration for political change, made no significant effort to enfranchise illiterates or to employ non-electoral means to power. The durability of Chile's circumscribed political system required extraordinary restraint by both reformers and conservatives.

DEPRESSION AND CRISIS, 1929–32

Chile was more profoundly affected by the world depression than any other country in the Western world. Foreign trade collapsed: by 1932 exports had tumbled to less than 12 per cent and imports to less than 20 per cent of their 1929 value. (The dollar value of exports in 1929 was not reached again until 1955.) Loans from the United States, which had created a veneer of prosperity in the late 1920s, plummeted from 682 million pesos in 1930 to 54 million in 1931 and then to zero in 1933. The heavily indebted government's budget shrank correspondingly, falling by roughly 50 per cent from 1929 to 1932, when it registered a resounding deficit of 189 million pesos.

Of all Chile's economic sectors, the depression struck mining earliest and hardest. The value of copper and nitrate exports dropped 89 per cent from 1927–9 to 1932. As world prices for farm goods plunged and consumption of food from central Chile by the northern mining provinces dwindled, the depression reverberated from the mineral into the agricultural sector. From 1929 to 1931, prices for farm products in Chile fell by nearly 50 per cent. Manufacturing suffered from the depression only belatedly and briefly: the index of industrial production (1927–9 = 100) fell from 117 in 1930 to 87 in 1931 but then rebounded to 99 in 1932, 109 in 1933 and 119 in 1934. Only one foreign and two domestic commercial banks collapsed, but bank reserves, deposits and loans shrank until mid-1931. By 1932, national unemployment had soared to more than 200,000, with nearly half of the jobs lost being in mining, where production dropped by more than 50 per cent. Throughout Chile, real salaries plunged some 40 per cent from 1929 to 1932. The sight of unemployed, hungry and angry workers demonstrating, begging and forming bread lines frightened the upper and middle classes.

As foreign exchange, savings and investment evaporated, landowners and industrialists bemoaned government inaction, although advocating different solutions to the crisis. Chile's dictator, Carlos Ibáñez del Campo, who since coming to power in 1927 had thrived on the mystique of his efficient management of the economy, at first clung to orthodox laissez-faire policies, maintaining the gold standard, pursuing a balanced budget, increasing taxes and pruning expenditure, which alienated bureaucrats, the armed forces and those employed in the public sector. Then in mid-1931, service on the foreign debt was suspended and exchange controls were imposed. These measures, however, did not go far enough to stem the economic collapse. In July, middle-class university students (both Catholics and Marxists), professionals and public employees took their protest to the streets. Such opposition, which could be silenced only with massive armed force, convinced Ibáñez to resign. Whereas in most of Latin America the depression destroyed civilian governments, in Chile it discredited military rule.

A wave of anti-militarism swept the country as a provisional government prepared for presidential elections. In September 1931 a mutiny by radicalized sailors in the northern naval squadron sharpened fears of revolutionary upheaval and further convinced the Chilean elites that a firm civilian administration would be more effective than the armed forces at preserving order. The short-lived naval uprising also persuaded many officers that the military should steer clear of political entanglements.

The fall of Ibáñez had left a vacuum in which traditional political parties splintered and scores of new contenders for power sprang up. Minuscule corporatist movements arose, but it was the Left that was most active as the Communists split decisively into Stalinist and Trotskyist branches and many tiny Socialist parties were established. Broadly speaking, the multi-party political spectrum was recast in 1931–2 into Left (Socialists and Communists), Centre (Radicals and *falangistas*/Christian Democrats) and Right (Liberals and Conservatives). To show solidarity against the threats of both militarism and Socialism, the Right and the Centre – representing most of the upper and middle classes – coalesced behind Juan Esteban Montero Rodríguez, a cautious Radical lawyer closely related to land-owning and banking interests. The convulsions of the depression moved the Conservatives and Liberals to prefer their old political enemies as insulation against more ominous alternatives. At a convention of the Left, disaffected Liberals and Radicals, the artisan-based Democrats and a handful of new Socialist groups nominated the populist paladin of 1920, and president of the republic from 1920 to 1925, Arturo Alessandri Palma, who, once again, campaigned as champion of the middle and working classes. Both the Stalinist and Trotskyist Communist parties also fielded candidates – Elías Lafertte Gaviño and Manuel Hidalgo Plaza, respectively – appealing to labour. Despite the depression, however, there was no evidence of dramatic voter radicalization in the 1931 election. Even after five years in hibernation under Ibáñez, the traditional parties easily dominated the contest: Montero won a landslide victory with 64 per cent of the votes – the first member of the Radical Party to be elected president. Thirty-five per cent went to Alessandri and only 1 per cent to the two Communist candidates combined.

The return of the established ruling groups to power, however, failed to remedy the economic disaster, calm the turmoil among leftists or dispel the general climate of fear. During the Tragic Christmas of 1931, clashes between rioting workers and panicky police and soldiers in two small northern towns ended in a massacre of the protestors. This violence increased elite fears of working-class insurrection and confirmed leftist beliefs that Montero's government represented only the gilded oligarchy. While the plodding president (nicknamed 'Don One-Step') dedicated himself to respecting the constitution and preaching austerity, production and employment sank to new depths.

In June 1932 Air Force Commander Marmaduke Grove Vallejo overthrew Montero and installed a putative Socialist Republic, which the rest
of the armed forces scrapped after only twelve days. Although confused
ideologically and ineffectual administratively, the ephemeral republic gave
birth to the Socialist Party of Chile and anointed the dashing Grove as 'the
Socialist caudillo' for the next decade. For one hundred days after Grove's
ouster, Ibáñez's former ambassador to the United States, Carlos Dávila
Espinoza, a journalist, presided over a second version of a Socialist republic, which came closer to corporatism and state capitalism. The armed
forces then ousted Dávila in September and called new presidential and
congressional elections for October.

While the president of the Supreme Court presided over an interim
government, Alessandri emerged as the leading candidate in the 1932
campaign. As in previous elections, the Radicals and Democrats provided
his official support, but many Liberals and neophyte Socialists also flocked
to his banner. He now appealed to all social strata as a reformist strong
man who could restore order after the exhaustion of other alternatives,
although he attracted more elite elements and fewer workers than in past
contests. He posed as the embodiment of national unity with the slogan
'The triumph of Alessandri is the triumph of civilian rule'.

Recovery of the economy and reconstitution of civilian authority were the
dominant issues at the end of 1932. In response to the depression, most
Chileans looked to state intervention, industrialization and moderate economic nationalism. Many on the Right argued for corporatist state regulation to control dissatisfied workers, while many on the Left pressed for
socialist state action to relieve the suffering masses. Import-substitution
industrialization protected by tariffs and accompanied by modest welfare
measures superficially blended these desires without endangering domestic
or foreign capitalists. Rightists, worried that military disruptions of constitutional order opened the way for leftist uprisings, set up paramilitary
Republican Militias to defend civilian government. Most leaders of the
armed forces, resenting such hostility and fearing divisions within the
ranks, now repudiated open political involvement. To avoid new nemeses
on the Left, many on the Right were willing in 1932 to support their former
adversary Alessandri. The 'Lion of Tarapacá' emerged victorious with 55 per
cent of the vote. Demonstrating that socialism was now an option for the
future, Grove leapt from obscurity to finish second with 18 per cent. In
April 1933 he founded the Socialist Party of Chile – an uneasy populist
grouping of Marxists, Trotskyists, Social Democrats and anarchist/anarcho-

syndicalists bridging the middle and working classes. Trailing the field in the poll were the president of the Conservative Party, Héctor Rodríguez de la Sotta with 14 per cent, the Liberal Enrique Zañartu Prieto with 12 per cent and the Communist Elías Lafertte with a mere 1 per cent. The president-elect had changed little from his days following the First World War as a liberal reformer. But the leftward slide of the electorate found him straddling the middle and therefore acceptable to the Right. Once in office, Alessandri governed with the Conservatives, Liberals, and the right wing of the Radical Party.

The 1932 congressional elections reflected the new tripolar alignment of the electorate, which persisted for four decades thereafter. The vote for the Right – mainly Conservatives and Liberals – which had been 76 per cent in 1912 and 52 per cent in 1925 had fallen to 37 per cent in 1932. Meanwhile, the Radicals and like-minded centrist groups won slightly more than 20 per cent of the 1932 vote, and the Democrats, Socialists, Communists and other leftists secured some 33 per cent. Chile's leading newspaper *El Mercurio* placed the transformed political landscape in the following perspective:

The Socialists of today are the Radicals of yesterday and the Liberals of the day before yesterday. The vanguard has changed in name, but its nature is the same. As much can be said of those stigmatized today as oligarchs; they are the same ones that yesterday were Conservatives and the day before yesterday Ultra-montanes. Between them both is the centre, which today is Radical and yesterday was Liberal. The names change: humanity does not.[2]

From the 1930s to the 1950s, it was the question of which forces the intermediate Radicals would accept as allies that provided the critical variable in Chilean politics.

THE SECOND PRESIDENCY OF ARTURO ALESSANDRI,
1932 – 8

President Alessandri's personal authority, electoral mandate and economic success reinvigorated constitutional legitimacy in Chile after 1932. At his inauguration, he pointedly refused to review the troops, although he stressed that a majority of the officers were honourable and deserved praise. He brought the military under control by rotating commands, retiring conspirators and rewarding loyalists. Scarred by public condemna-

---

[2] *El Mercurio*, 9 June 1932.

tion of their role in the dictatorship and the depression, most of the armed forces preferred to abstain from open politics. They snuffed out an attempted coup in 1933 and remained loyal to the constitution for the next four decades. Alessandri also re-established order by wielding extraordinary executive powers against rightist and leftist agitators. He briefly jailed Grove, and between 1933 and 1936 he used the heavily armed Republican Militia as a bulwark against military or socialist adventurers. As the decade wore on, he increasingly relied on the parties of the Right and the economic elite as the mainstays of his government.

Economic reconstruction benefited from the gradual revival of the international market, especially the demand for copper and, to a lesser extent, nitrates. The inadvertent Keynesianism of the short-lived governments between Ibáñez and Alessandri, which had abandoned the gold standard and fanned inflation, also facilitated recovery. By 1932, the peso had fallen to one-fifth of its 1929 value. Although monetary depreciation slowed under Alessandri, the amount of money in circulation more than doubled from 1933 to 1940. His government tried to strike a balance between growth and stability. Exchange controls, protective tariffs, tax incentives and credit expansion by the Banco Central encouraged urban enterprises to lead Chile out of the depression. Despite the generally orthodox beliefs and policies of Gustavo Ross Santa María, the finance minister, the Alessandri administration favoured manufacturing, construction and mining, which lowered the number of unemployed from nearly 300,000 in 1932 to less than 15,000 in 1935. After slashing public works expenditures during 1932–4, the government launched new construction programs during 1936–8. By 1939, Chilean factories produced nearly 60 per cent more goods than in 1930.

Despite renewed growth, issues of economic nationalism as well as social justice continued to fuel leftist opposition to the Alessandri administration. Although the president dissolved Ibáñez's controversial nitrate cartel, he left majority control of the industry in the hands of the Guggenheims. He also disappointed nationalists by using the government's earnings from nitrates to resume partial service on the burdensome foreign debt (suspended from 1932 to 1935) and by refusing to take over the U.S.-owned and mismanaged Chilean Electric Company. Leftist nationalists – including many left-wing Radicals – urged the government to hold out for further reductions of repayment rates in its protracted negotiations with U.S. bondholders over the 1920s debt, to complain more vociferously about high tariff barriers in the United States and to defend exchange discrimination in favour of import-substitution domestic industries and against U.S. interests eager to extract dollars from Chile. Despite some disagreements and pressure from the emerging Popular Front for more energetic anti-imperialist actions, Alessandri maintained good relations with the United States, even as Great Britain and Europe (especially Germany) recaptured a larger portion of Chilean trade. Both Left and Right shared his desire for expanded commerce with the Colossus of the North, and Roosevelt's Good Neighbor policy improved attitudes towards the United States across the political spectrum. On the other controversial foreign policy issue in the 1930s – the Spanish civil war and the rise of conflict in Europe – Radicals, Socialists and Communists excoriated the administration for adopting a posture of neutrality towards the Spanish conflagration that was biased in favour of Franco. Although most Chileans probably shared the Left's sympathy with the Spanish Loyalists, they also endorsed Alessandri's desire to avoid involvement in European conflicts, in accord with long-standing foreign policy principles.

Critics also attacked Alessandri's conservative programmes as prejudicial to the workers, whose wages and salaries trailed behind the cost of living. Social security policies gave white-collar employees benefits far superior to those delivered to manual workers. Alessandri did institutionalize labour–industrial relations through implementation of the legal code of 1924, but he accepted landowner demands for the restriction of union rights to the cities. While holding down the price of basic foodstuffs to quell urban labour discontent, the government compensated landed elites with continued dominion over the rural work-force.

Despite dissatisfaction with restrictions on food prices and exports, many *latifundistas* tolerated Alessandri's support for urban industry because they also possessed economic interests in the cities. The more sophisticated agriculturalists realized that urban expansion would gradually increase consumption of foodstuffs, raw materials and excess labour in the countryside, which they hoped would curtail pressures for land reform. At the same time, agrarian elites retained special access to public credits and railways, extremely low taxes (always beneath 2 per cent of total government revenues), influence over government agencies concerned with farming and numerous seats in Congress thanks to the compliant peasant electorate. Naturally, urban industrialists and financiers exuded even greater enthusiasm for Alessandri's administration, which presaged many of the sectoral preferences of future Popular Front governments. Recognizing the erosion of the rightist parties, the Chilean upper class relied increasingly on its corporate organizations and their links with the state. While the SNA and the SFF became more active, the founding in 1933 of the Confederación de la Producción y del Comercio epitomized this capitalist assertiveness. It co-ordinated all the elite economic interest groups in opposition to the new Left and in favour of low taxes and ample credits from the government.

The political parties representing the upper class sought to hang on to power mainly through gradual liberalization and endorsement of increasingly statist measures. The Conservatives now joined with the Liberals against the new spectre of populism and socialism in the hope that greater employer and governmental paternalism would preserve social peace and thus undercut the Left. Within the Conservative Party, young reformers – notably Manuel Garretón Walker, Bernardo Leighton Guzmán and Eduardo Frei Montalva – wanted to go even farther with semi-corporatist programmes for social welfare to outbid the Marxists for the loyalty of the masses. Inspired by reformist Catholic thought from Europe, they created the Falange, which became an independent centrist party in the 1940s and was transformed into the Christian Democrat Party in the 1950s. In the 1930s and 1940s, many Liberals also moved beyond Manchester individualism towards more reformist positions consonant with state capitalism.

A rash of minor right-wing parties also sought a path between the tarnished laissez-faire past and a dreaded socialist future. These corporatist and regionalist movements included the Agrarian Party, the Popular Corporative Party, the Republican Union, National Action and, most significant, the Movimiento Nacional Socialista (MNS) led by Jorge González von Marées. The MNS spliced together reformist ideas – such as administrative decentralization and land redistribution – from European fascists and Latin American populists, notably Peru's *apristas*. These 'creole Nazis' clashed with the Marxists in the streets and competed unsuccessfully with the Socialists for middle-class allegiance. Neither the MNS nor the more democratic and reformist Falange ever captured more than 4 per cent of the votes in national congressional elections.

Both the Right and the Left courted the middle class. Heavily dependent on government programmes and employment, the middle sectors supported state expansion. In an oligopolistic economy with few industrial openings and many executive posts filled by foreigners, the middle groups sought mobility and security by taking charge of the bureaucracy and political parties.

In the 1930s the Radical Party, like the middle class as a whole, debated whether to become the progressive wing of the Right or the moderate wing of the Left. Far more than the rightist parties, the Radicals, although always divided and opportunist, converted from classic liberalism to welfare state interventionism, officially recognizing the class struggle generated by capitalism and vowing to ameliorate it. After initially supporting Alessandri, they gravitated to the Popular Front, which allowed them to become senior rather than junior partners in a multi-party coalition. Their inclusion also blurred polarization and provided a safety valve for class conflict.

The depression and its aftermath enhanced the attractiveness of multi-class coalitions for workers in the cities and mines. At the beginning of the 1930s, the few existing unions were feeble and wallowing in internecine feuds. From more than 100,000 members (or so it was claimed) in the early 1920s, the Communist-led Federación Obrera de Chile (FOCh) had shrunk by nearly 90 per cent, leaving a residue mainly among nitrate and coal miners. As the mines revived, so did the Partido Comunista Chileno (PCCh), adding unions of transportation and dock workers as well as a few industrial labourers. The anarcho-syndicalist Confederación General de Trabajadores (CGT) was even more devastated than the FOCh and failed to revive, maintaining fewer than six thousand members by the early 1930s. Erstwhile CGT supporters in construction, printing, leather, maritime and a few industrial trades for the most part drifted to the Socialist Party, as did legal unions surviving Ibáñez's regime and new associations, which gathered into the rising Confederación Nacional Sindical (CNS). Dominated by the Socialists, the CNS attracted principally industrial labourers and white-collar employees. Significant non-aligned unions, such as the railroad workers and bakers, also recovered from the damage wrought first by Ibáñez and then by the depression. Fledgling Catholic unions, however, experienced little success.

In the 1930s this fragmented urban labour movement gained strength and unity. Thanks to the lack of opposition of Alessandri and encouragement from the Popular Front, the number of unions and their members more than tripled from 1930 to 1940. Although monitored by the government, this growth took place independently of it as unions obtained firmer legal standing through more intimate collaboration with state agencies and leftist political parties. The older Democrat Party, which had nurtured many of the Communist and Socialist leaders, gradually lost its worker and artisan clientele to the advancing Marxists. Increasingly opportunist, the Democrats split between the Right and the Popular Front. Their share of the congressional votes shrivelled from 14 per cent in 1932 to 6 per cent by 1941 and subsequently vanished.

By combining the combative slogans of Marxism with the charismatic populism of Grove, the PS became the leading party of labour in the 1930s. It also developed a strong following among urban professionals, intellectuals and students, who came to dominate an organization based on the working class. The Socialists appealed to the workers with revolutionary imagery and to the middle strata with an evolutionary approach. Although committed to class struggle in theory, in practice the party increasingly emphasized nationalist, reformist, electoral and coalition politics. Outdistanced by the Socialists in the labour movement and at the polls, the Communists began to change their strategy and broaden their base. They edged away from sectarian demands for an immediate proletarian revolution, a combative stance dictated by the Comintern from 1928 to 1935. The PCCh also accepted more members from the middle class, symbolized by Carlos Contreras Labarca, a lawyer, who served as secretary-general of the party from 1931 to 1946. Meanwhile, most of the Trotskyist rebels had by 1937 joined the Socialist Party.

Despite sporadic Marxist recruitment, incipient unionization and occasional outbursts of discontent, rural workers remained largely isolated from the ferment on the Left. The most violent instance of agrarian unrest occurred in 1934 at Ránquil, where the national police (*carabineros*) defended traditional landowners by slaughtering scores of protesting *campesinos*. The Marxists' failure to capitalize on oppression in the countryside and to galvanize rural labour kept the Left reliant on coalitions with centrist groups. The Right preserved its dominance over the rural electorate.

In 1934–5 the Socialists had anticipated what became the Popular Front by assembling a congressional Bloc of the Left, which included left-wing Democrats, Trotskyists and a handful of maverick Radicals. For their part, the Communists had already begun to tone down their doctrinaire, proletarian revolutionary positions when late in 1935 the Comintern endorsed the Popular Front strategy. The PCCh now stressed electoral over insurrectionary tactics, class coalitions (even with 'the petty bourgeoisie and the progressive national bourgeoisie') over conflict, industrialization over socialization, nationalism over internationalism. As a result the party's electoral base grew from barely 2,000 voters in 1931 to more than 53,000 by 1941. As Alessandri increasingly shifted to the right, the PCCh began winning converts to the idea of a popular front. In 1935–6 the Communists concentrated on wooing the Radical Party, convincing many of its wavering leaders by delivering enough votes in a 1936 by-election to capture a senatorial seat for a Radical millionaire landowner. Supplying the Popular Front with crucial respectability, organization, voters and money, the Radicals argued that their party, 'within the Left, is called upon to discharge the role of a regulating force, one which makes possible the desired transformation by means that preserve democratic rights and avoid social explosion'.[3] The Communists' success with the Radicals left the Socialists little choice. Left-wing Socialists feared that the Popular Front would deceive the workers with bourgeois demagoguery, but party leaders concluded that the pact was necessary both to avoid fascism and to acquire power. Inspired by similar experiments in Spain and France, the Socialists, like the Communists, now expanded their following by diluting their ideological zeal.

The new Confederación de Trabajadores de Chile (CTCh) also enlisted in the Popular Front. Founded in 1936 as a result of new leftist unity, the CTCh banded together middle- and working-class unions, incorporating the FOCh, the CNS, the Association of Chilean Employees, most independents and even a few peasants, although the shrinking CGT spurned affiliation. Like the Marxist parties, the CTCh improved labour solidarity but restrained militancy. It curbed worker demands in order to facilitate Popular Front electoral victories, as politicians who owed first loyalty to their party came to dominate the confederation. Among the members, the Socialists held a slim majority and the secretary-generalship. Through the CTCh, workers helped launch and sustain the Popular Front, beginning with a major strike in 1936 by railroad labourers that provoked government reprisals against the leftist press and parties as well as the workers, thus cementing the coalition.

Largely representing the middle class, the Masonic lodges also helped to weld the Popular Front together. Eminent leaders of the Radicals, Socialists and Communists found common ground through their membership in the Masons, whose grand master promoted prudent reform coalitions as an antidote to revolutionary or reactionary dangers. At the same time, the national student federation and many intellectuals lent support to the Popular Front. Outstanding writers active in the campaign included Pablo Neruda, Vicente Huidobro, Volodia Teitelboim, Ricardo Latcham, Luis Galdames and Ricardo Donoso.

[3] *Hoy*, no. 278 (18 March 1937), p. 10.

As the largest member party, the Radicals assumed leadership of the Popular Front. They dominated its national executive committee and its platform, which bore the redistributive populist slogan of 'Bread, roof, and Overcoat', coined by the 1932 Socialist Republic. The Popular Front's program promised to enhance democratic freedoms, generate economic modernization under state guidance, promote economic and cultural nationalism and ensure social welfare for the middle and working classes. It pledged to respect and improve electoral rights and civil liberties. It advocated protection for industrialization and redistribution of under-utilized agricultural lands. Demanding 'Chile for the Chileans', the coalition suggested scaling down payments on the foreign debt and nationalizing some foreign-owned mines, industries and public utilities. Phrased in vague terms, the platform offered disadvantaged groups better incomes, housing, health, education and representation. Since this social democratic program differed more in tone than in substance from the public pronouncements of the Right, the actual policies of the Popular Front would obviously be determined by which members of the coalition carried them out. Most observers agreed with the U.S. Embassy's evaluation that 'the platform of the Popular Front is sufficiently vague so that the Conservative Party itself could operate under it and later point with pride to its well-kept promises.'[4]

In the 1937 congressional elections, the political extremes scored impressive gains. The Conservatives and Liberals combined won 42 per cent of the vote; together with minor party collaborators and a few renegades from the Radicals this gave the Right a thin electoral and congressional majority. At the same time, both the Socialists (11 per cent) and the Communists (4 per cent) approximately doubled their 1932 share of the vote, while the Radicals once again won about 18 per cent. Thereafter, the disappointed Popular Front redoubled its efforts to build an electoral majority.

Following a bruising battle with the Socialists, the Radicals installed their candidate as the Popular Front's presidential nominee. Pedro Aguirre Cerda, a teacher, lawyer, wealthy wine grower and Mason, came from the right wing of the Radical Party, which had resisted the formation of the Popular Front. His advocacy of industrialization was one of the few policy objectives he shared with the left of the party. His moderate appeal

---

[4] U.S. Department of State Archives, Record Group 59 (hereafter cited as USDOS), Santiago, 29 October 1938, 825.00/1085.

mellowed the reformist content of the coalition at the same time as it brightened its electoral prospects, illustrating the inescapable dilemmas of such evolutionary coalitions for the revolutionary Marxists.

In his campaign Aguirre Cerda succeeded by appealing to the middle and working classes without unduly frightening the wealthy. His bland, compromising character also served to hold the quarrelsome Popular Front together. The diminutive candidate's dark complexion prompted the Right to scorn him as 'El Negro' and the Left to embrace him as 'Don Tinto'. The key to his eventual victory, however, came from the Marxists' ability to mobilize the workers against the traditional ruling parties, raising the consciousness of labourers and convincing them not to sell their votes to the Right. Although the Radicals supplied the largest single block of votes for the Popular Front, it was the growing identification of the workers with the Socialists and Communists which transformed the political scene in Chile.

The Right contributed to the Popular Front's momentum by nominating as its candidate Alessandri's stern minister of finance, Gustavo Ross, to the dismay of moderate Liberals and the Falange. Whereas Aguirre Cerda represented the moderate face of the Popular Front, Ross exemplified the rapacious image of the propertied class. The Popular Front branded him the 'Minister of Hunger' and the 'last Pirate of the Pacific'. In addition to the Conservatives and Liberals, the SNA, the SFF, the Chamber of Commerce, the leading banks and corporations and many clergy openly worked and prayed for his election. U.S. businessmen in Chile also preferred Ross, who sounded the campaign theme of 'order and work'. Although issuing no formal platform, the Right differed from the Popular Front mainly in its emphasis on production over redistribution, efficiency over import substitution and control of foreign investors over nationalization. The conservative forces tried to lure the middle class and timid Radicals away from the Popular Front by warning that the Marxists would destroy religion, family, property and social harmony. While the Right hammered away at the atrocities of communism, the Left drummed up the horrors of fascism. Ross and Aguirre Cerda each vowed to save Chilean democracy from the other.

Rather than rely on programmes or oratory, the Right expected to triumph through its seasoned party machinery. One of Ross's campaign managers assured the U.S. ambassador that the parties would buy enough working-class votes to vanquish the Popular Front, even though he conceded that Aguirre Cerda would win handily in an honest election. At least in the cities, however, Popular Front vigilance and rising working-class political consciousness complicated such customary bribery.

Even more than the Right's tactics, the existence of a third alternative obstructed the Popular Front's path to the presidency. The personalist campaign of former dictator Ibáñez had no chance of success but withheld potential supporters – especially in the middle class – from Aguirre Cerda. Ibáñez's platform echoed the Popular Front's by trumpeting state planning, economic nationalism and social welfare, but his ambition and his support from González von Marées' MNS rendered the two reform movements irreconcilable. However, a few weeks before the balloting, youthful Nazis staged a foolhardy putsch against the Alessandri government. The botched coup shocked public opinion less than did the administration's massacre of the perpetrators. Discredited by the incident and alienated from the Right, the *ibañistas* switched their support to Aguirre Cerda. The incongruous alignment of Nazis behind the anti-Fascist Popular Front showed again the need of Chilean politicians, like those elsewhere, to subordinate ideological to electoral considerations.

The Popular Front won a narrow victory over the Right in 1938 with 50.3 per cent of the vote. When Aguirre Cerda beat Ross in the far northern and southern provinces and in the cities, the conservative forces learned that votes from the central latifundia zones could no longer guarantee supremacy. As in every other Chilean electoral victory by reformist or left-wing presidential aspirants – Alessandri in 1920, González Videla in 1946, Allende in 1970 – tense days passed between the counting of the ballots and the ratification of the results by Congress. Many rightist leaders grudgingly accepted the defeat because of assurances of moderation from the victors, but others, warning that Aguirre Cerda would become the 'Kerensky of Chile', conspired to overturn the result through charges of electoral corruption and by inciting a take-over by the armed forces.

The Popular Front legitimized its claim to the presidency by restraining its jubilant followers and discrediting rightist rumours of impending anarchy. It simultaneously encouraged the view that it would merely introduce a Chilean 'New Deal' if allowed to take office but that it could unleash effective mass resistance if denied: 'Chile will not be a second Spain. We will scotch fascism here before it can lift its head.'[5] As Aguirre Cerda warned the opposition, 'I am the second Chilean President from the Radical Party. . . . I will be the second and the last if those of the other

[5] Ibid.

side do not know enough to listen to reason and to make concessions, as the great leaders of their own group have advised. . . . Either I open a regulating channel for the desires of the people or after me comes the flood.'[6] Those arguments convinced a minority of leaders of the Conservatives, Falange and Liberals to acknowledge his right to the presidency. These rightists calculated that the social and political costs of reversing the Popular Front's fortunes might exceed the price of bowing to its victory: 'Since we cannot count on either the masses or the armed forces,' it was argued, 'it suits us [the Conservatives], even more than our adversaries, to maintain constitutional democracy.'[7]

Three public announcements from establishment groups were critical at this juncture. First, although the Alessandri government abstained from official recognition until the Right's charges of electoral irregularities could be adjudicated, the minister of the interior, Aguirre Cerda's godfather, acknowledged the Popular Front victory when the results first came in, and this declaration was communicated to Chilean legations abroad by the minister of foreign affairs. Second, a northern bishop sent Aguirre Cerda a congratulatory telegram and, in subsequently becoming archbishop, eased relations between the Church and the Popular Front. Third, and most important, the commanders-in-chief of the army and the national police proclaimed that the Popular Front's election had already been accepted by the military and public opinion and that denying the coalition office would ignite more civil violence than they were prepared to confront. Implying that they opposed communism but not reformism, the armed forces thus convinced most recalcitrant rightists to combat the Popular Front through the regular channels – Congress and the bureaucracy – which they still dominated. Thus, at the end of 1938 Arturo Alessandri peacefully transferred the presidential sash to Pedro Aguirre Cerda of the Popular Front.

THE POPULAR FRONT, 1938–41

With the Popular Front victory in the 1938 elections, the Radicals realized their long-standing dream of taking all key government positions away from the Right. At the same time the centrist domination of the incoming administration reassured the upper and middle classes. The Left obtained only minimal representation: the Socialists were given a few minor cabinet

---

[6] USDOS, Santiago, 9 November 1938, 825.00/1093.
[7] Rafael Luis Gumucio, *Me defiendo* (Santiago, 1939), p. 65.

posts – Health, Development, and Lands and Colonization – the Communists, in order to shield the government from rightists' charges of Marxist control, none. Although capturing few patronage plums, the Communists, Socialists and the CTCh reaped a large number of new recruits during the Popular Front period. In a clientelist political system, many middle- and working-class Chileans eagerly clambered aboard the bandwagon; the CTCh reportedly doubled its membership in the year following Aguirre Cerda's victory.

Through the Popular Front, the Marxist forces claimed a regular place in the political system. The Socialists and Communists had progressed from participation in elections in 1932 to participation in government six years later. Yet a decade of intense leftist mobilization of the middle and working classes had produced an administration far less advanced and daring than its composition and rhetoric implied. The very coalition politics which had allowed the Marxists to gain influence in high national offices also inhibited the enactment of the programmes for which they had sought those offices. Predictably, the inauguration of a Popular Front president did not herald sweeping structural transformations. Rather, it ushered in a new political era with the Socialist and, to a lesser extent, Communist forces institutionalized as part of the established bargaining system, with government legitimacy based on support from the urban masses through the brokerage of the centrist groups and with state capitalism accelerated in the name of industrialization.

Like Alessandri, indeed, like all Chilean presidents in the 1930s and 1940s, Aguirre Cerda essentially pursued a model of paternalistic state capitalism in which government collaborated with private enterprise in the construction of a mixed economy. Aiming to catch up with the more industrialized West, Chile's Popular Front mobilized the labour movement behind national economic development more than working-class social conquests. Compared with the Right, however, it placed greater emphasis on state intervention, industrialization and the needs of labour. Economic policy was in any event influenced more by international than by internal factors. As elsewhere in Latin America, the onset of the Second World War accelerated domestic production of manufactured consumer items, widened the scope of the central state and augmented dependence on the United States instead of Europe. All these trends dampened Marxist campaigns for bold redistributive measures at the expense of domestic and foreign capitalists.

The Popular Front's primary economic instrument became the new

Corporación de Fomento de la Producción (CORFO), fashioned originally to promote recovery from the earthquake of 1939. CORFO allocated public credits to all sectors of the economy, but especially industry and construction. From the end of the 1930s to the early 1950s, this quasi-autonomous agency accounted for nearly one-third of total investment in capital equipment and nearly one-fourth of total domestic investment. While supplied mainly from national sources, almost one-third of its investment funds flowed from abroad, principally the U.S. Export–Import Bank. When those loans, which had to be spent on imports from the United States, were extended in 1940, Chile dropped retrospective tax claims against the North American telephone and copper companies.

Although hailed by the Popular Front as a breakthrough for state socialism and economic nationalism, CORFO evolved into a vehicle for state capitalism linked to private and foreign vested interests. In a trade-off between the twin goals of industrialization and social reform, the Popular Front sided with the former. The elites were initially suspicious of this leap forward in state activism, but they soon became the primary beneficiaries. At the same time, Chile's dependence on U.S. capital increased. Under the Popular Front government, the United States nearly doubled its Chilean sales and tripled its purchases, as British and German commerce dwindled; discussions between Chile and the United States about lowering trade barriers, however, made little headway.

Under Alessandri, the government had counted on credit inflation from the Central Bank to spark economic recovery and full employment. Under Aguirre Cerda, credit expansion to fund import-substitution industrialization pushed inflation still further, as did the war. During 1939–42, the cost of living jumped 83 per cent, surpassing the entire price rise from 1931 to 1939. By imposing ceilings on prices of agricultural produce, the government effectively transferred income to the urban sector. The index of industrial production rose over 25 per cent while agricultural output virtually stagnated, a pattern which persisted throughout the 1940s.

While the right-wing parties fought tenaciously against the Popular Front mainly because it jeopardized their political livelihood, other elite groups tried to conciliate, co-opt or neutralize the Radical governments of the 1940s. One traditional institution which reached a modus vivendi with the Popular Front was the Roman Catholic Church. The Vatican replaced the reactionary archbishop of Santiago with José María Caro, the northern bishop who had congratulated Aguirre Cerda on his election. In his new office, Caro advocated reformist positions close to those of the indigenous Falange, bestowing upon the Chilean Church a reputation as the most progressive in Latin America. The archbishop even stunned the landed elite by urging unionization, higher wages, profit-sharing and better living conditions for rural labourers. Such an enlightened stance was designed to revive clerical influence among the working classes and counter the spread of Marxism. At the close of the 1930s, some 98 per cent of Chileans still baptized their children, but barely 10 per cent attended mass on Sundays and only some 50 per cent were married in the Church.

The landowners in the SNA also sought a truce with the more conservative elements in the Popular Front. The president of the SNA and of the Confederación de la Producción y el Commercio, Jaime Larraín García Moreno, encouraged the rural elites to provide better treatment for their workers in order to pre-empt Marxist proposals for agrarian reform: 'It is impossible to stop social evolution. We must put ourselves on the side of social evolution in order to channel it'.[8] Many landed Radicals now joined the SNA for the first time, which facilitated co-operation with the Popular Front government. Cristóbal Sáenz Cerda, the Radical landowner who had won the first by-election for the Popular Front in 1936, became vice-president of the SNA and a spokesman against agrarian reform in Aguirre Cerda's cabinet. As a fellow large landowner, the president also helped to bury reforms for the peasants through his own cordial relations with the rural upper class.

During the first year of Aguirre Cerda's administration, Marxist unionization of farm workers threatened to disrupt the tacit agreement between landowners and the Popular Front. Although no precise and reliable statistics are available for either rural or urban unions, in late 1939 the Communists boasted nearly four hundred rural associations with almost sixty thousand members and growing daily. The CTCh gave *campesino* organization a high priority and enrolled thousands, and the Federación Nacional del Campesinado, led by Emilio Zapata, a Socialist, superseded the smaller Liga Nacional de Defensa de los Campesinos Pobres (1935) and escalated rural mobilization and strikes. In former conservative strongholds the Popular Front began winning rural by-elections, both by Marxists rallying agricultural workers and by Radicals buying up estates.

[8] Erico Hott Kinderman, *Les sociedades agrícolas nacionales y su influencia en la agricultura de Chile* (Santiago, 1944), pp. 21–2.

Aguirre Cerda made a critical concession to the landlords by establishing a moratorium on peasant unionization and strikes, even though some 35 per cent of the active population worked in the countryside compared with less than 20 per cent in urban industry. In terms of political economy, the government, despite its ideological affinities, chose to favour least the group least able to put pressure on it. Marginalizing rural workers in order to reduce demands on limited resources appeared especially necessary to politicians when wartime shortages restricted the government's campaign for industrialization and benefits for the urban middle and working classes. The suppression of *campesino* activism also averted disruptions of food supplies to the mines and cities, which would have further accelerated agricultural imports. Holding down the cost of basic foodstuffs and peasant demands slowed inflation and mollified urban constituents, whereas higher food prices would have engendered more urban strikes and thus hindered industrialization.

In spite of protests by the Left, all of the Popular Front parties and the CTCh acquiesced in the government's suspension of agricultural unionization. The Communists and Socialists deplored this surrender to the SNA but bent to the administration's wishes to cool conflicts with the Right. By co-operating with the Radicals at the cost of leaving the workers largely unorganized, the Marxists remained dependent on segments of the middle groups. Consequently, the compromises and dilemmas inherent in populist multi-class coalitions and policies persisted.

The industrialists and the SFF welcomed CORFO and Aguirre Cerda's support for their tepid brand of economic nationalism. Although still apprehensive about state intervention, most manufacturers came to realize that the Popular Front's activism boosted private enterprise. As the Radical Party boasted, 'Never have industry and commerce had larger profits than during the government of the Left'.[9] The more far-sighted industrialists saw that better organization, representation, health, housing and education for workers defused social conflict. Moderate reforms for workers increased their productivity and consumer capacity more than their cost to employers, while inflationary credit policies also kept wages from rising commensurately with productivity. Since Chile had relatively cheap but not proportionately inefficient labour, the Popular Front's guarantee of social peace made welfarism and industrialism compatible.

The middle class was another leading beneficiary of the Radical govern-

[9] Isauro Torres and Pedro Opitz, *Defensa de los gobiernos de izquierda* (Santiago, 1942), p. 3.

ments in the 1940s. The gap between white-collar employees and manual workers widened as the middle sectors received more employment, income, health, housing, education, social security and other benefits than did the lower strata. They also accumulated many new political offices, partly thanks to the decline of bribery at the ballot box. Bureaucratic expansion mainly benefited followers of the Radical Party, which came to represent a majority of public employees. Although criticized by the elites, this growth of central government assuaged middle-class aspirations without impinging on the fundamental privileges of the upper class.

Continuing working-class support for the Popular Front and its successors in the 1940s was not easily explained by material gains or class consciousness. Through inflation and increasingly indirect taxes, the subordinated classes paid for the government's pumping up the bureaucracy and industry. The few labourers who experienced real wage gains were concentrated in urban, skilled and unionized occupations; most workers saw their standard of living stagnate or deteriorate in the 1940s, as income distribution became more regressive.

Organizational advances for labourers exceeded their material progress, as the number of legal unions nearly tripled during the administration of Aguirre Cerda. From 1941 to 1949, the total number of union members increased more than 40 per cent. Nevertheless, most union stalwarts were still miners, artisans or middle-class employees, because manufacturing growth did not foster as large an industrial proletariat as the Marxist parties had hoped. From 1940 to 1954 the percentage of the economically active population grew twice as much in services as in industry. The CTCh reined in worker militancy in order to provide support and tranquillity for Aguirre Cerda, and the government, in turn, ensured that a rising number of labour–management disputes were settled in favour of workers (from 184 in 1938 to 266 in 1939). The Popular Front argued cogently that backing the administration was at least preferable to a rightist government and, in the long run, more in the best interests of labour than were destabilizing demands for immediate payoffs.

In contrast to the generally accommodationist approach of the upperclass interest groups, the right-wing parties opposed the Popular Front implacably, erecting a congressional barricade against nearly all of Aguirre Cerda's initiatives. Rightist legislators and newspapers constantly charged the regime with incompetence, corruption, extremism, illegality and illegitimacy. Amidst such political polarization, only the tiny Falange sustained a compromising centrist position. In August 1939 extreme right-ists and *ibañistas* convinced General Ariosto Herrera Ramírez, an anti-Communist and admirer of Mussolini, to pronounce against the Popular Front, but loyal military officers, backed by Popular Front party militias and union cadres, suppressed the uprising. The abortive coup persuaded many of the Right and Left to modulate their rhetoric and retreat from the brink of armed conflict.

Aguirre Cerda laboured constantly to hold the squabbling coalition together. In the tussle for advantage, the Radicals entrenched themselves in the state apparatus and laid the groundwork for a decade of domination. Even the left wing of their own party complained about the Radicals' bureaucratic feast, favouritism for wealthier party members (especially from the right wing and the capital city) and lack of interest in social reforms.

All of the Popular Front parties grew, but the Communist Party did so most spectacularly by pursuing moderate policies and muzzling worker discontent. It temporarily revived the rhetorical radicalism of the early depression years during the period of the Nazi–Soviet pact when Popular Front co-operation in the cause of anti-fascism received less emphasis. However, Germany's attack on the Soviet Union quickly bought the PCCh back into full collaboration with its coalition partners opposed to the Axis. Despite such deviations, Communist involvement in the coalition government generally furthered the harnessing of the Left and labour as non-revolutionary and subordinate participants in electoral, congressional and bureaucratic politics.

The Socialists acquired sinecures in the government hierarchy at the cost of postponing worker mobilization and structural reforms. For example, they disbanded the Socialist militia and downplayed peasant unionization. Dissidents, who soon broke away from the party, complained that the PS was becoming an employment agency devoted to electoral and bureaucratic advancement as an end in itself. The Socialists grappled with a trickier dilemma than did their allies. The Radicals could concentrate on pragmatic administration with fewer ideological qualms and less erosion of their social base, blunting the Socialists' initiatives in the executive branch and outbidding them for middle-class allegiance. Conversely, the Communists could dedicate themselves to recruiting the working class with less responsibility for a mediocre administrative performance. Not surprisingly, the PS never resolved the paradox of how to lead the masses towards socialism through the bourgeois democratic state without succumbing to reactionary resistance or getting stuck in the half-way house of incremental reformism.

Early in 1941 the Socialists withdrew from the Popular Front party coalition while remaining in Aguirre Cerda's cabinet. They shattered the original coalition not so much because of discontent with the paucity of social reforms introduced by the Radicals but largely because of discord with the Communists. The Socialists resented Communist competition over unions and opposed the Stalin–Hitler pact. Their increasingly negative posture toward the PCCh reflected a correspondingly positive attitude towards the United States. This rapprochement resulted from the Socialists' animosity towards fascism, their participation in the national government, desire for industrialization and quest for better economic relations with the United States under the stringencies of wartime. Many Socialist leaders came to appreciate the limited choices available to policy-makers in a highly dependent economy, and they became more eager to acquire credits from the Export–Import Bank than to nationalize foreign enterprises or press worker demands. When they berated the Communists for obstructing co-operation with the United States, consorting with Fascists externally and fomenting labour unrest internally, the PCCh retorted with charges that the Socialists were selling out to North American imperialism. Unable to convince the Radicals to break with the Communists, the PS and a majority of the CTCh left the Popular Front and ran independently in the 1941 congressional race.

Although Aguirre Cerda compiled a laudable record of reform compared with past administrations, his achievements fell far short of his campaign promises. The Popular Front – especially the Marxists – determined finally to put through its program by breaking the conservative control of Congress in the 1941 mid-term elections. Fearing substantial losses and hoping to curtail leftist mobilization by other means, the Conservatives and Liberals threatened to undermine the legitimacy of the balloting by abstaining. To ensure rightist participation, Aguirre Cerda's administration temporarily restricted union political and strike activities, muffled the leftist press, banned Marxist militias and called out the armed forces to prevent intimidation, violence or corruption at the polls. As the original Popular Front parties swept into control of both houses of Congress with 59 per cent of the votes, both the Radicals and Socialists secured more than 20 per cent while the Communists significantly increased their vote from 4 per cent in 1937 to almost 12 per cent. The Conservatives and Liberals together now accounted for only 31 per cent. Most dramatic were the Popular

Front's gains in rural zones, which showed that the Right's fears of Marxist activism in the countryside and of the continuing leftward movement of the electorate had been well founded.

Even following the Popular Front's congressional victories, wartime economic constraints still discouraged substantial reforms. Marxist desires for a broad consensus against fascism also favoured compromises rather than conquests. More importantly, Aguirre Cerda died from tuberculosis in November 1941, nine months after the elections, having observed at one of his last cabinet meetings:

We promised the people to pull them out of misery, to raise their social, economic, and moral level. Apart from the intelligent and constructive action of some of my ministers, we have wasted time here with long debates and discussions, without ever arriving at practical and effective solutions for the great problems. It burdens my soul with profound sorrow, because I imagine that the people, whom I love so much, could think that I have deceived them.[10]

THE CONTINUATION OF RADICAL RULE, 1942–52

Although not now based on a formal alliance among the reformist parties, Popular Front politics endured after the death of Aguirre Cerda for another decade on an informal basis. The Radical Party nominated Juan Antonio Ríos Morales, a businessman identified with the anti-Communist right wing of the party, as Aguirre Cerda's successor without constructing or consulting any multi-party coalition. Nevertheless, to avert the return of the Right behind the irrepressible Ibáñez, Communists, Socialists, members of the CTCh, Democrats, Falangists and even some renegade Liberals, including Alessandri, gave their support to Ríos. His Alianza Democrática (AD) secured 56 per cent of the vote in the extraordinary 1942 election.

Ríos devoted his government to national unity, social stability and economic growth. He perpetuated the late president's emphasis on industrialization but soft-pedalled his accompanying concern with social welfare and reforms for urban labour. Whereas his predecessor's slogan had been 'To govern is to educate', Ríos proclaimed, 'To govern is to produce'.

In response to wartime scarcities, especially of capital goods (total imports fell to 13 per cent of national income), Ríos gave priority to maintaining economic productivity. The general index of production rose

[10] Arturo Olavarría Bravo, *Chile entre dos Alessandri*, 4 vols. (Santiago, 1962, 1965), vol. 1, p. 555.

from a base of 100 in 1938 to 108 in 1942 and 112 in 1945, while industry went from an index of 112 in 1942 to 130 in 1945. Between 1940 and 1945, industrial output increased by more than 9 per cent annually. The upper and middle classes constituted the major beneficiaries of Ríos's policies, since the cost of living galloped ahead of workers' wages. The general price index climbed roughly three times as much from 1942 through 1945 as it had between 1938 and 1941. During 1940–5 monetary national income soared by 120 per cent while real national income inched up only 8 per cent.

As the Socialists and Communists had demanded, Chile finally broke relations with the Axis powers in January 1943. Following Pearl Harbor, Chile had hesitated to back the Allies strongly because the United States could not guarantee its security against a Japanese attack. At the same time, Alessandri and many other rightists had lobbied effectively for maintaining Chile's neutral stance. Pressures and inducements from the United States as well as the ground swell of domestic public opinion against the Axis, however, finally overcame traditional reluctance to become embroiled in conflicts outside South America. Even after severing relations, Chile was never satisfied with the amount of aid and lend-lease military equipment it received, and neither was the United States content with the extent of Chilean action against Axis agents and firms operating there. Nevertheless, Chile subsidized the Allied cause by accepting an artificially low price for its copper exports to the United States while paying increasingly higher prices for its imports. The war gradually boosted Chile's mineral exports and foreign exchange accumulation, while U.S. trade, credits and advisers facilitated state support for capitalist enterprises. For example, U.S. loans were granted to CORFO projects in steel, oil and fishing. Not unlike that of Ibáñez in the 1920s, Ríos's basic policy was to develop the Chilean economy through external alignment with the United States.

Ríos' wartime cabinets included Socialists, Democrats, Radicals and Liberals (including the president of the SNA). Dismay over shared responsibility for an increasingly conservative administration further ruptured the PS, while the PCCh again abstained from taking cabinet seats and continued its expansion in the unions. Yet under the banner of anti-fascist unity, both Marxist parties renounced strikes and held back labour demands. Even with a majority in Congress from 1941 to 1945, the original Popular Front parties passed very little of the social legislation long promised to urban and rural workers.

The governing coalition's diminishing ardour for reform coincided with declining electoral support. Between the 1941 and 1945 congressional elections, the Radical vote fell from 21 to 20 per cent while the increasingly dispirited and divided Socialists saw their share reduced from 21 to 13 per cent, and that of the Communists fall from 12 to 10 per cent. Meanwhile the combined Conservative–Liberal share of the vote increased from 31 to 44 per cent, demonstrating the resilience of traditional party strength.

Because of the failing health of Ríos, another right-wing Radical, Alfredo Duhalde Vásquez, took over as interim chief executive at the end of 1945. Duhalde overreacted to Communist-led strikes in the nitrate and coal mines, supported by solidarity rallies in Santiago. His marshalling of troops against the strikers and demonstrators produced bloodshed, widespread opposition to his shaky stewardship and unusually bitter battles between Socialist and Communist unions.

The same Marxist parties which had forged labour unity in 1936 demolished it in 1946, when the end of the Second World War and the onset of the Cold War unleashed pent-up hostilities between them. The Communists had acquired a majority in the CTCh and refused any longer to obey a Socialist secretary-general. As the PCCh seized control of most of the confederation, the PS seceded with its followers, so that organized labour, still dependent on party leadership, was weaker at the end of the 1940s than at the start of the decade.

Both Moscow and Washington contributed to this division. In accord with a harsher line from the Soviet Union, the Communists tried to tighten their grip over unions even at the cost of splitting the national federation. They set out to crush the Socialists, who, by the same token, became determined to drive the PCCh out of the Chilean and Latin American labour movement. Having drawn closer to the United States during the war, the PS now aligned with the AFL–CIO and its international crusade against Communism. Even with support from U.S. government and U.S. labour officials for the remainder of the 1940s, the Socialist's smaller branch of the CTCh lost ground to the Communists. The PS retained the greatest strength among copper, public transportation, railroad, textile and chemical workers, while the PCCh dominated nitrate, coal, construction, port, baking and scattered industrial unions.

The extraordinary presidential election of 1946 to replace Ríos demonstrated the political metamorphosis from ideological and social struggles in the 1930s to opportunist manoeuvring for party advantage in the 1940s. A left-wing Radical, long considered a firebrand and a friend of the

PCCh, Gabriel González Videla, revived, it is true, in the optimistic post-war atmosphere the reformist promises and expectations of 1938. The Communists enthusiastically joined his campaign, and most Socialists, although officially endorsing their secretary-general Bernardo Ibáñez Aguila to avoid a formal alliance with the rival PCCh, also ended up voting for González Videla. The Conservatives countered with Social Christian representative Eduardo Cruz-Coke, backed by the reformist Falange, while the Liberals tried to capitalize on Chile's most durable political family name by nominating Arturo's son, Fernando Alessandri Rodríguez.

A sense of political malaise, however, was reflected not only in party fragmentation and the dearth of fresh options but also in reduced turn-out at the polls. Whereas 88 per cent of the registered voters cast ballots in 1938 and 80 per cent in 1942, only 76 per cent bothered to do so in 1946. The dwindling appeal of Popular Front politics was also evidenced when González Videla eked out only a 40 per cent plurality over Cruz-Coke (30 per cent), Alessandri (27 per cent) and Ibáñez (3 per cent). If the Conservatives, Liberals and Falange had put up a single candidate, the Right would probably have won. As in 1938, the candidate of the Left had to walk a tightrope from election to inauguration. González Videla ensured his congressional certification by granting the Liberals, who were just as likely as the Conservatives to be large landowners, new legal restrictions on peasant unionization, which lasted until 1967. He also pasted together the most bizarre administration in Chilean history, seating Liberals in the cabinet alongside Communists and Radicals.

As a result of these political compromises, González Videla shelved his campaign pledge to transform Chile from a 'political democracy' into an 'economic democracy'. Instead, he promoted industrialization, technological modernization in agriculture and improved transportation, all through increased state intervention and the expansion of the public sector. The government's share of national income and expenditures grew even more under González Videla than it had under Aguirre Cerda and Ríos, rising from 16 per cent of GDP in 1945 to 18 per cent in 1950. Nevertheless, the pace of industrial expansion slowed down, and the general growth rates of real production and real per capita income slid below wartime levels. From a base of 100 in 1938, the general price index climbed to 238 by 1946 and then accelerated to 417 by 1949, intensifying the siphoning of real national income away from wage-earners. This inflation was fuelled by inadequate output from agriculture as well as by deficit spending from government for manufacturers and the middle class.

Economic ties with the United States tightened as productivity in the mining sector and prices for minerals, especially copper, scaled new heights. Total export revenues rose from U.S. $329 million in 1938 to $406 million in 1945 and $547 million in 1952, while total import expenditures went from U.S. $240 million to $187 million and $430 million. Chile's foreign trade had almost recovered from the impact of the depression by the end of the Radical era. Foreign investment – nearly 70 per cent from the United States – also increased during the post-war period, rising from $847 million in 1945 to $1,025 million in 1952; foreign loans to CORFO continued to foster industrialization.

Chile's deepening dependence on the United States – now pressuring Latin America to enlist in a global cold war – helped to turn González Videla against his Communist and labour allies. The shift away from the Left also reflected growing conservatism among the middle class and the Radical Party. The middle sectors increasingly preferred to use the bureaucratic state rather than multi-class coalitions and co-operation with labour to pursue their interest and provide protection against inflation. Many in the middle strata – particularly in the wealthier and professional levels – came to look more favourably on co-operation with the traditional elites, the Right and the United States.

The Radical governments of the 1940s, especially the González Videla administration, continued to benefit the middle class far more than the workers. Although precise figures vary, the best estimates for the Radical era agree on the increasingly regressive distribution of income. According to one calculation, real national income rose some 40 per cent from 1940 to 1953, while the real income of the upper class went up 60 per cent, that of the middle class 46 per cent and that of the workers only 7 per cent. Another estimate for the period from 1940 to 1957 concluded that the per capita income of the upper class climbed from twelve to fourteen times that of the workers, and the per capita income of the middle class rose from four to five times that of the workers. The Radical Party itself estimated that the average daily wage of a factory worker would buy 9 kilos of bread in 1938 and 11 kilos in 1950, while the average monthly salary of a white-collar employee would purchase 292 kilos in 1938 and 633 in 1950. Indeed, average real wages for industrial workers, measured in 1950 escudos, improved only slightly between the First World War and the 1960s: 30.4 escudos in 1914–16; 26.9 in 1938–40; 32.3 in 1951–3; and 34.0 in 1960–1. Despite minimal gains, labourers in the factories and mines fared much better than their counterparts in services or farming, who saw their wages plunge after the Second World War. Average annual real wages per manual worker in 1940 pesos rose from 4,451 pesos in 1940 to 6,304 in 1952 in industry and from 9,024 to 10,499 in mining, while those in services fell from 3,489 to 2,613 and those in agriculture from 3,422 to 2,824, making the total average wage increase per worker a paltry rise from 4,353 pesos in 1940 to 4,361 in 1952. During the same period the average salary for white-collar employees climbed from 11,011 pesos to 16,811. By the end of the 1940s, approximately 70 per cent of the active population still received less than the minimum income defined as necessary for survival by the government.[11]

In order to continue subsidizing the middle class and high-cost industry, González Videla clamped down on the mounting post-war protests of the Marxist parties and of organized labour. During their initial months in the administration, the Communists made rapid progress on the labour front, spearheading union demands and renewing organization of *campesinos*. They also secured 17 per cent of the vote in the 1947 municipal elections, which compared with 10 per cent in the 1945 congressional elections and was triple their tally in the municipal elections of 1944. The conservative political and economic groups now brought to a head their incessant campaign to convince the Radicals to jettison their Marxist partners. Each government in the 1940s had tilted farther to the right than the one before it. The Radicals finally caved in completely to rightist pressures because they were losing votes while the PCCh was gaining and because they wanted to pre-empt any military plot against the government by ejecting the Communists. Moreover, years of state involvement in the growth of the modern sector had woven a web of common interests between rich property owners and Radical leaders, many of whom had always been apprehensive about collaboration with the Communists. The decision was made to outlaw the PCCh and to stifle urban and rural labour demands in a period of economic uncertainty. Particularly during the 1947 recession, it became attractive to the government to quash labour interference with a policy of industrialization dependent upon U.S. co-

[11] Most of these figures are taken from Héctor Varela Carmona, 'Distribución del ingreso nacional en Chile a través de las diversas clases sociales', *Panorama Económico*, 12, no. 199 (1959), pp. 61–70; idem, 'Distribución del ingreso nacional', *Panorama Económico*, 13, no. 207 (1959), p. 405; Flavián Levine B. and Juan Crocco Ferrari, 'La población chilena', *Economía*, 5 nos. 10–11 (1944), pp. 31–68; Partido Radical, *14 años de progreso, 1938–1952* (Santiago, 1952), esp. pp. 37–47; Corporación de Fomento de la Producción, *Geografía económico de Chile*, 4 vols. (Santiago, 1950, 1962), vol. 2, pp. 224–324; idem, *Cuentas nacionales de Chile: 1940–1954* (Santiago, 1957); Markos J. Mamalakis, *Historical Statistics of Chile*, 2 vols. (Westport, Conn., 1979, 1980), vol. 2, p. 315; Aníbal Pinto Santa Cruz, *Chile, un caso de desarrollo frustrado* (Santiago, 1962), pp. 136–9, 185–198.

operation. It also enabled the government to control inflationary pressures at the expense of the workers.

In April 1947 the Communists were expelled from the cabinet, and the final break between González Videla and the Communists came in August. They retaliated with protests and strikes, notably in the coal mines, which the government countered by deploying troops. When rightist groups, particularly the paramilitary Acción Chilena Anticomunista, called for sterner measures, González Videla in April 1948 banned the PCCh under the newly enacted Law for the Defence of Democracy and then severed relations with the Soviet Union, Yugoslavia and Czechoslavakia. Although González Videla turned against the Communist Party mainly because of domestic political and economic considerations, Cold War ideological pressures and financial incentives from the United States significantly contributed to that decision. After the Communist Party was declared illegal, an appreciative U.S. government stepped up its loans, investments and technical missions and also signed a military assistance pact with Chile.

While the Communists went underground – where they were to operate for a decade – the splintered Socialists continued to flounder, seeking fresh leadership, strategies and popularity under the guidance of new Secretary-General Raúl Ampuero Díaz, who rekindled the party's ideological commitment to revolutionary Marxism. In the 1949 congressional elections, however, in which women voted for the first time, the combined fractions of the PS netted only 9 per cent of the ballots; the Radicals mustered 28 per cent and the Right 42 per cent. A host of minor parties accounted for the remainder of the vote.

By the end of the Radical era, most Chileans were disenchanted with Popular Front politics. The contradictions of the 1940s had peaked with the González Videla administration, when a president promising to elevate the workers and secure 'economic independence' had ended up suppressing labour and embracing the United States. Disillusioned with shop-worn party programmes and slogans, Chileans groped for fresh political options at the outset of the 1950s.

Populist developmental strategies had proved tenable during the 1930s and 1940s. Import-substitution industrialization satisfied industrialists with protection and credit. Although penalized, agriculturalists welcomed expanding urban markets, low taxes and controls over rural labour. The middle class and the armed forces appreciated state growth and moderate nationalism, while the more skilled and organized urban workers received consumer, welfare and union benefits superior to those accorded other lower-class groups. These allocations postponed any show-down over limited resources and temporarily made Right and Left willing to compromise. Political institutionalization and accommodation stayed ahead of mobilization and polarization because the unorganized urban and especially rural poor remained effectively excluded. None of the reformist coalition governments ever mounted any assault on the fundamental privileges of domestic or foreign oligopolists, and severe obstacles to later development were left intact. Although operating through distinctive party mechanisms, Chilean politics produced few economic or social changes at variance with general patterns in Latin America. In the twilight of the Radical era, however, populist development strategies and Popular Front politics lost their dynamism. They came to be seen by the Right as an impediment to non-inflationary economic growth and by the Left as a diversion from essential structural change.

THE RETURN OF IBÁÑEZ, 1952 – 8

In the 1950s new battle-lines were being drawn up among seemingly incompatible ideological and social alternatives. On the Left, resurgent Marxists presented more militant projects for the construction of socialism and disdained alliances with centrist parties. Equally zealous Christian Democrats displaced the Radicals in the Centre and offered proposals for 'communitarian' reforms that bisected the poles of communism and capitalism. And the Right gradually closed ranks in defence of neo-capitalist and semi-corporatist visions of reconstruction. All three alternatives used the hiatus of the personalist presidency of Carlos Ibáñez (1952–8) to stake out firm new positions for future electoral combat, which would result in a victory for the Right in 1958, for the Centre in 1964 and for the Left in 1970, after which the military would brush aside all democratic competition. The second presidency of Ibáñez, then, served as the last gasp of the politics of the past and the seed-bed for the politics of the future.

The new directions taken by the parties in the 1950s corresponded to significant changes in the economic, social and political terrain. Under Ibáñez it became evident that import-substitution industrialization was hard pressed to transcend the stage of replacing light consumer goods from abroad or to provide the employment, productivity and national independence expected of it. As the growth of population and the cities increased, rural-to-urban migrants, agricultural workers and women emerged as social and political forces of greater consequence. The previously narrow electorate expanded enormously, mainly because the enfranchisement of women breathed new life into rightist and centrist parties. The percentage of the population registered to vote in presidential contests rose from approximately 10 per cent in the 1930s and 1940s to 18 per cent in 1952 and 21 per cent in 1958. This increase was also a result of improving literacy and the electoral reforms of 1958, which introduced an official secret ballot as well as stiff penalties for abstention or fraud. As elsewhere in Latin America, escalating and intensely politicized competition over indequate resources reduced the likelihood of broad populist coalitions, overloaded delicate political institutions and apparently pushed Chile towards a zero-sum game. Like the Radicals before him, Ibáñez entered office as a reformer governing with leftist parties and departed from it as a conservative surrounded by rightist groups, jettisoning his programme for economic nationalism and social justice along the way. Although the crises from 1958 on were not inevitable, the lack of attention by President Ibáñez to festering problems rendered subsequent demands for overdue changes less manageable.

In the 1952 presidential campaign, the old warhorse Ibáñez posed as a personalist alternative to the politics of spoils practised by the existing parties. Wielding the symbol of a broom, he promised to sweep out the rascals, represent all Chileans above petty partisanship, halt inflation and defend economic sovereignty. Thus, the 'General of Victory' attracted a ground swell from the discontented middle and working classes. His only firm party support, however, came from the tiny Agrarian Labour Party and Ampuero's fraction of the Socialists, which was attracted to the Argentine *peronista* model and hoped to use Ibáñez's mystical, nationalist appeal to recapture the masses for the Left. On his own momentum, the former dictator drew support from all points on the political spectrum and finished first with 47 per cent of the vote. His most surprising source of electoral support came from rural workers and Marxists, as the Left gathered new converts in the countryside with calls for land reform.

Ibáñez was trailed in the poll by the Conservative–Liberal candidate Arturo Matte Larraín (28 per cent), Pedro Enrique Alfonso Barrios for the Radicals (20 per cent) and the dissident Socialist Salvador Allende Gossens (5 per cent), formerly minister of health under Aguirre Cerda. Allende's token effort unfurled the banner of Socialist and Communist unity against centrist reformers that would become the strategy of the Left after infatuation with Ibáñez faded and the prohibition of the Communist Party was rescinded. Instead of heterogeneous coalitions of the middle and working classes behind programmes of industrialization, the Marxists began emphasizing mobilization of urban and rural labourers behind concerted demands for collectivist social and economic changes.

The rejuvenation of the Left was fed by President Ibáñez's failure to remedy economic dependence, stagnation, inflation and working-class poverty. Although posturing as an economic nationalist in tune with rising public resentment against U.S. influence, Ibáñez tried mainly to liberalize trade and stem inflation. Faced with declining export revenues and rising domestic prices, he began the return to economic orthodoxy that would be accelerated under his successor, Jorge Alessandri. He tried to reduce the emphasis on industry and restore some incentives to mining and agriculture. Although copper prices shot up briefly during the Korean War, after 1946 the general trend in mineral production and employment was downwards, the share of the labour force engaged in mining dropping from 6 per cent in 1940 to 4 per cent by 1960. In the 1950s, imports grew more rapidly than exports, paving the way to subsequent deficits and indebtedness. Ibáñez tried to resuscitate the mines by reversing the discriminatory government policies of the previous fifteen years and entering into a 'New Deal' with the copper companies in 1955 that lowered tax rates on the U.S. firms in order to stimulate investments and sales. During the remainder of the decade, however, copper exports rose only slightly, few new investments materialized and the primary result was higher profits for the U.S. copper firms, Anaconda and Kennecott. Ibáñez made similar attempts to reinvigorate the nitrate industry. Continuing severe dependence on the mining sector was also spotlighted by friction with the United States over possible copper tariffs and by the fact that in 1958 every one-cent fall in the world price of copper reduced Chilean foreign earnings by some $7 million.

Agriculture also remained in the doldrums. Productivity per worker declined 20 per cent under Ibáñez as farming came to account for barely 12 per cent of the GDP. The resultant gap between supply and demand boosted food imports and prices. The proportion of the active population in agriculture fell from 37 per cent in 1940 to 31 per cent in 1960, when farm workers received only 11 per cent of total wages paid in Chile. After sinking by 18 per cent from 1940 to 1952, real wages for agricultural labourers plummeted by another 38 per cent between 1953 and 1960. Many of those workers who had finally broken the grip of the landowners to vote for Ibáñez in 1952 thereafter switched to the Marxists or the

Christian Democrats, who promised to recast rural property and power relationships.

Stagflation also afflicted industry. Whereas industrial production per inhabitant had increased 6 per cent annually during 1946–52, it rose by less than 1 per cent annually during 1953–9. Import-substitution industrialization stalled as Ibáñez gave manufacturers less support for their efforts to move beyond the replacement of light consumer goods. When this dynamic sector of the economy lost its momentum, Chileans noted that it had brought neither the promised prosperity nor economic independence, especially given the manufacturers' heavy reliance on imported raw materials, equipment, technology and capital. Import substitution had also failed to absorb the burgeoning work-force – industrial employment only crept up from 17 per cent of the active population in 1940 to 18 per cent in 1960. Consequently, many Chilean intellectuals began advocating nationalization and redistribution – to transform ownership and income patterns – instead of merely the subsidization of domestic manufacturing. These critics observed that per capita income had grown by only 1.4 per cent annually during 1940–60 and that the gap with the industrial powers was not being narrowed. Per capita income in 1954 in Chile was still less than $150 compared with nearly $2,000 in the United States. They also criticized support for high-cost, oligopolistic industry on the grounds that it contributed to inflation.

A key reason for the industrial slow-down under Ibáñez was in fact the attack on inflation. Based on recommendations from the U.S. Klein–Saks mission, the administration restricted public spending, credit and currency emissions and imposed ceilings on prices, wages and salaries. It also lifted some controls on foreign exchange and trade. These drastic measures reduced the rise in the cost of living from 88 per cent in 1955 to 38 per cent in 1956. They also triggered the worst recession since the depression, convincing many Chilean economists that inflation was a necessary concomitant of growth and that orthodox stabilization medicines were inimical to national development. This controversy heated up the debate between 'structuralists', who blamed endemic inflation mainly on foreign trade dependency, archaic modes of production (especially in agriculture) and political struggles over government largesse among entrenched vested interests, and 'monetarists', who attributed rising prices principally to classic financial causes such as currency expansion and deficit spending. Whereas the former, with greater influence among Christian Democrats and Marxists, argued for the transformation of backward economic structures rather than financial belt-tightening, the latter, who held more influence with Ibáñez and the Right, contended that development would have to be delayed and distorted until financial practices were sanitized and monetary and wage–price increases were checked. Although the rate of inflation dipped to 17 per cent in 1957, it rebounded to 33 per cent in 1958, whilst economic growth and per capita income continued to sag. Amidst the debate as to whether stability and growth were compatible or conflictual, Chile was enjoying neither.

The resounding failure of Ibáñez's economic policies produced mounting social discontent and friction. According to one estimate for the years from 1953 to 1959, slower economic growth dragged the workers' portion of national income down from 30 to 26 per cent and that of the middle strata from 26 to 25 per cent, while the share of property-owners, financiers and top executives rose from 44 per cent to 49 per cent. In response to their shrinking purchasing power and rising unemployment (which leapt from 4 to 10 per cent in Santiago during 1952–8), workers manifested their discontent through the ballot box, demonstrations and agitation. Mainly in protest against the widening chasm between workers' incomes and the cost of living, strikes escalated from an average of 85 per year in the period 1939–46 to 136 per year in 1946–52 to 205 per year during the Ibáñez years. Although still concentrated in the cities and mines, such labour activism increasingly penetrated the countryside. At the same time, squatter slums proliferated as rural–urban migrants poured into the metropolitan areas, especially Santiago, creating mounting pressures for political representation, employment and housing. The unsatisfied demand, from both the working and middle classes, for dwellings led Ibáñez to create a government housing corporation, but an estimate for 1960 still placed the housing deficit at more than 500,000 units. A reasonably scientific poll of Santiago residents in 1957 turned up a shortage of housing and money as the chief worries of the inhabitants, a majority of whom felt their standard of living was deteriorating and unlikely to improve.[12] Thus, Ibáñez left the presidency with accumulated and compounded social ills, inequalities and complaints unattended to and crying out for attention from new political contenders.

There had, of course, also been considerable progress in the decades since the depression. For example, life expectancy at birth had increased

---

[12] Information on the sample survey as well as other aspects of the second Ibáñez period can be found in Federico G. Gil, *The Political System of Chile* (Boston, 1966), pp. 28–31.

from forty-one years in 1932 to fifty-seven years in 1960, while daily per capita protein intake had risen from sixty-nine grams before the Second World War to eighty grams by the end of the 1950s. Literacy among those fifteen years or older had risen from 75 per cent in 1930 to 80 per cent in 1952 and 84 per cent in 1960, and school enrollment from the primary grades through the universities had climbed from 743,125 in 1940 to 958,958 in 1950 to 1,506,287 by 1960. Chileans in the 1950s took justifiable pride in having one of the best-educated and healthiest populations in one of the most democratic countries in the hemisphere. They also, however, gazed with apprehension on the millions of workers and peasants whom decades of unfulfilled promises had left mired in poverty. Out of the urban slums and rural shanties were emerging renewed and intensified pressures on the inherited political order. The disappointments of the Radical years and of the return of Ibáñez convinced many Chileans that more comprehensive and dramatic cures would be required. As a result, electoral support flowed away from Ibáñez to the advancing Christian Democrats and the revivified Marxists, who offered competing concepts of reform to the masses.

Two splinter groups from the Conservative Party, the Falange and the Social Christians, fused to found the Partido Demócrata Cristiano (PDC) in 1957. Exuding youth and dynamism, they attracted new followers with their innovative wedding of Catholic and reformist appeals. Energized by the personal magnetism of Eduardo Frei, the Christian Democrats began dislodging the Radicals as the dominant centrist party. Their rise reflected the changing contours of Chilean society, as they carved out significant constituencies among the middle class, urban squatters, rural workers and women.

The Marxists achieved greater success, as they had in the 1930s, with a unified national trade union movement. Inspired by the ravages of inflation, the major labour unions replaced the defunct CTCh with the Central Unica de Trabajadores Chilenos (CUTCh) in 1953. Within this conglomeration of white- and blue-collar, Marxist and non-Marxist unions, the Socialists and especially the Communists quickly took command, primarily on the basis of their enduring support in older unions in mining, construction and manufacturing. In 1956–7 the Socialists and Communists formed an electoral alliance known as the Frente de Acción Popular (FRAP). This new approach grew out of the experimental Allende presidential campaign of 1952 and the subsequent Socialist call for a workers' front. FRAP rejected coalitions dominated by the upper or middle class, the Right or the Centre, and instead emphasized more intense dedication

to urban and rural workers and to socialist programmes for radical nationalization and redistribution.

The stage was set for the 1958 presidential contest by the congressional
elections in 1957. The various Socialist factions increased their share of the
poll from 10 per cent in 1953 to 11 per cent while the Christian Democrats' vote jumped from 3 to 9 per cent. With the waning of Ibáñez's
popularity, the Radicals saw their share of the vote increase from 14 to 22
per cent, the Conservatives from 10 to 18 per cent and the Liberals from
10 to 15 per cent. Following the reunification of the Socialists and the re-
legalization of the Communists immediately after the 1957 elections, the
Left joined the Centre and the Right in harbouring high expectations for
1958. The Conservatives and Liberals banked on the family reputation of
the austere businessman Jorge Alessandri Rodríguez, son of the deceased
Arturo. In the Centre, the Radicals nominated Luis Bossay Leyva and the
Christian Democrats Eduardo Frei. The FRAP, supported by some smaller
parties and *ibañistas,* campaigned for Allende.

Alessandri won the 1958 presidential election with 31.2 per cent of the
vote. Advocating more draconian state intervention to restructure the
national economy and society than any previous major candidate in Chilean history, Allende with 28.5 per cent came within a hair's breadth of
victory. Had not Antonio Zamorano, a former priest and FRAP deputy
with a following among the poor, taken 3.3 per cent of the vote, and had
not only 22 per cent of women compared with 32 per cent of men voted
for the FRAP, Allende might easily have won. The leftists' impressive
showing, including major inroads in rural districts, convinced them to
maintain their independent approach and awakened the United States to
the possibility of a democratically elected Marxist president in the Americas. The 1958 election also set patterns for the future by more clearly
defining electoral options in three main ideological camps, by revealing a
strong class bias behind those three positions and by establishing the
Christian Democrats, whose candidate, Frei, collected 20.5 per cent of the
vote, as the successors to the centrist Radicals, who secured only 15.4 per
cent. For the first time since 1932, it was the historic parties of the Right
which occupied the presidency. The era of Popular Front politics and
populism was over. Beginning in 1958 Chile became a laboratory for
contemporary developmental models, with each of the three political
camps – Right, Centre and Left – taking its turn in power until, in
1973, the armed forces imposed their own solution to Chile's economic,
social and political problems.

4

CHILE SINCE 1958

Since 1958, Chile has been ruled by four administrations (three elected, the fourth and longest imposed by a military coup), profoundly different in their ideologies and political aims, social basis and economic policies. The government of Jorge Alessandri, elected in 1958, was conservative and pro-business. Its support came from the private sector of the economy, from landowners (and the substantial peasant vote they still controlled), from sectors of the urban poor still ignored by the Marxist parties (Socialist and Communist) and by the Christian Democrats, and from the urban middle class, disillusioned with the Radicals, who had dominated political life from the Popular Front of 1938 to the election of Ibáñez in 1952, and not yet won over to the Christian Democrats. Alessandri proved incapable of dealing with Chile's persistent and increasing economic and social problems, and in 1964 Eduardo Frei, a Christian Democrat, was elected president.

Promising a 'revolution in liberty' the Partido Demócrata Cristiano (PDC) offered economic modernization combined with social justice and reform and the pursuit of class harmony. Even though the PDC enjoyed almost unprecedented electoral and congressional support (though without a majority in the Senate), the contradictions produced by trying to secure all those objectives, coupled with increasing ideological conflict and political strife, proved too much even for the able technocrats brought into the state apparatus. The threat of further reform and the electoral collapse of the Right in 1965 pushed the divided right-wing parties, Liberals and Conservatives, into the new and influential National Party. At the same time, mounting social conflict and the challenge posed by the PDC pushed the frequently discordant Socialist and Communist parties into strengthening – and broadening – their fragile alliance; the Frente de Acción Popular (FRAP) formed the axis of a new coalition of six parties of the Left, Unidad Popular (UP). The PDC, caught between the now stronger Right and Left, and weakened by small but damaging defections from its own ranks, offered a profound self-criticism in its electoral programme of 1970 and chose as its candidate the radical Radomiro Tomic, who pledged to accelerate the reforms partially implemented by the outgoing PDC administration. The National Party nominated former president Alessandri on a platform emphasizing authority, law and order. The UP coalition chose, though not without some unseemly public wrangling, Senator Salvador Allende to face his fourth presidential campaign on a programme of profound economic, political and social change. Allende was elected by a very narrow margin over Alessandri. The tasks Allende faced were more formidable than those of his predecessors, and the support he had was far less firm. Allende's government was by no means unique in its inability to deal with Chile's economic problems, especially inflation. However, political and ideological polarization and conflict reached levels of intensity which no constitutional political system could survive. Interference by the United States compounded Allende's problems, and no doubt there were grave errors of political leadership. The breakdown of democracy took place on 11 September 1973 with a brutal military coup.

A military junta in which General Augusto Pinochet, the last commander-in-chief of the armed forces in the UP government, soon took the leadership, combined political authoritarianism with an economy guided by the precepts of the monetarist school of economists—a return to the rule of market forces after a long period of state direction of the economy. Like the previous experiments, this one faced the obstacles that had plagued previous governments – over-dependence on earnings from copper exports, too high a level of external indebtedness, too low a level of new investment in productive activities and too low a level of productivity in agriculture. The economy did recover in the late 1980s, thanks to careful macro-economic management and favourable international prices. This recovery, however, has to be seen in the light of two severe recessions, and the social cost was great. Even economic recovery could not counteract the loss of popular support and an increasingly mobilized and active opposition. In a plebiscite held in October 1988, only 43 percent of the electorate voted for President Pinochet to remain in office for another eight years, while 55 percent opposed him.

SOCIAL CHANGE AND ECONOMIC INSTABILITY

In 1960 Chile had a population of 7.6 million; it had risen to 11.7 million by 1983 and to 12.5 million by 1987. Most of this population increase was absorbed by the cities, the urban population increasing from 68 to 82 percent. The population of Santiago doubled between 1952 and 1970, when it reached 2.8 million inhabitants; it had risen to more than 4 million by 1983.

Agriculture contributed 13.2 per cent to gross domestic product (GDP) in 1950, 10.1 per cent in 1960, a low of 7.1 per cent in 1981 and 8.6 per cent in 1986. Whereas 25.7 per cent of the economically active population was employed in agriculture in 1967, by 1980 this figure had fallen to 16.3 per cent, although it rose to 20.6 per cent by 1987 as the expansion of export agriculture generated more rural employment.[1] The political power of the traditional landowners declined sharply as the agrarian reform process, begun in a very mild way under Alessandri, accelerated with a new law and the legalization of rural unions under Frei. Virtually all large estates were expropriated under the UP government. The struggle of landowners to block reform and increasing peasant demand for land redistribution transformed a generally peaceful rural world into one of sharp class and political conflicts between 1967 and 1973.

Although the social structure of Chile became increasingly urban, employment in modern manufacturing enterprises generated only a relatively small proportion of total employment. Manufacturing, which contributed 21.9 per cent of GDP in 1950, increased its share to 24.7 per cent in 1970 but fell to 20.6 per cent in 1986; and the proportion of the economically active population engaged in manufacturing declined from 18.0 per cent in the mid-1960s to 16 per cent in 1980 and to 13.6 per cent in 1987. Moreover, most workers were not employed in large factories. Excluding the large artisanal sector, in 1978 21.2 per cent of the manufacturing work-force was employed in small-scale industry (10 to 49 workers), 30.2 per cent in medium-size industry (50 to 99 workers) and only 48 per cent

[1] Chilean statistics are a political minefield. This chapter relies heavily on the World Bank Report, *Chile: An Economy in Transition* (Washington, D.C., 1980), Markos Mamalakis, *The Growth and Structure of the Chilean Economy* (New Haven, Conn., 1980) and, especially, *Estudios CIEPLAN*. It is difficult to construct series because of changes in official methods of calculation – not least for price increases. Moreover, the official planning agency, ODEPLAN, from time to time revises its past estimates.

in large-scale industry (more than 100 workers).[2] In 1950, mining occupied 5.1 per cent of the work-force and in 1980, 3 per cent; the service sector (including government services), 23.8 per cent in 1960 and 28.1 per cent in 1980; and commerce 10.5 per cent in 1960 and 14.9 per cent in 1980.[3]

The relatively large size of the Chilean 'middle class' has often been noted; and though the term 'middle class' is very imprecise, it is not without meaning. White-collar workers (*empleados*), for example, considered themselves members of the middle class, and they were distinguished from blue-collar workers by separate legal codes, special privileges and higher earnings. This was a large group in 1970; it accounted for 24 per cent of the work-force in manufacturing, 49 per cent of the service sector and 29 per cent of the commercial sector. However, a much wider range of occupations fall into the category of middle class – small businessmen, professional groups, teachers, shopkeepers, managers and so on. Some groups were powerful, others were not; some formed part of the state sector, others worked in private enterprises. These middle-class sectors constituted a very influential segment of society; the political allegiance of the more Catholic sectors tended towards the PDC and the Right, whilst more secular elements provided the basis for the Radical Party and an important source of support for the Socialist Party. Others were attracted by the independent image of Alessandri in two presidential elections (1958 and 1970). In many ways the key political struggle in Chile was for the support of this sector of society.

One reason for the proliferation of political parties in Chile was the fragmentation of the electorate into a variety of social groups. Their perception of distinct interests and their increasing ability to make organized demands on the economic system help to account both for the way in which economic issues became highly politicized and for a general feeling that the economy was in serious difficulty. Yet poor economic performance should not be exaggerated. The overall annual growth rate per capita from 1960 to 1970 was 2.6 per cent, and there were periods of high growth thereafter despite a decline in the overall rate. In 1983 GDP per capita was lower than in 1970. Only by 1988 was it higher (by 10 per cent).

All four administrations in the period after 1958 pursued very distinct

[2] Guillermo Campero and Jose A. Valenzuela, *El movimiento sindical chileno en el capitalismo autoritario* (Santiago, 1981), p. 44.
[3] See Ricardo Lagos and Victor Tokman, 'Global Monetarism, Employment, and Social Stratification', *World Development* 12, no. 1 (1984), pp. 43–66.

economic policies to deal with problems that recurred with monotonous regularity. Each government tried to implement a growth model that avoided excessive inflation or foreign indebtedness. In this there was nothing new. Chile has had a long history of what Aníbal Pinto has called 'frustrated development'.[4] All these governments hoped to maximize earnings from the basic export mining sector, but found themselves victims of fluctuating international prices. Each government sought to attract new investment into the manufacturing sector and to increase the productivity of the neglected agricultural sector. Each government achieved some success in its efforts to stabilize the economy, but that success was only temporary and obtained at high cost. Alessandri's price stabilization of 1960–1 was financed by reckless foreign borrowing. The PDC found that its social reforms intensified demands and cost too much for the early economic achievement to be maintained. The Allende government achieved stabilization and growth for only a short period. The limited success of the military government before the sustained recovery after 1985, reflected in the high growth rates between 1977 and 1980, was based on massive foreign borrowing and by the use of the recession of 1975 as base year for calculations.

Nothing indicates more clearly the instability of the Chilean economy than the fluctuating rate of inflation. The rate in Alessandri's first year was 33.1 per cent; this was reduced to 5.4 and 9.4 per cent in the two succeeding years, but it accelerated again to 45.9 per cent in 1963. The Frei government gradually brought it down to a low of 17.9 per cent in 1966, but it rose again in 1970 to 34.9 per cent. Under Allende, although the rate fell to 22.1 per cent in 1971, thereafter it accelerated sharply and rose to 605.9 per cent in 1973. Only by 1977 did it fall below three figures, to 84.2 per cent and in 1978 to 37.2 per cent.[5] Inflation reached a low point of 9.5 per cent in 1981, rose again to 20.7 per cent in 1982 and then fell to 12.7 per cent in 1988.

The persistence of inflation in Chile was clearly much more than an economic phenomenon. In 1950 an International Monetary Fund (IMF) mission pointed out the non-monetary causes of inflation: 'Ideally the Chilean inflation could be ended by cutting off its sources one by one. Individual acts of investment, the Government budget, foreign transac-

---

[4] Aníbal Pinto, *Chile, un caso de desarrollo frustrado* (Santiago, 1962).

[5] Calculating the real rise in the consumer price index is very difficult when price movements are so erratic. However, the question is important since it affects politically sensitive issues such as the level of real wages. The most careful and accurate estimates are those of René Cortázar and Jorge Marshall, *Indice de precios al consumidor*, in *Estudios CIEPLAN*, no. 4 (1980), pp. 159–201.

tions, proposed wage increases and price increases could all be investigated and any plans inconsistent with a stable price level nipped in the bud. But this is a counsel of perfection'.[6] The reasons that these painful choices were not made in the competitive political world of Chile were analyzed and the gravity of the problem outlined by President Frei in his outgoing speech in 1970:

> The country is destined to tackle inflation either by consensus which is the democratic approach or by coercion: but an inflationary process like that which Chile has been experiencing over recent decades will lead inevitably to a grave social and economic crisis. The problem is more than merely technical. From the technical point of view the procedures for containing inflation are well known. But what happens here is that the patient calls the doctor and then he doesn't want to take the medicine. The problem is mainly political. . . . Everyone wants the sacrifices to be made by others than themselves. Every year I presented laws which would have enabled us to control inflation and every year they were rejected. Then the very people who had rejected these laws and fomented conflicts were the very ones who said that the government was to blame for inflation. It is a game with sinister overtones.[7]

One reason for the political importance of inflation was the central role of the state in almost every aspect of economic activity. The state came to control a growing share of the GDP in this period, rising from 38 per cent under Alessandri to 43 per cent under Frei and 53 per cent under Allende. The state's share of investment was even higher. There were, of course, differences in emphasis. Under Alessandri state activity was intended largely to support business; under Frei it was more actively concerned with the modernization of the economy; under Allende it emphasized redistribution and nationalization; and under Pinochet its role in theory was to be subsidiary to an economy shaped by market forces. Nevertheless, even under the military government, a very important part of economic activity continued to be controlled by the state; the top eight firms in Chile in 1980 were still in state lands, even though they were expected to operate as private firms, and much of the financial system was taken over by the government during the recession of 1982–3.

There were, however, limitations on the ability of the state to control the economy. One obvious factor which complicated economic planning in

---

[6] Quoted in Oscar Landerretche, 'Inflation and Socio-political Conflicts in Chile, 1955–1970' (unpublished D. Phil. dissertation, Oxford 1983), pp. 33–4.

[7] Quoted by Laurence Whitehead in Rosemary Thorp and Laurence Whitehead (eds.), *Inflation and Stabilisation in Latin America* (London, 1979), p. 68. Whitehead adds, 'Needless to say, between 1970 and 1973 Frei's party adopted exactly the strategy he criticised in his opponents'.

Chile was the external vulnerability of the economy. Any economy in which imports were so crucial, and exports so unstable, would tend towards instability unless changes in international prices could be absorbed into the domestic price structure, but the absence of sufficient resources for subsidies (e.g., to agriculture) and the oligopolistic character of much of the economy did not permit such flexibility in relative prices. Between a quarter and a third of total tax revenue came from the copper sector and from imports. After being very unstable in the 1950s, copper prices rose throughout the 1960s only to fall sharply in 1971–2. They rose briefly in 1973–4 but then fell sharply to real values well below those of the 1950s. Only in the late 1980s did prices rise substantially – even to record heights in 1988.

The problem of fluctuating export revenues was patched over by heavy foreign debt, which was in itself to become a major burden on the Chilean economy. The foreign debt grew rapidly from Alessandri's period onwards, especially from the raising of foreign loans to cover the fiscal deficit. The proportion of export revenues taken up by servicing the foreign debt was already varying between 40 and 60 per cent of export revenues by the late 1960s. The level of public and private foreign debt rose from U.S. $598 million in 1960 to $3 billion in 1970 and to an estimated $20 billion by 1986. Chile's per capita indebtedness was estimated in the early 1970s to be one of the highest in the world. Debt equity swaps helped to reduce the Chilean debt – in sharp contrast to the rest of Latin America – but it was still around $18.5 billion in 1988.

Chile was economically dependent on the United States, and this was to cause serious difficulties for the Allende government. Almost 40 per cent of Chilean imports came from the United States (including 90 per cent of supplies for copper mining). Most of the overseas credits that Chile obtained came from the United States. And the United States was Chile's main international public creditor, accounting for 50 per cent of the Chilean debt in 1970. The United States was by far the largest source of foreign investment in the Chilean economy—largely in mining until Frei's 'Chileanization' and Allende's nationalization and then increasingly in other sectors, though not on the scale of Mexico or Brazil. The United States also provided large loans from AID and extensive military aid.

Although Chile's economic relationship with the external world created problems for policy-makers, other countries had similar economic relationships without suffering from the same degree of persistent inflation and instability. The factors propagating inflation – disequilibria in the public finances, expansion of banking credit, excessive wage and salary increases and so on – reflected the national, as well as the international, political economy of Chile. The state of public finances in Chile has been referred to as 'fiscal anarchy'.[8] Throughout the period of civilian government there was the wide-spread practice of approving budgets that ignored important costs foreseen at the outset of the fiscal year. These costs, often the result of pressure from a powerful group, were then passed on by the printing of more money and an increase in the rate of inflation. Moreover, the fiscal budget did not include the autonomous and semi-autonomous agencies that sent their budgets to the Ministry of Finance, which approved and modified them without discussion in Congress. In effect, these agencies, which accounted for half of total public expenditure, were free to determine the size of the deficit which the state would have to finance.

One of the major bottlenecks in the Chilean economy was the inadequate rate of capital formation. Chile's disappointing growth rate was due in large measure to the low rate of savings, normally about 12 per cent of GDP when other Latin American countries achieved rates of more than 20 per cent. Even following the economic recovery of the late 1980s, savings rose to only 17 per cent of GDP. Most investment in Chile, even during the Pinochet years, was public. The share of total public investment in gross domestic capital formation rose from 46.6 per cent in 1961 to 74.8 per cent in 1969, while private direct investment grew at an annual cumulative rate of only 3.2 per cent. All three civilian governments tried different methods to stimulate private investment. Alessandri offered substantial benefits to the private sector, but the response was lukewarm; Frei tried a forced savings scheme from workers' contributions, but union resistance undermined his plans, aided by opposition from employers who were also expected to contribute; and Allende faced a virtual private investment boycott.

Various factors explain the private sector's reluctance to invest. The small size of the market set limits on the extent of industrialization possible in an economy like that of Chile. Industrialists imported a large proportion of their inputs and faced problems of price variation and supply difficulties. It is often noted that the concentration in most industrial sectors permitted large profits with only limited new investment. Another

---

[8] Ricardo Ffrench-Davis, *Políticas económicas en Chile, 1952–1970* (Santiago, 1973), p. 199.

explanation stresses entrepreneurs' lack of expectation of stable growth: quick profits from speculation looked more secure than investment in long-term growth or reinvestment in land. The absence of a well-organized capital market and frequently erratic interest rates discouraged long-term investment and encouraged reliance on borrowing from abroad. Bank credit was highly concentrated, and those who enjoyed access to it in effect received a substantial subsidy. Such a high level of concentration led to an inefficient use of resources, permitted enormous speculative gains and discriminated against small enterprises, and the low real cost of credit under civilian governments generated inflationary pressures.

As agricultural development lagged behind population growth, Chile became an increasingly heavy importer of food. The cost of food imports rose from an equivalent of 9 per cent of the value of non-agricultural exports in 1956 to 22.2 per cent in 1965 and to more than 30 per cent by 1972. There are many reasons for this dismal performance of agriculture, some of them contradictory. One argument is that urban food prices were kept low by means of controls that suppressed income and profits for farmers and reduced the incentive and the possibility of investing. A counter-argument suggests that food prices rose faster than the costs of agricultural inputs and that the real reason for the dismal performance of agriculture was the grossly unequal distribution of land tenure.[9] Exchange rates were generally overvalued, making food imports relatively cheap and Chilean food exports relatively expensive. Government policy towards agriculture was divided among competing agencies. Like the industrial sector, credit was concentrated in a very few hands and marketing facilities were inadequate. Until the Agrarian Reform Law was passed by the PDC government, the land tenure system concentrated the best agricultural lands in large, inefficient estates. But simple redistribution of land alone could not increase productivity, which depended on a series of other measures that civilian governments could not afford in either political or financial terms. In any case, the process of reform lasted only a relatively short time before it was ended by the military coup. Though agriculture suffered initially under the military regime, increased investment, a more realistic exchange rate after 1983, government help and protection and low agricultural wages eventually led to growth, especially in the export sector.

[9] This is the argument of the classic article by Osvaldo Sunkel, 'La inflación chilena: Un enfoque heterodoxo', *El Trimestre Económico* (Mexico), (October 1958).

The economy exhibited features of concentration other than that of income and credit even before the process intensified after 1973. The industrial and construction sectors were highly concentrated, and overlapping membership and ownership confined economic power to a relatively small circle. This pattern of a small number of large firms and a huge number of small enterprises and artisanal workshops (as late as 1963 almost half of industrial employment was in some seventy thousand artisanal firms) was not efficient. Industry needed a high level of protection, charged high prices and was heavily dependent upon imports while having a poor export performance. The removal of protection by the Pinochet government did not lead to a notably more efficient industrial structure—though it did lead to a record number of bankruptcies.

Although not excessively inequitable by international standards, Chile's income distribution pattern was still sufficiently imbalanced to supply ample ammunition to reformers. Income differentials did narrow in the post-war years: between 1954 and 1968 the share of the poorest 20 per cent rose from 1.5 to 4.9 per cent of total incomes and that of the richest 10 per cent fell from 49 to 35 per cent. Although this trend was initially accelerated under the Allende government, the gains were eroded first by inflation and thereafter by government policy under the military. Unemployment fell from 7.3 per cent in 1960 to a low of 3 per cent in 1972. But it was consistently in double figures during the military government, rising to a high of about 30 per cent in 1983. Unemployment fell sharply in the late 1980s, but low wages and a decrease in state provision of basic services meant that some three to four million Chileans were living below the poverty line.

The Chilean economy was a battle-ground between economists of the structuralist and the monetarist persuasions, both of which had an opportunity to apply their theories. Monetarists first experimented in a mild way in 1956–7 and then in a very extreme way between 1975 and 1983. Structuralist ideas informed the Frei government in 1965–7 and influenced the analysis of UP policy-makers as well. The costs of the monetarist experiment were reflected in a decline in economic activity, recession and unemployment. The economic and social costs of the structuralist reforms proved to be incompatible with the need for short- and medium-term stabilization. Even with strong authoritarian government, those bearing the social cost of the monetarist experiment were not permanently passive, and the Pinochet government was incapable of permanently repressing discontent.

THE CRISIS OF CONSTITUTIONAL POLITICS

Since the election of Arturo Alessandri in 1932, Chile had experienced a long period of constitutional government. However, political conflicts frequently entered the institutional arena in the form of clashes between president and Congress. These clashes were not simply the product of a reforming president facing a hostile Congress: Jorge Alessandri's conservative administration (1958–64) had to resort to measures to by-pass Congress. The system of proportional representation used for elections made it virtually impossible for a president to have a majority in both chambers of Congress; the fact that elections were staggered rather than simultaneous compounded the problem; and since presidents could not offer themselves for immediate re-election, there was inevitably a lame duck period towards the end of a presidential term of office.

Although the major problem of political management for the executive lay in the party system, the administrative system itself was an obstacle to effective rule: it was fragmented; it exhibited marked degrees of independence, especially in the decentralized agencies; and it often developed close links with the sector it was supposed to oversee to the detriment of overall planning. The fifty or so decentralized or autonomous agencies employed almost 40 per cent of public employees in Chile, and in many ways they were a law unto themselves. The PDC, for example, constantly found its housing policies undermined by the activities of these agencies.

The party system permeated all layers of political life, from the remote *municipio* to the national Congress. Trade unions of all sorts enjoyed close and often traditional links with the political parties: with the Socialist and Communist parties in the case of blue-collar workers, with the Radicals and PDC in the case of white-collar workers. Employers associations, associations of landowners, university student movements, neighbourhood associations and even football clubs were subject to competition for support from the political parties. In a remote coal-mining area like Lota, for example, the municipality and the trade union seemed to be extensions of the Communist Party, and the only alternative forms of social organization were the evangelical chapels.[10] Such a party system could function only as long as ideological commitment was qualified by compromise. It needed a basic political consensus – or else the inability of those who did not accept

---

[10] See Penelope Pollitt, 'Religion and Politics in a Coal Mining Community in Southern Chile' (unpublished Ph.D. dissertation, Cambridge, 1981).

Table 4.1. *Percentage of votes for major parties in congressional elections (deputies), 1957–73*

Party	1957	1961	1965	1969	1973
Conservative	17.6	14.3	5.2	20.0	21.3
Liberal	15.4	16.1	7.3		
Radicals	22.1	21.4	13.3	13.0	3.7
PDC	9.4	15.4	42.3	29.8	29.1
Socialist	10.7	10.7	10.3	12.2	18.7
Communist	–	11.4	12.4	15.9	16.2
Others	24.8	10.7	9.2	9.1	11.0

Source: Adapted from Arturo Valenzuela, *The Breakdown of Democratic Regimes: Chile* (Baltimore, 1978), p. 35. The Conservatives and Liberals formed the National Party in 1966. The Communist Party was illegal until 1958.

the consensus to disrupt the political system. During the period from 1958 to 1973 the consensus weakened while the capacity for disruption increased.

The Chilean party system had a number of unusual features. Electoral competition was intense, and apart from the 42.3 and the 35.6 per cent for the PDC in the congressional election of 1965 and the municipal election of 1967, no party gained more than 30 per cent of the popular vote in any election under the 1925 constitution. Moreover, despite the huge increase in the size of the electorate, it was divided into three relatively stable blocs – Right, Centre and Left – as the distribution of support for the major parties in five congressional elections held over twenty years shows (Table 4.1). Of course, this tells us nothing about the relations of the parties and movements inside those blocs, nor about the nature of competition between them. And it begs the question about the definition of the 'Centre'. But it does show how difficult it was to create majority government.

It is not possible to establish a simple correlation between social class and support for a particular party. In the first place, the existence of so many parties undermined the claim of any one of them to represent a particular class. The organized working class, for example, was divided between Socialists and Communists, with a not inconsiderable number supporting the PDC. The urban poor, not subject to the politicizing influence of trade union membership, spread its vote (or abstention) quite widely, including support for parties of the Right. Moreover, the Socialist Party received considerable support from middle-class groups, especially university-trained professionals. Middle-class groups were at home in the PDC, Radical Party or the National Party. This distribution of social class amongst political parties was by no means unique to Chile. Nor was it peculiar that the ideological inflexibility of the party militants and party elites increased quite markedly after 1964. There were, after all, enough deep social cleavages in Chile to provide the basis for the politics of class confrontation.

One change that did take place in this period was the reduction in the number and importance of minor parties. The percentage of the vote received by the five largest parties increased from 52.5 per cent in 1957 to 78.6 per cent in 1961, to 85.6 per cent in 1965 and to 90.9 per cent in 1969, although there was a small decline in 1973 to 87.8 per cent.[11] It would, however, be an exaggeration to attribute this process of concentration solely to an increase in ideological hostility among the parties; there were also changes in the electoral laws which made it virtually impossible for small parties to win seats in Congress.

It would also be an exaggeration to trace a simple development in Chile during this period from the politics of compromise and clientelism to the politics of exclusion and polarization. Yet it is undeniable that from the mid-1960s onwards political parties in Chile became more ideologically dogmatic and intransigent and that party relationships deteriorated. One element in this process was the replacement of a pragmatic party, the Radical Party, from the central position in Chilean politics by an ideological party, the PDC. The PDC had a much more coherent project of national transformation than the Radical Party, and it attempted to exclude other parties from power rather than construct alliances. On the Left, the Socialist Party adopted a much more intransigent line at its congress in 1967, which expressed a preference, if not for the *via armada*, at least for the *via insurreccional*. This line was never the choice of Allende, but represented the victory of pro-Cuban groups in that divided and factional political party. Yet at the same time, the party elected a moderate, Aniceto Rodríguez, as secretary-general. Although the Communist Party was less intransigent that the Socialist Party, by its very nature it could not be other than opposed to the PDC and the Right. The days of

[11] Arturo Valenzuela, 'Origins and Characteristics of the Chilean Party System: A Proposal for a Parliamentary Form of Government', mimeo (1984), Table 3. This section on parties owes a great deal to the insights of Valenzuela.

Eurocommunism had not yet dawned. On the Right, the rise of the technocrats of the Chicago school saw the growing influence of a political dogma which was more doctrinaire than that of the PDC. The traditional politicians of the Right saw their influence decline with the growth of both the technocrats and the neo-fascist groups organized in movements like Patria y Libertad.

The evolution of the Chilean political system up to the coup of 1973 supports Linz's proposition that 'the conditions leading to semi-loyalty or even suspicion of semi-loyalty by leading participants in the political game, opposition and government parties alike, account for the breakdown process almost as much as the role of the disloyal oppositions'.[12] It was the combination of the growth of extremism with the 'semi-loyalty' of the major parties that was to create the conditions for the breakdown of the democratic system in 1973.

THE CONSERVATIVE AS TECHNOCRAT: THE PRESIDENCY OF JORGE ALESSANDRI, 1958–1964

Although his candidacy was backed by the parties of the Right (Conservative and Liberal), Jorge Alessandri was elected president in 1958 as an independent. One reason for this was tactical. The combined Liberal and Conservative vote was unlikely to win a plurality. By presenting himself as an independent, Alessandri would draw on the multi-class support of those who identified party politics as corrupt and narrowly sectoral. The traditional Right in Chile was to face this dilemma in subsequent presidential elections: by itself it could not hope to win, and yet alliance with the Centre (now represented more by the PDC than the Radicals) was very uncomfortable. However, Alessandri's stance as an independent also represented his genuine belief in the virtues of technocracy over party politics. He hoped in government to avoid the political compromises and concessions of previous administrations.

Alessandri was a prominent businessman who held important positions in a number of firms, including a monopoly on paper processing, and was closely associated through the Alessandri–Matte economic conglomerate with three large private banks. Before becoming a senator in 1957 he was the president for fifteen years of Chile's major business association, the Confederación de la Producción y el Comercio. His father had twice been

---

[12] Juan Linz and Alfred Stepan (eds.), *The Breakdown of Democratic Regimes: Crisis, Breakdown and Reequilibration* (Baltimore, 1978), p. 38.

president of the republic. His two brothers were senators (both Liberals), and one had been a presidential candidate in 1946. Alessandri had served as finance minister in the last Radical administration and had been forced to resign in 1950 when white-collar unions opposed his proposed wage freeze.

Alessandri's proposals in the 1958 campaign were far less specific than those of major rivals – Allende (FRAP, Socialist–Communist), Frei (PDC, Christian Democrat), Bossay (Radical) – but his general stance was in favour of economic liberalism. His electoral platform advocated less government control over the economy, including the suppression of controls over prices, credits and foreign exchange and a policy of price stabilization. An essential part of his strategy was the opening of the economy to foreign economic interests by making the conditions for foreign investment more attractive. However, Alessandri and his economic team were not monetarists. He rejected a policy of credit restriction and saw no need for a reduction in economic activity or an increase in unemployment in order to combat inflation. His policy was to create the right conditions for the private sector to develop the economy. Since this could not be achieved overnight, the government was initially prepared to increase state investment and to try to attract foreign capital and loans both to finance government expenditure and to assist the process of domestic capital formation. In effect, the short-term economic policy of Alessandri was a mixture of liberalization and reflation of the economy, with public investment playing an important role. Wage and salary increases were to be held down to prevent inflation (redistribute income to profits). Tax increases could be avoided by foreign borrowing.

In spite of the initial support that Alessandri received from the dominant economic sectors, his position was not an easy one. The economy he inherited from the previous administration was weak: the balance of payments was in deficit, unemployment had risen to 9 per cent in the cities, there was a large fiscal deficit in spite of a low level of investment and the economy had suffered a long period of stagnation. Nor was his political position very strong. He had gained less than one-third of the popular vote (see Table 4.2), and his supporters controlled only about one-third of the seats in Congress. So he eventually had no alternative but to seek coalition allies, especially since some of his measures proved to be very unpopular with the FRAP and the PDC.

Alessandri's attempt to reactivate the economy enjoyed initial success but soon ran into difficulties. Overall growth rates were quite positive. In

Table 4.2. *The 1958 presidential election*

Candidate	Vote	Percentage
Alessandri (Conservative–Liberal)	389,909	31.2
Allende (Socialist–Communist)	356,493	28.5
Frei (Christian Democrat)	255,769	20.5
Bossay (Radical)	192,077	15.4
Zamorano (Independent)	41,304	3.3
Blank/void	14,798	1.1
Total	1,250,350	100

Source: Arturo Valenzuela, *The Breakdown of Democratic Regimes: Chile* (Baltimore, 1978), p. 40. The abstention rate was 16.5%.

fact, the annual increase in GDP per capita of 2.7 per cent for the period from 1959 to 1964 was far more impressive than the 0.3 per cent of the previous period, or even the 2.0 per cent of the next five years.[13] But inflation, which declined from 33.3 per cent in 1958 to 7.7 per cent in 1961, rose sharply to 44.3 per cent in 1963. Nevertheless, unemployment fell from 9.0 per cent in 1959 to 5.5 per cent in 1963, and industrial output rose steadily throughout the period. There was also substantial investment in the road network and in housing construction for the working and middle classes.

The breakdown of economic policy came on the external front. By 1961 the fiscal deficit had risen to 5 per cent of the GDP, and this growing deficit was financed by foreign loans. Exports did not rise as anticipated, and the deficit on the current account balance of payments rose to 55 per cent of the value of exports in 1961. Most of the foreign loans were short-term financial loans, and the policy of freezing the exchange rate could not be sustained. The result was a massive devaluation of 33 per cent in 1962. The period of stabilization was over, and one of the major legacies of the Alessandri administration was a crippling level of debt. In 1960 total public debt was U.S. $589 million, equivalent to 20 per cent of GDP. Over the next five years the level rose to just over U.S. $1 billion, or 26 per cent of GDP, though only a modest amount went into long-term investment. If paid, the total servicing of foreign capital (including profit remittances) would have amounted to 70 per cent of exports in 1965.

[13] World Bank Report, *Chile,* p. 11. The government seems to have absorbed the effects of the 1960 earthquakes even though they destroyed an estimated 9% of GDP, mostly in buildings.

Foreign financing of private sector activities to expand working capital also grew rapidly during this period – from $63 million in 1960 to $219 million by the end of 1965.

Alessandri's policies soon ran into political difficulties. The attempt to hold down wages led to union protests, culminating in a series of strikes in 1960. In November there was a national strike and a series of demonstrations all over the country, in which two workers were killed. Many of the strikers were white-collar workers and government employees, and this discontent was translated into adverse results in the March 1961 congressional elections, even though Alessandri softened his policy on wage restraint.

The 1961 elections were the first to be held after significant changes in the electoral law. For the first time there was a single official ballot and increased penalties for electoral fraud and bribery. Landowners could no longer manipulate peasant voters by ensuring that they took the correct party list along with them to the ballot box, although, of course, the political influence of landowners over peasants was not ended overnight. The vote was also made compulsory. The results were a set-back for the Right: for the first time, the PDC polled more than the combined vote of the Conservatives and Liberals and – just as troublesome – the FRAP won nearly a third of the seats in the lower house and elected thirteen out of forty-five senators.

The illusion of technocratic administration was replaced by the realities of party politics as the Radicals were brought into the cabinet. Moreover, influenced by the newly founded Alliance for Progress, the government took several reformist measures that, although modest in themselves, paved the way for further and more drastic remedies. Reform of its relationship with the (largely U.S.-owned) copper companies was placed firmly on the political agenda, even though this was partly a device of the landlords to deflect attention away from the issue of agrarian reform. Taxes on the copper industry rose by 10 to 15 per cent, and there were moves to increase drastically the amount of copper refined in Chile to 90 per cent and to increase overall production. Although Alessandri replaced the Conservative minister of mines who made these proposals, it was clear that the pressure for nationalization would grow. The first steps towards land reforms were also taken, under pressure from the United States, which was anxious to avoid another Cuba in Latin America. Law 15020 was a modest measure, and very little land was expropriated. But it did establish two agencies that were to play a crucial role in transforming the countryside, the Corporación de Reforma Agrícola (CORA) and the Instituto de Desarrollo Agropecuario (INDAP).

Alessandri's economic policies were no doubt in the long-term interests of the economic elite, which certainly benefited from them. But for its part the elite failed to transform itself into a modernizing autonomous sector: it preferred protection and monopoly profits to the bracing effects of competition. The political consequence of this was the continued dominance of traditional conservatism and the maintenance of the Right in an essentially defensive posture. This left the way open for the PDC to adopt the task of modernizing capitalism and reforming the traditional land structure, a measure bitterly opposed by the Right. Morever, the Right had failed to free itself from reliance on a candidate who made a personal appeal above parties; in 1970 it was to turn again to Alessandri.

Although Alessandri remained personally popular with the entrepreneurial sectors, their support for the government declined. And as inflation started to accelerate after the 1962 devaluation, popular opposition mounted. The strikes called that year by the Central Unica de Trabajadores (CUT) were widely supported, especially in the shanty towns that surrounded Santiago. In the demonstrations against the government, six people were killed and many were wounded and arrested. The government once more gave in to the striker's demands, thus accelerating inflation and reaffirming the Left's new-found strength and confidence. In the 1963 municipal elections the real victors were the PDC, whose vote rose from 15.4 per cent in the 1961 congressional elections to 22 per cent in 1963; both Communists and Socialists registered small gains.

The scene was now set for the 1964 presidential election. The Right could not hope to do well. Inflation was running at nearly 50 per cent; the balance of payments was still critical; real wages and salaries had fallen, especially those of government employees and the poorest members of the work-force, who received little more than the government minimum wage, which fell by 14.2 per cent in 1963. The announced right-wing presidential candidate, Julio Durán, saw his alliance (Radicals, Liberals and Conservatives) come a poor third in a by-election in the rural and normally Conservative province of Curicó. The election was unexpectedly won by the FRAP candidate, with 40 per cent of the vote to the PDC's 27 per cent. The forthcoming presidential election began to look like a contest between those two forces. In such circumstances the Liberals and Conservatives reluctantly supported the least undesirable candidate, Eduardo Frei, who won with 56 per cent of the vote (Table 4.3). The shadow of Cuba loomed large over the

Table 4.3. *The 1964 presidential election*

Candidate	Vote	Percentage
Frei	1,409,012	55.7
Allende	977,902	38.6
Durán	125,233	5.0
Blank/void	18,550	0.7
Total	2,530,697	100

Source: Arturo Valenzuela, *The Breakdown of Democratic Regimes: Chile* (Baltimore, 1978), p. 40. Abstention was 13.2%.

subsequent electoral campaign, and the United States provided considerable financial and technical support for the PDC.[14]

THE REVOLUTION IN LIBERTY: THE PRESIDENCY OF EDUARDO FREI, 1964–70

I am convinced that the failure of the 'revolution in liberty' was inevitable, essentially because of the contradiction between its *programme for economic development* based on and reinforcing the capitalist structure of the Chilean economy and its *programme for social development*. The latter, mobilizing the people in defense of their interests, increased the many contradictions in Chilean society, particularly those related to the functioning of capitalist economy in an underdeveloped country. (Radomiro Tomic, PDC presidential candidate in 1970)[15]

Tomic's statement reflects the judgment of hindsight. It is far removed from the sense of excitement that swept the PDC when its triumph in the 1964 presidential elections was announced. The electoral euphoria of 1964 was reinforced by the results of the congressional elections of March 1965, when the honeymoon with the new administration had not yet worn off. The PDC gained 42.3 per cent of the vote, a massive increase compared with its last congressional election showing in 1961, when it gained only 15.4 per cent. The PDC took 82 of the 147 seats in the lower house; and

[14] According to the U.S. congressional report, 'The CIA spent more than $2.6 million in support of the PDC candidate. . . . More than half of the PDC's candidate's campaign was financed by the United States, although he was not informed of this assistance.' Staff Report of the Select Committee to Study Governmental Operations with Respect to Intelligence Activities, *Covert Action in Chile, 1963–1973* (U.S. Senate, Washington D.C., 1975), p. 9.

[15] Radomiro Tomic, 'Christian Democracy and the Government of the Unidad Popular', in Federico Gil, Ricardo Lagos and Henry Landsberger (eds.), *Chile at the Turning Point: Lessons on the Socialist Years, 1970–1973* (Philadelphia, 1979), p. 214.

in the Senate (where only half the seats were up for re-election) it increased its number from 12 to 21, although it lacked an overall majority.

The PDC's historical roots dated from the break of the Falange from the Conservative Party in the 1930s. At first a party of socially committed students from Chile's Catholic University, it remained a small, though sometimes influential, body until the 1950s, when it started to gain popular support. Hierarchical in structure and led by men from the upper and middle classes, it nevertheless began to attract considerable support from the urban poor, neglected by the Socialist and Communist parties, which concentrated on trade unions, as well as backing from large sectors of the middle class, disenchanted with the Radicals.

Naturally a party which enjoyed such widespread support across the social spectrum, and whose growth had been so rapid and so recent, contained several divergent groups. Even before the divisions assumed a more solid form in the splits between the *Oficialistas, terceristas* and *rebeldes*, there were differences in the pace and direction of social and economic change. The most conservative group was concerned to modernize the capitalist system and intensify the process of industrialization. A second group emphasized income redistribution and the organization of the poor. The most radical group, the *rebeldes*, was more concerned with profound transformations of such areas as the agrarian landowning system and the concentration of economic power, especially in the banking and financial system, and with the development of communitarian forms of ownership. Frei's presidency saw a constant struggle among these sectors.

Even so, for a multi-class party with such divisions over policy, the degree of unity was surprisingly high – much higher than that in the Socialist or Radical Party. This was due in part to a common sense of ideological purpose, not unlike that of the other relatively united ideological force in Chilean politics, the Communist Party. Perhaps it had something to do with the mores of obedience and hierarchy that came from its identification with the Catholic Church. Perhaps it also derived from the feeling that the electorate had entrusted the party with a mission that was not to be diluted with alliances with other parties. There is little doubt that many members felt that they had become the natural governing party of Chile – which gave rise to a degree of sectarianism that many Christian Democrats came later to regret.[16]

---

[16] Thus, according to Andrés Zaldívar, a leading member of the PDC and a former finance minister, 'We are guilty of a great deal of sectarianism . . . we made a fundamental error in not having sought alliances with the Radicals, and others of social-democratic tendencies'. Florencia Varas, *Exilio en Madrid* (Santiago, 1983), p. 56.

The U.S. government, also hoping that the PDC would become the natural governing party, gave consistent support to Frei's government. It should not be assumed that policy was unduly influenced by the United States. Frei pursued an independent foreign policy, marked by several important initiatives towards Latin American unity, and he was one of the few Chilean politicians to emerge as a statesman of world repute. Yet between 1962 and 1969 Chile received well over a billion dollars in direct, overt U.S. aid – more aid per capita than that to any other country in the hemisphere. Such help reinforced economic dependence on the United States and partly explains the favourable terms offered to U.S. multinationals, including, initially at least, the copper companies. But it was also to prove a source of internal dispute within the PDC.

In contrast with the two previous administrations, the PDC did not propose a policy of price stabilization as top priority. Rather, the emphasis was on stabilization through structural reform to encourage both economic growth and income redistribution. This would lead to the eventual creation of a communitarian society in which class conflict would be eliminated. Three reforms were regarded as of utmost priority. The first was the 'Chileanization' of the copper sector – a project of partnership between the state and the U.S. companies. Massive investment in copper was needed to provide the revenue for imports. The second was an agrarian reform combined with rural unionization and organization. The old large estates would be replaced initially by communally run farms which would increase production and secure a base for the PDC in the countryside. The third was a programme of organization of the popular sectors, especially shanty town dwellers, and of women. This programme of *promoción popular* would end the marginalization of these sectors. Of lesser urgency, but no less important, were measures to 'democratize' the union movement and break the hold of the Marxist parties, a massive educational reform and a constitutional reform to strengthen the executive branch.

The Frei government benefited from very high copper prices, although this was due partly to a change in the pricing policy by the government itself. Tax revenues from the large foreign companies averaged U.S. $195 million per year from 1966 to 1970 – a considerable increase over the level of $80 million under Alessandri's administration. Exports rose from $676 million in 1964 to $1,139 million in 1969, and although imports rose quickly too, a deficit of more than $4 million in 1964 was converted into a surplus of $183 million by 1969. GDP growth, however, was slightly lower than in the Alessandri period, at an annual per capita increase of 2 per cent. The external debt doubled during the period of PDC rule to reach a little more than $2 billion in 1969. Perhaps the greatest disappointment was the failure to curb inflation. The rate did come down from 40.4 per cent in 1964 to 17.9 per cent in 1966 but it thereafter rose gradually to 34.9 per cent in 1970.

Real progress was made in dealing with the problems of poverty. Compared with the end of the Alessandri period, when the figure was about 42 per cent of GNP, the wage and salaried sector received closer to 51 per cent at the end of the Frei presidency. Government policy encouraged this transfer, especially in the rural sector, where real wages rose by 40 per cent. Total enrollment in education rose by 46 per cent from 1964. A quarter of a million new houses were built, mostly for the poorest sectors of society. The PDC administration also increased the efficiency of the state apparatus. Taxes rose as a percentage of the GNP from 12.8 per cent in 1964 to 21.2 per cent in 1970. The government introduced a wealth tax and carried out a property tax reassessment.

The PDC period is notable for an impressive growth in state participation in the economy. Public expenditure as a proportion of the GNP rose from 35.7 per cent in 1965 to 46.9 per cent in 1970. The share of the state in public investment and in the banking sector also grew rapidly. As in the Alessandri period, however, this increase in public investment reflected the weakness of private sector investment and an overall failure to improve the level of new investment in productive sectors of the economy. The PDC spent more on social reforms than was justified by the increases in state revenue. Tax revenue continued to finance only about three-quarters of total government spending in 1965. Expenditures on housing, agriculture and education increased sharply: on housing alone they rose by 70 per cent in real terms in 1965. Once the process of expansion had started, it became difficult to restrain, especially as initial expenditures aroused popular enthusiasm for more. Fiscal problems were also caused by large salary and wage increases, especially for civil servants. But this enthusiasm was not shared by the private sector. Private sector investment fell, as investors feared the extension of the redistributive reforms of the PDC. The two greatest obstacles to the achievement of successful stabilization were the failure to raise the level of national savings and the increases in remunerations over the planned level. The former aspiration of the union movement – readjustments in line with inflation – now became the starting point for negotiations.

The 'Chileanization' of copper was regarded as the keystone of the government's policy. The objectives were to double the production of copper in the Gran Minería by 1972, to set up a series of joint ventures between the Chilean government and the U.S. companies, to increase the amount of copper refined in Chile, to integrate the copper industry into the Chilean economy and to give the Chilean government a more active role in international marketing. The Kennecott Company, whose Chilean holdings represented only a small part of its international operations, took the initiative in order to push the government into a quick deal; the government, anxious to show a successful initiative, responded quickly. The agreement proved to be a triumph for a firm that had a poor record of investment in Chile. The company secured an estimate for the value of the 51 per cent share in the El Teniente mine purchased by the government that was far higher than the book value (the real value was assessed at U.S. $160 million, compared with the book value of $66 million). Moreover, tax on sales was reduced, providing the company with a considerable increase in profits. This, combined with an underestimation of the price of copper, meant that the profits on the 49 per cent of the shares owned by the company were higher in 1967 and 1968 than they had been for the complete holdings in the preceding six years. It was agreed that the Chilean government would invest $110 million obtained from the U.S. Export–Import Bank; CODELCO, the Chilean copper corporation, would invest $27 million; and the company would invest $92 million, just $12 million more than it received as compensation. Moreover, Kennecott maintained management control as a condition of the Export–Import Bank loan to Chile.

The political outcry at the leniency of the deal with Kennecott, and the reluctance of the Anaconda Corporation, whose Chuquicamata and other mines were an important part of its overall operations, led to a more prolonged and difficult negotiation – 'nacionalización pactada'. Anaconda, which had also made record profits from its limited agreements with the government, agreed in 1969 to transfer 51 per cent of its assets to the government at once and the remainder over three years; and a new agreement over prices increased government revenue. The initial compensation was based on the book value, but the rather less favourable agreements for transferring the remainder were overtaken by the nationalization of the Gran Minería under the Allende government. The Anaconda deal was still regarded as too favourable to the company – not least by important sectors of the PDC itself.

The main benefit of these agreements with the U.S. mining companies was a considerable increase in productive capacity. The process was not as rapid as anticipated, but by the end of the 1970s, the production of copper had doubled, thanks in part to the investments made during this period. Moreover, the Chilean government gained considerable experience in the marketing, pricing, and control of the product. The local economy benefited as the value retained in Chile rose from an annual average (in constant 1979 prices) of U.S. $513 million in 1960–4 to $953 million in 1965–9 and as companies made more local purchases in Chile. Fiscal revenue rose from an annual average, in the earlier period of $225 million to $511 million.

Many factors made agrarian reform an urgent priority, although proposals had existed since the 1940s. The Catholic Church became an advocate of land distribution. The U.S. government, through the Alliance for Progress, advocated reform as a way of countering the possible growth of rural guerrilla movements. The political power of landowners had been eroded by social, demographic and economic changes. The level of food imports was far too high for a country with Chile's agricultural potential. The traditional agrarian structure was seen as a bottleneck on industrial production.

The PDC put great emphasis on land reform. In the words of a leading PDC theoretician, it was to be 'drastic, massive and rapid'. The major problem was seen as the highly inequitable distribution of land. In the agricultural provinces of Chile between Coquimbo and Llanquihue, where 92 per cent of Chilean farms were located, latifundia occupied more than half (55.3 per cent) of the land area in 1965; minifundia, making up a total of 82 per cent of farms, occupied only 9.7 per cent of arable land. Concentration of credit and resources was similarly inequitable. But the original proposals for expropriation were diluted by Congress. The landowners, organized in the Sociedad Nacional de Agricultura (SNA) were no longer such a powerful political group, but they still exercised influence and could count on support from other sectors of the propertied classes. The basic unit guaranteed to efficient landowners was to be eighty irrigated hectares, and depending on local conditions, as much as four times that amount could be held. There were a number of favourable conditions regarding retention of animals and equipment, as well as compensation for improvement, all of which the Left considered far too generous. Although the law allowed for the creation of collective *asentamientos* on expropriated properties, this was seen as a transitional form to the preferred PDC solution – a large number of efficient medium-sized and small family farms. Little would be done under these proposals for the *minifundistas* or landless labourers, the most numerous groups in the countryside.

The reform proceeded more slowly than the government expected, but nevertheless by 1969 substantial advances had been made. More than 1,300 farms had been expropriated, with a land area of more than 3 million hectares, representing about 6 per cent of all arable land in Chile and including about 12 per cent of all irrigated land. About 650 *asentamientos* were created to incorporate some twenty thousand families, and another two thousand families were given land directly. The problem was not so much that the results were poor, but rather that the initial target was set too high – reflecting perhaps the over-enthusiasm of an inexperienced team.

Perhaps of equal political significance was the encouragement the government gave to rural unions with the law of 1967. In 1964 rural unions barely existed. By 1969 there were more than 400, with 100,000 members. In addition, there were 22 rural co-operatives with 30,000 members and 59 committees of small producers with 37,000 members. However, it was not only the rural poor who organized. The 1967 law allowed for employers' unions, and with the help of the SNA there were by 1970 nearly 10,000 members organized in local and provincial groups; at the national level the Confederación Nacional de Empleadores Agrícolas (CONSEMACH) brought together a third of the large and medium landowners in the country. The scene was set for organized conflict.

Agricultural production grew at a reasonable rate during the PDC years, even though crops were badly hit by the severe drought of 1968. The production of field crops rose at an annual average rate of 5 per cent from 1965 to 1970 (compared with 2.3 per cent for the preceding period). Livestock production reached an annual average of 5.5 per cent growth compared with a historical rate of less than 2 per cent. But imported foodstuffs still constituted a heavy drain on the balance of payments (accounting for a little less than 20 per cent of the value of exports for the 1965–70 period), in spite of an increase in agricultural exports of 40 per cent. The historical neglect of Chilean agriculture would take more than one presidency to put right, especially when two harvests were badly affected by drought.

The Frei government could not sustain its early pace of reform and began to lose the political initiative. In an attempt to restrain inflation, it tried to claw back some of what it viewed as excessive wage payments through a forced savings scheme to which both employers and workers would contribute. It was intended that the resulting funds would be used to establish worker-run industries, increase savings and restrain consumer demand. However, the proposal, put forward in 1967, brought the government into headlong collision with both the unions and the Right, and the plan had to be withdrawn. The PDC was dismayed that despite rises in industrial profits and wages neither employers nor workers gave institutional support to the government (although as voters, sections of the working class gave considerable backing to the party). Industrialists, always mistrustful of PDC rhetoric about the communitarian society, became increasingly alarmed after the *oficialistas* lost control of the party apparatus in 1967. They were also concerned about possible alterations in the constitutional status of property after this had been redefined in 1967 in order to allow the Agrarian Reform Law to be implemented: they feared that once large farms had been expropriated, the same might happen to large firms. Moreover, they were worried that in the competition for scarce investment resources, an increasing share would go to the state to the detriment of the private sector.

Relations between the PDC and the unions were never good. The trade union movement, mostly dominated by the FRAP parties (though the PDC had made inroads into the white-collar sector at the expense of the Radical Party), resented proposals to do away with the closed-shop and single-plant union system, and eventually the CUT. These proposals were seen, not unreasonably, as an attempt to divide the union movement. The PDC government increased the number and importance of unions quite considerably, but then tried to control them, which was not at all popular amongst the more radical wing of the PDC. This group had gained control of the party apparatus in July 1967 and, alarmed at the decline in the party's vote in the municipal elections of that year to 35.6 per cent (from 42.3 per cent in 1965 congressional elections), was urging an intensification of the reform process.

The urban labour force in unions doubled in the six years of the PDC government. Peasant unions grew rapidly to include more than 120,000 members by 1970. Shanty towns became organized and increasingly militant in this period. The number of strikes increased from 564 in 1964 to 977 in 1969 (and to 2,474 in 1972). In the countryside where there had been only 3 strikes in 1960 and 39 in 1964, there were 648 strikes in 1968 and 1,580 in 1970. Seizures of farms, urban land sites for housing and factories also increased. In 1968, 16 farms were invaded by their workers; in 1970 there were 368 invasions. In the same period the number of urban land seizures rose from 15 to 352, and the number of factory seizures from 5 to 133.

Former Conservatives and Liberals, and some distinctly undemocratic members of the nationalist Right, united in the National Party and began to take the offensive. In the 1967 municipal elections the National Party gained an impressive 14.3 per cent of the vote, and this rose to 20 per cent in the 1969 congressional elections. In 1969, however, the Marxist parties took 28.1 per cent of the vote, and the Radical Party, now in political alliance with them, another 13 per cent. Within the PDC itself, the defeat of the Left in 1968 after an active campaign by the president, returned an executive of the party loyal to Frei. But even this was insufficient guarantee to the Right that the now-divided and uncertain PDC could stop the Marxists.

Political activity became increasingly bitter as the PDC government came to an end. The Right was infuriated with the administration's reforms, especially with the agrarian reform, and having little positive policy of its own to offer, increasingly emphasized authoritarian, non-democratic solutions to the political stalemate. The Left had been profoundly affected by the Cuban Revolution, and its attachment to Marxism was, in the case of some sectors of the Socialist Party, increasingly couched in the language of the guerrilla struggle and popular insurrection.

The victory of President Frei's supporters in the internal party elections in 1968 can also be seen as a turning point. Although the margin of victory was by no means large, a section of the party youth, a small but influential group of congressmen and the party theoretician of agrarian reform, Jacques Chonchol, left the party to set up the Movimiento de Acción Popular Unitario (MAPU). Whatever chance there might have been of an agreement between the PDC and the FRAP in the forthcoming presidential elections was clearly no longer possible. Perhaps it was never feasible, given both the PDC's opposition to coalitions and the hostility of the Marxist Left to Christian Democracy. Indeed, it has been argued that by presenting itself as the natural governing party, by eschewing the usual bargaining politics employed by Centre parties and by undermining the power of Congress (in the reform of 1970), the PDC helped to undermine the consensus that made party agreement possible in a multi-party system.

The period preceding the 1970 elections was marred by increasing polarization and violence, the worst example of which occurred when police fired on a group of squatters in the southern town of Puerto Montt, killing nine people. The seizure of urban land sites and farms increased. A revolutionary break-away group from the Socialist Party, the Movimiento de Izquierda Revolucionario (MIR), went underground and began to incite subversion. Even the military began to reflect the uneasy atmosphere with an uprising of the Tacna regiment – the so-called *tacnazo*. The object of the uprising was unclear, but it seemed to be a combination of economic grievances of the military and a warning to the government not to let the process of 'subversion' continue.

The presidential campaign of 1970 was fought among three evenly balanced movements. Former President Alessandri was the first to announce his candidacy, backed by the National Party and a group of dissident Radicals. At first he seemed to take the political initiative and was well ahead in the polls, which was a factor in discouraging the Right from repeating its tactic of 1964. But Alessandri's age (seventy-four) showed in the campaign, especially on television, and he had little new to offer in terms of policy or programme. His strength was his personal standing above party politics – though no one doubted his commitment to the economic ideas of the powerful groups associated with the National Party.

Radomiro Tomic, the candidate of the PDC, had been the former ambassador to Washington and was identified with the leftist segment of the party. Tomic's programme was not noticeably less radical than that of Allende. He promised, for example, to complete the agrarian reform by expropriating all the large estates 'from the Andes to the sea'. His attacks were directed at the National Party and the Right, rather than at the parties of the Left united in the UP.

Salvador Allende, a senator and at sixty-two the presidential candidate of the Left for the fourth time, only narrowly secured the nomination of the Socialist Party – a foretaste of the difficulties he was to have with his party in government – for the Socialist Party had changed over the decade. It was more hostile to political alliances and deals and more concerned with doctrinal purity. It was more Leninist in its conception of the role of the party, less committed to a gradual process of building socialism and more to a vision of a permanent popular revolution. But it was still divided internally over many issues, and it had to work within a political coalition that covered a wide spectrum of political positions.

Allende's victory with 36 per cent of the vote (Table 4.4) did not represent a great swing to the left or any radicalization of the electorate. It was more the product of party relationships and hostilities than a great shift in opinion. Nevertheless, the UP government set itself the task of

Table 4.4. *The 1970 presidential election*

Candidate	Vote	Percentage
Allende	1,070,334	36.2
Alessandri	1,031,159	34.9
Tomic	821,801	27.8
Blank/void	31,505	1.1
Total	2,954,799	100

Source: Arturo Valenzuela, *The Breakdown of Democratic Regimes: Chile* (Baltimore, 1978), p. 40. Abstention was 16.5%.

producing the shift in public opinion necessary for it to transform its programme into practice.

The pace of politics during the next three years was prefigured by the frenzied activity that occurred before Allende could assume the presidency. In order to secure the congressional ratification necessary for a candidate who had not achieved a majority of the votes, Allende agreed to sign a Statute of Democratic Guarantees proposed by the PDC.[17] At least one major U.S. corporation, the International Telegraph and Telephone Company (ITT), tried to 'destabilize' the incoming administration and to persuade the PDC not to support Allende's ratification. An attempt was made by the extreme Right, encouraged by the CIA, to kidnap the commander-in-chief of the armed forces, General René Schneider, in order to spread panic. The plan went tragically wrong when Schneider resisted and was killed. Capital flight heralded the difficulties the incoming government was to have with the business sector.

THE 'VIA CHILENA AL SOCIALISMO': THE PRESIDENCY OF SALVADOR ALLENDE, 1970−3

I won't be just another president. I will be the first president of the first really democratic, popular, national and revolutionary government in the history of Chile. (From Salvador Allende's victory speech)

[17] The statute called upon Allende to respect political and civil liberties and to guarantee the existence of political parties, freedom of the press, freedom of education, freedom of the unions from state control and freedom of the armed forces from political interference. As Arturo Valenzuela points out, the very need to ask the president-elect to guarantee that he would, in effect, respect the constitution was a measure of how far political trust had eroded. Valenzuela, *The Breakdown of Democratic Regimes: Chile* (Baltimore, 1978), p. 49.

The central policy objective of the Unidad Popular forces will be the search for a replacement of the present economic structure, doing away with the power of foreign and national monopoly capital and of the latifundio in order to initiate the construction of socialism. (From the programme of the Unidad Popular)

The UP government led by Salvador Allende transformed the atmosphere of public life in Chile. Old concepts, like party membership, changed from being seen as a simple expression of party preference to a position in the class war. The general consensus about the validity of the constitutional system was broken. Political violence, until then rare in Chile, grew in intensity and frequency. New movements, loosely identified as *poder popular*, expressed an intensification of popular demands that not only alarmed the opposition, but also weakened the political authority of the government. All aspects of life became politicized, and politics became polarized — it was impossible not to be either for or against the government. The terrible brutality with which the government was overthrown on 11 September 1973 is sad testimony to the level which political passion had reached.

The UP government promised to nationalize the economy, to implement a massive programme of income redistribution, to end the dominance of the latifundia, to transform the political system through the creation of a unicameral legislature, to develop popular participation in the running of the economy, in the making of political decisions and in the administration of justice and to pursue a genuinely independent foreign policy. Although this programme was little short of revolutionary, the government intended to implement it within the bounds of a pre-existing constitutional system. That system would, of course, be modified, but for the majority of the UP coalition there was no question of revolutionary illegality or insurrection. The government argued that the implementation of the programme would adversely affect only a tiny minority of landowners and only a small fraction of the highly concentrated economic elite. In the industrial sector, for example, the government initially intended to nationalize 76 companies. These crucial companies accounted for about 44 per cent of total manufacturing sales, but even added to those the state already owned or controlled, the nationalized sector was to consist of only about 130 out of 30,500 industrial firms.

There was considerable vagueness about the methods of implementing such a sweeping set of policies within the existing institutional framework. How were they to be implemented and over how long a period, and how were the short-, medium- and long-term measures to be related?[18] The implementation of UP policies depended on a number of interrelated assumptions about the success of its economic policies, about the firmness of political support for the government and about the behaviour of the opposition. The assumptions turned out to be unrealistic.

The UP government was a coalition of six parties, and the programme itself was a compromise document drawn up to accommodate the distinct tendencies within the coalition, from the social democratic moderation of the Radical Party to the Leninism of the leftist segment of the Socialist Party. Most important were the differences between the Socialists and the Communists over the speed of implementation of the programme and the political balance between popular mobilization on the one hand, and the need to assure middle-class sectors, on the other.[19] The endless debate on the way to create the Chilean road to socialism produced uncertainty about policies and fuelled suspicions on the Right that the road to socialism would prove to be a Marxist cul de sac from which there would be no return.

The difficulties Allende faced as president were compounded by the lack of discipline and the factionalism of his own Socialist Party. Ever since the party had declared in its 1967 congress that 'revolutionary violence is inevitable and necessary', there were important sections of the party that supported, in theory at least, the *vía insurreccional* rather than the *vía pacífica*. And there were groups outside the Socialist Party, notably the MIR, which practised what some of the leftist Socialists preached. The ambivalent attitude of some leading Socialist politicians towards the activities of the MIR and the legitimacy of revolutionary violence embarrassed the Allende government and gave an opportunity to the Right to create fears about the intentions of the UP as a whole. Such fears were not allayed by the tone of the propaganda of either the Left or the Right. The murder of Edmundo Pérez Zujovic, a leading Christian Democratic politician, by an extreme leftist group in June 1971 sharply intensified the climate of political fear and hostility.

---

[18] The question that defeated the UP, according to the left-wing Socialist senator Carlos Altamirano, was not what to do, but how to do it. This is not very different from the point made by Sergio Bitar, a minister of mining in the UP government, that one of the major defects of the government was its inability to implement a clear strategy. Carlos Altamirano, *Dialéctica de una derrota* (Mexico, 1977), p. 44, and Sergio Bitar, *Transición, socialismo y democracia: La experiencia chilena* (Mexico, 1979), p. 15.

[19] Joan Garcés, one of Allende's close political advisers, strongly criticized the lack of 'confidence, respect and discipline' of the parties towards each other, towards the government and towards Allende himself. Garcés, *Allende y la experiencia chilena* (Barcelona, 1976), pp. 228, 455–5.

The Socialist Party never shed its suspicions of the Partido Comunista Chileno (PCCh) The PCCh was a long-established party in Chile, firmly rooted in the labour movement, very disciplined, a strong supporter of Moscow on international issues, but not without flexibility on domestic issues. Its moderation and caution were not acceptable to sectors of the Socialist Party. There appeared to be a dual leadership at the core of the UP. The Radical Party tended to side with the caution of the Communists, but it split three ways and lost its political significance. The other two ideological parties of the UP, the MAPU and the Izquierda Cristiana (IC), also suffered losses and the MAPU split into two separate parties. The Acción Popular Independiente (API) of Senator Rafael Tarud was a personalist party of little political significance.

One major problem caused by the existence of so many parties was the imposition of a quota system in apportioning government posts. Places were to be distributed according to a more or less fixed schedule, favouring the smaller parties; but subordinates were to be of different parties than their immediate superior. This system was designed to stop any one party from colonizing a ministry. In practice the results were damaging. Party authority superseded administrative authority; the control of the executive over the governmental machine was weakened; and the effect on the professional civil service, whose co-operation was essential if such an ambitious reform programme was to be successfully carried out, was very adverse.

These divisions would have been damaging enough if the UP had enjoyed a majority in Congress, but it was a minority. As a result of the 1969 elections, the UP had eighteen Senate seats; the opposition thirty-two. The PDC had twenty senators; the largest UP party, that of the Communists, only six. In the lower house the government had fifty-seven seats; the opposition ninety-three. The PDC had forty-seven seats and the National Party thirty-three, whereas the Communists had twenty-two and the Socialists fourteen. The gains that the UP made in the 1973 elections only slightly reduced the opposition majority. Thus, the UP government faced a congress that became increasingly hostile. Unless an agreement could be reached with the PDC, the only hope for the UP was that its economic policies would be so successful that there would be a massive swing in its favour. But after a year of initial success, the economy began to deteriorate.

The initial action of the government on the economic front was a massive wage and salary increase. Although the rate of inflation in 1970 was 35 per cent, the wage increase averaged 55 per cent. There were differential increases for the poorest sectors, but in effect there was a wage explosion rather than a redistribution of income from the rich to the poor. The poor did better, relatively, than the rich; but the top income-earners did not suffer. Price controls were established, and the government set up an elaborate system of distribution networks through various agencies, including local committees on supply and prices (Juntas de Abastecimientos y Precios – JAPs) to make sure local shopkeepers were following the rules.

The copper mines were nationalized, with support from the opposition, by July 1971; and during the first year more than eighty enterprises from important commercial and industrial sectors were taken over. Land reform was also accelerated, but the government had to work within the confines of the law passed by the preceding government. Almost as many farms were expropriated in the first year as in the whole period of PDC government, many as a result of land seizures. By late 1971 virtually all of the financial sector was under government control, transferred to the Area de Propiedad Social (APS).

Government-led expansion produced a high rate of economic growth in 1971. Because of unused capacity in industry, stockpiles, rapid growth in imports and a high level of international reserves, the government achieved a lower rate of inflation than the previous year. The GDP in 1971 grew by 7.7 per cent overall, gross industrial production went up 11 per cent and a good harvest increased agriculture's share of GDP by 7 per cent. Unemployment fell from 8.3 per cent in 1970 to 3.8 per cent by the end of 1971. Wages and salaries rose to 61.7 per cent of income in 1971, as compared with 52.2 per cent in 1970 and an average of 48.4 per cent for the decade of the 1960s.

On the external front the government announced its intention to maintain a fixed exchange rate. The Left had been a fierce critic of the crawling peg system of devaluation of the Frei government, arguing that it increased costs and fuelled inflation. But as a result the escudo started to become increasingly overvalued. Other warning signs were beginning to appear before the end of Allende's first year in office. Central government expenditures rose sharply, more than 66 per cent in nominal terms in 1971 over the previous year, from 21 to 27 per cent of GDP, but government current revenue declined from 20 to 18.5 per cent of GDP. The fiscal deficit rose to 8 per cent of GDP compared with 4 per cent in the preceding year. The money supply more than doubled, and the huge expansion of credit went mostly to the public sector. During 1971 the average price of copper fell by 27 per cent, and since production also fell slightly in the three major mines, the value of copper exports fell by 16.5 per cent. Although international reserves were high, so was the outstanding debt. The trade balance turned from a U.S. $95 million surplus in 1970 to a deficit of $90 million in 1971. Traditional sources of external finance in the United States virtually dried up, and the government was forced to turn to other sources – Europe, Latin America and the USSR. Chile's reserves fell by three-quarters in 1971, and in November the government was forced to announce the suspension of debt service, pending renegotiation.

All of the problems already visible in 1971 – capacity limits in industrial and other sectors, breakdowns in the distribution system, industrial conflict, the growth of a black market, the decline in private investment, uncontrolled monetary expansion, the exhaustion of international reserves – accumulated and multiplied with terrible force in 1972 and 1973. By the time the UP government came to an end, real GDP per capita and real wages were falling, agricultural output was down sharply (perhaps to the levels of the early 1960s, though the workings of the black market make calculation difficult), inflation was out of control, several years of debt service had to be rescheduled, net international reserves were more than U.S. $200 million in the red and the balance of payments was heavily in deficit. Government revenue fell sharply while expenditure grew. With the growth of the black market and congressional obstacles to tax changes, the central government deficit rose to record heights: 22 per cent of GDP in 1973. The money supply grew by 576 per cent from the end of 1971 to August 1973; total expansion of the money supply under the UP government was 1,345 per cent.

Although the government devalued in December 1971, and at intervals thereafter, such a high rate of inflation kept the escudo seriously overvalued. After a fall in export revenues with declining copper prices in 1972, there was a recovery in 1973. But imports continued to grow faster; total food import costs were almost four times what they had been in 1970 (and accounted for more than one-third of total imports as compared with only 14 per cent three years earlier). This reflects rising international prices as well as the result of rising incomes of the poor and declining production.

Agrarian reform accelerated during 1972. More than 60 per cent of irrigated land had been taken into the hands of the state for redistribution. There was, for such a massive process, remarkably little violence and destruction of property. But there was also a giant disincentive to invest and serious decapitalization, leading to a decline in production in 1972 and 1973. In the industrial sector, the take-overs by the state continued, and the threat of expropriation as well as spontaneous take-overs by workers led to the virtual cessation of investment by the private sector.

Analysis of the economic policy of the UP government tends to concern itself with what went wrong, why things turned out so badly. However, one of the major and enduring achievements of the UP government was the nationalization of the large copper mines. The decision to transfer these assets to the nation needed a constitutional amendment, and this was passed with the support in Congress of all the parties. The UP government promised compensation to the companies at the book value of their assets but warned that they would be penalized for earning excessive profits in the past. After some complicated legal wrangling, the government decided that the amount owed by a number of companies exceeded book values. Some payment for certain mines was offered, but nationalization was fiercely contested by the companies and created difficulties for Chile's international trade. Although there were initial problems in the transition, and though unit costs did rise appreciably, overall production did increase; the combination of the measures taken by the PDC and UP governments helped to ensure both a considerable expansion of copper production in the 1970s and that earnings from copper remained in Chile and were not exported.

Other reforms of the UP period, such as the distribution of free milk to schoolchildren, were admirable on many grounds. There was a positive attempt to reform the tax system although it was left rather late and faced too much hostility in Congress. The schemes for worker participation in industry and for co-operative ventures in agriculture were imaginative and in less troubled times might have made a positive contribution both to production and to a genuine extension of participation. But the times were troubled, and the reforms were caught up in a political controversy that destroyed them.

The strength of the opposition was not enough by itself to explain the economic reversal. There was a lack of co-ordination between the economic team and the politicians, between the political strategy of gradual change and consensus and the radical economic strategy of redistribution. The apparent lack of concern of the government about the gathering economic storm denoted an unjustified optimism about long-term prospects and an unjustified lack of concern about short-term management.

The strategy of Pedro Vuskovic, the minister of the economy, was based on the reflationary effects of a massive redistribution of income. Vuskovic was the key economic strategist and exercised considerable influence over Allende. The major intention of his strategy was to widen the political base of the UP, and the vote in the 1973 election showed that the political base was indeed remarkably firm, although the strategy had not increased support dramatically (and it had intensified the opposition to the government). Consumption demand, however, was not held down to a level consistent with foreign exchange earnings or the desired level of investment. The huge increase in purchasing power soon ran up against supply limitations, resulting in the growth of the black market, hoarding and inflation. Redistribution did not affect the upper income-earners – except by reducing the relativities – and everyone benefited in terms of increased purchasing power. It has been argued that the income explosion was the principal factor behind the economic crisis.[20]

The government's policy would have had more chance of success if a policy of wage restraint had been possible, but this was in practice very difficult: in 1971 wages and salaries already accounted for that share of GNP that they were supposed to reach in 1976. The government's attitude towards wage demands was generally supportive. After all, this was a government supported by, and working in the interests of, the working class. Parties of the UP jostling for influence sought in some cases to increase their support by encouraging wage claims; and opposition parties desiring to increase the government's economic difficulties also promoted excessive wage demands. How could the government contain these pressures? The use of repressive measures that had been implemented in the past was completely unacceptable on political grounds. But the result was disastrous. The large unplanned deficit of both traditional state enterprises and recently nationalized ones was due mainly to the combination of wage increases and price controls. In 1972 the government proposed a wage and

---

[20] José Serra and Arturo León, *La redistribución del ingreso en Chile durante el gobierno de la Unidad Popular* Documento de Trabajo no. 70, FLACSO (Santiago, July 1978), p. 61. They also criticize the unjustified confidence on the external front that led to a year's delay in seeking debt renegotiation; an erroneous policy of maintaining a fixed exchange rate; and excessive permissiveness in relation to social expenditures. The extent to which income redistribution based on wage increases really benefits the very poor (many of whom do not receive wages) is open to question. See the perceptive discussion of Alejandro Foxley and Oscar Muñoz, 'Income Redistribution, Economic Growth and Social Structure', *Oxford Bulletin of Economics and Statistics* 36, no. 1 (1974), pp. 21–4.

Table 4.5. *Strikes in 1971 and 1972*

	Number of strikes	Total days of strike	Total workers involved	Total man-days lost
Private sector				
1964	564	–	138,476	–
1969	977	–	275,405	972,382
1971	2,377	18,153	251,966	1,281,834
1972	2,474	11,097	262,105	1,177,186
Public sector				
1971	322	1,088	50,431	132,479
1972	815	2,881	135,037	476,965

Source: H. Landsberger and T. McDaniel, 'Hypermobilisation in Chile', *World Politics* 28 (July 1976), p. 520, using the official figures in the annual presidential address to Congress.

salary increase of 22 per cent for the public sector; the average of the actual increases obtained was 47.7 per cent (and the private sector level was not far short).

Wage and salary increases were not obtained without a struggle in the private or even the public sector, and the period saw a sharp increase in the number of strikes (Table 4.5). Many of these strikes in 1971 and 1972 were preludes to take-overs of factories or farms by the workers and enjoyed the active support of local government officials even if central government became increasingly worried.

The incorporation of enterprises into the APS, the state sector of the economy (Table 4.6), created many problems. Many more firms were taken over than intended (though some twenty-five that were planned to be nationalized managed to escape). By 1973 the manufacturing enterprises of the APS accounted for more than 40 per cent of total industrial production and employed 30 per cent of the industrial labour force. In addition, the state sector accounted for 93 per cent of total bank credit, 90 per cent of mining production and 28 per cent of food distribution. Intended to be run jointly by representatives of workers and managers, they were not meant to represent a threat to small and medium-sized enterprises, though that was how they were in fact perceived.

Apart from the question of worker participation, which had mixed results, the major function of the APS according to Vuskovic was to generate a surplus and increase capital accumulation. But independent

Table 4.6. *State sector, 1970–3*

	Number of firms			
	Nov. 1970	Dec. 1971	Dec. 1972	May 1973
State ownership[a]	31	62	103	165
Under intervention or requisition	–	39	99	120
Total	31	101	202	285

[a]Includes both social and mixed areas (i.e., jointly run by state and private sectors) and six new industries created after 1970.

Source: Stefan de Vylder, *Allende's Chile: The Political Economy of the Rise and Fall of the Popular Unity* (Cambridge, 1976), p. 149.

action by the workers, following from the worker take-over of the major Yarur textile plant in April 1971, meant the dominance of political rather than economic criteria in the process of nationalization. Many of the firms taken over were small or medium enterprises, and these nationalizations often occurred against Allende's wishes.

In spite of government appeals for restraint, workers in the APS began to demand special benefits, such as discounts on produce and wage increases well above the rate of inflation. Management of the APS was divided according to party lines, and considerations of party policy often overrode those of economic efficiency. Different parties had distinct strategies and used their control over certain enterprises to implement the strategies they believed in. Rather than provide a surplus for the economy, the state sector as a whole was responsible for a large part of the huge fiscal deficit, although this was a product of running the traditional state enterprises rather than the newly nationalized concerns.

The UP government abandoned the strategy of Vuskovic in July 1972 when he was replaced as minister of the economy by Carlos Matus, an Allende Socialist, and Orlando Millas, a Communist, became minister of finance. Matus and Millas tried a more coherent strategy in order to reduce the gap between supply and demand. But relaxation of price controls and devaluation sent inflation spiralling upwards. The government lost any capacity for long-term planning: survival on a day-to-day basis was all that could be achieved.

The opposition did its utmost to sabotage the UP's economic plans and undoubtedly contributed decisively to its economic difficulties. The opposition in Congress refused to accept tax reforms and readjustments, and in 1972 substantially increased the fiscal deficit by its refusal to finance the budget. Nor did the opposition confine itself to congressional activities. There was sabotage of production, and massive strikes such as the so-called bosses strikes of October 1972 and June 1973, which severely damaged the economy.

The question of North American interference is controversial. The CIA was authorized to spend U.S. $8 million to secure the overthrow of Allende; and given the black market price of dollars this was probably worth closer to $40 million. In addition, U.S. loans were cut off; the United States used its influence to block loans from the World Bank and Inter-American Development Bank; it tried to obstruct renegotiation of the Chilean debt; short-term credits from U.S. banks dried up; and the North American copper companies took legal action against Chile to block exports of copper to Europe. There was, of course, substantial borrowing, particularly from other Latin American countries, and important financial aid was given by the USSR and other Communist countries in 1972 and early 1973. But the credits for long-term development, including a total of U.S. $500 million from the Soviet bloc, were nearly all unspent at the time of the coup. There may not have been a blockade by the United States, but there was a virtual boycott, and the effect on an economy so tied to the U.S. economic system could not but produce serious dislocation.

The political centre disappeared in Allende's Chile. The Radical Party disintegrated into three factions. Under electoral pressure, pushed by its own right wing and with the defection of several progressive congressmen to form the IC, the PDC moved, in 1972, into a working relationship with the National Party. His own moderation made Allende increasingly isolated as his supporters developed new forms of political organization, outside the control of the executive, in the so-called *poder popular*.

Why could the conflict not have been contained inside the institutional system? Probably because neither side was sufficiently committed to that system and because the expectations of all the parties were too high. The opposition indulged in a series of measures designed to obstruct the executive, which, if not illegal, certainly violated the conventions of the congressional system. The government, for its part, employed measures of dubious legality. There was intensive use of constitutional censures of ministers in an attempt to create administrative confusion and conflict among the branches of government. Restrictions on legislative initiatives were avoided by turning proposed laws into projects to amend the constitution. The major conflict there was over the proposal by two PDC senators, Juan Hamilton and Renán Fuentealba, to restrict the executive's powers to take firms into the APS beyond those agreed between the executive and Congress. The opposition tried to devise measures to blunt the executive's long-established powers of veto over congressional proposals. This culminated in the famous debate on 22 August 1973 in which the Chamber of Deputies declared unconstitutional and illegal the policies of the president and, by a vote of 81 to 47, invited the military to defend the constitution.

The government, for its part, used some unorthodox measures to implement its policies – such as the use of a 1932 decree to facilitate the takeover of enterprises. Whatever the rights and wrongs of these questions of interpretation of the constitution, the effect was to politicize the judicial system by seeking legal arbitration of disputes that had previously been decided by agreement among the politicians. This did nothing to help solve issues of principle or to ensure the impartiality of administrative procedures.

If the UP's project of social transformation was possible only with the support of the majority of the people, it could have come about through elections, a plebiscite on constitutional reform or an agreement with the PDC. The municipal elections of April 1971 gave a total of 48.6 per cent of the vote to the UP, 48.2 per cent to the opposition and the rest blank or void. However, the municipal elections did not alter the balance of political power. In some ways it was a bad result for the UP. It gave the government no new power, but it helped to create a sense of false confidence, and it bolstered arguments against a deal with the PDC. The congressional elections of March 1973 were also to some degree inconclusive. The UP obtained 44.2 per cent of the vote (the Socialists 18.4 per cent and the Communists 16.2 per cent) and the opposition parties 54.2 per cent (the PDC 28.5 and the National Party 21.1 percent) with 1.6 per cent blank or void. Such a result could not resolve the political impasse one way or the other. But it did show that the opposition could not get the two-thirds majority in Congress it needed to impeach Allende – a conclusion not lost on those favouring a coup.

A plebiscite on the constitution, dissolving the existing chambers and re-electing a unicameral people's assembly, was debated several times in the UP coalition. It was considered immediately after the municipal elections of 1971, but rejected by Allende and the Communists on the grounds that it would force the opposition to unite. It was considered again in the last months of the government, but although now favoured by Allende, it was rejected by the parties, some of which sought cooperation with the PDC, others of which anticipated conflict and wanted time to prepare.

There were always members of both the PDC, not least of all Tomic, and the UP who argued for co-operation. There were frequent attempts to come to agreement on a common programme right up to an attempt at mediation by the cardinal-archbishop of Santiago in mid-August 1973. But attempts at co-operation always broke down. The Socialist Party opposed such agreements on the grounds that they would be betraying the central objectives of the UP and would alienate its supporters. Patricio Aylwin, a leading PDC senator, similarly felt that to co-operate with the UP would be a betrayal, unless there were concrete concessions to the PDC.[21] Indeed, hostility of some PDC leaders towards co-operation with the UP actually led them to welcome a military coup. The tragedy is that at certain stages, when, for example, the agreements were reached in June and July 1973, there was acceptance of so many substantive points previously in dispute that little remained apart from an act of political will by both sides to put these agreements into practice. One continuing element working against co-operation was the press of both Left and Right. Violent attacks on politicians of both camps and wildly exaggerated reports of plots and counterplots all contributed to the creation of a siege mentality. Agreement between the PDC and UP became increasingly unlikely as social and political developments pushed them into antagonistic positions. The UP found it easier to accept a military presence in the cabinet to resolve the October 1972 crisis than to revive talks with the PDC.

Although UP theorists speculated on the problems of winning over the middle class, it seemed to be assumed that the loyalty of the working class could be taken for granted. This was not the case. There were substantial elements of the working class whose political allegiance was elsewhere; and those sectors of the working class whose loyalty to the ends of the UP government was firm nevertheless developed organizations and undertook actions that further reduced the possibility of an institutional and constitutional resolution of the political crisis.

The difficulties experienced by the government in restraining wage in-

[21] According to Tomic, 'The strategy of the UP was never to collaborate with the Christian Democrats but to divide and destroy them'. According to Altamirano, the PDC only appeared to want to negotiate in order to confuse the UP and to keep the democratic senators of the UP quiet. Tomic, 'Christian Democracy', p. 190. Altamirano, *Dialética*, p. 98. See also Garcés, *Allende*, p. 213.

Table 4.7. *The CUT national election, 1972*

	Votes	Percentage
Manual workers		
Communists	113,000	38
Socialists	95,900	32
Christian Democrats	47,400	16
MAPU members	22,000	7
FTR[a] members	5,800	1
Radicals	5,600	1
Total	291,400[b]	
White-collar workers		
Christian Democrats	61,000	41
Communists	33,000	22
Socialists	29,000	19
Radicals	11,000	7
Total	146,000[c]	

[a]An MIR group.
[b]Includes votes for other small parties and invalid votes.
[c]Includes minor parties' votes and invalid votes.

Source: Official CUT figures. Slightly different figures are published by Manuel Castells, *La lucha de clases en Chile* (Buenos Aires, 1974), p. 427. But since the counting took about six weeks and was disputed, it is not surprising that such discrepancies exist.

creases demonstrate the extent to which the CUT was unable to restrain its constituent unions. Much more than before, the CUT became part of the system of government, but its weaknesses remained an impediment to the exercise of central control. The Chilean trade union movement had always been a very decentralized one; federations and even plant unions had a tradition of robust independence which they were not willing to surrender. And a substantial proportion of union members belonged to parties of the opposition, as the results of the 1972 elections to the executive of the CUT show (Table 4.7).

Although the parties of the UP took about 70 per cent of the total vote, the PDC had a plurality in central Santiago with 35,000 votes against about 30,000 for the Communists and 25,000 for the Socialists, and the PDC controlled the regional branch of the CUT for Santiago Province. Many PDC unionists were to the left of their party leadership, and some collaborated with the UP unionists in the participation schemes. But they were obviously not going to be more modest than UP unionists in demanding wage increases and other benefits for workers, and this led to damaging strikes such as the El Teniente copper mine dispute of April 1973, which not only meant an unwelcome loss of export earnings but was also a blow to the government's authority.

Even if the unions had been solidly behind the UP, they would still have been only a minority of the total work-force. Women workers, for example, were largely unorganized, and their electoral behavior showed them to be more opposed to the UP than men. The participation of women in the electorate had grown more rapidly than men, and by 1970 they constituted half of the electorate. While it is clear that the UP was closing the gap between the electoral behaviour of men and women in urban working-class areas, in the 1973 elections 61 per cent of women's votes went to the opposition compared with 51 per cent of men's.

The political allegiance of shanty town dwellers was always something of a problem for the UP. Only a small proportion were organized in unions; the extreme Left MIR had more support here than amongst other social sectors; the PDC also had strong backing; and normal mechanisms of government control were much weaker in these areas. By mid-1973 there were 275 *campamentos* in Santiago, in which about one-sixth of the capital's population lived. Many of the *campamentos* had been established by seizures of land; such activities were expected of the urban poor in a political climate for once sympathetic to their aspirations, but the *tomas* contributed to loss of governmental authority. Very few of these inhabitants would benefit, for example, from participation in the work-force of the APS: according to government figures, only about a quarter of the economically active labour force was employed in the state sector. The government, therefore, had to deal with the grievances of those outside the state sector in other ways – price controls and state distribution agencies, for example, and subsidized transport. The problem was that the UP did not have enough resources to deal with all these pressing demands at the same time.

The countryside presented a different set of problems for the government. As it stood, the reform law could do little for substantial sectors of the poor – the landless labourers and the *minifundistas*. In the late 1960s *minifundistas* held 80 per cent of all land holdings, but these made up only 10 per cent of total arable rural land, even though they employed 40 per cent of the work-force. The major beneficiaries from the reform process were the resident labourers on expropriated estates. The problems facing the government were immense. In the first place there were a large number of land seizures (*tomas de tierra*) – perhaps 1,700 during the first year and a half of the UP government. Many were directed at the medium-sized properties that the government was pledged to defend, and whilst the MIR was active in the *tomas*, the parties of the UP did not encourage land seizures. The proportion of the rural labour force involved was relatively small – perhaps 20 per cent – but the opposition press seized on the *tomas* to wage a propaganda war against the government. Second, many of the beneficiaries of the reform, the *asentados*, had no desire to see their benefits diluted and became strong supporters of the PDC. Third, the government's alternative organizations, Centros de Reforma Agraria (CERAs) and the *consejos campesinos* did not really take root amongst the peasantry. They were essentially state-promoted agencies, and many of them indeed were taken over by the opposition. Social conflict in the countryside was complex. The process of agrarian reform and peasant unionization had not eliminated conflict but rather transferred it to a different level from the simple *hacendado*–peon conflict. In any case the period was too short, and the pressures too great, for the reforms either to increase productivity or to resolve the remaining inequalities in the countryside.

Thus, the opposition counted on the support of many urban and rural workers – most obviously white-collar workers and the beneficiaries of the reform process in the countryside. Pro-government supporters in the working class were increasingly taking their own initiative, decreasingly controlled by central party or union bureaucrats, increasingly mobilized and militant. Activities such as farm and factory seizures created problems for a government anxious to preserve its image as constitutional and hopeful of winning majority support for its policies.

Popular power and popular participation were fundamental aims of the UP, but the exact form that participation was to take was never entirely clear, and there were differences of emphasis between the Socialists and Communists. The local UP committees, for example, never really developed. A People's Assembly held in Concepción in July 1972 was opposed by the Communist Party and did not have Allende's approval. The more successful forms of participation were those that responded to local pressures and involved community and work-force. The most radical expression of *poder popular* developed in the *cordones industriales* that developed dramatically in response to the 'bosses' strike' in October 1972.

'*Poder popular*' was the name given to the host of organizations – *comandos comunales, comandos campesinos, cordones industriales* – that grew up to defend local communities, farms and factories. They organized the defence of their communities and undertook the tasks of maintaining production and supplies. But *'poder popular'* was a misleading name, for the movement included only a minority of the work-force, was defensive in character and was not co-ordinated above the local level. Nevertheless, it was an impressive demonstration of determination to defend the gains made by workers under the UP government.

The maximum expressions of *poder popular* were the *cordones* in the working-class belt surrounding Santiago that brought together local inhabitants and workers in a joint effort to run the enterprises and administer services in the area. As economic paralysis threatened Chile with the October 1972 truckers' strike, these organizations sprang up, on the basis of a number of existing organizations, in defence of the government. In October 1972 perhaps 100,000 people were active in the Santiago *cordones.* They rejected party affiliations; they were not supported initially by nor were they responsive to, the CUT; and they alarmed not just the opposition but also the Communist Party and the government. These were short-lived, crisis-based organizations, and their decline after October 1972 was not reversed, except in response to another opposition strike in June 1973, when in a single day they took over about 250 factories. This time the take-overs had the support of the government and the CUT. But this only served to intensify opposition accusations that the government was acting illegally; and further accusations that arms were being distributed to the workers (though there is no evidence of this) led to clashes between workers and the army and police in their search for arms. It was far too late to construct a parallel *poder popular* movement in order to take over state power, even if this was envisaged by the government. The general slide into anarchy continued.

In some ways as impressive as the growth of the popular sectors and their organizations was the parallel expansion of the *gremios.* These were associations of non-manual employees and professional groups, ranging from doctors, lawyers and architects to lorry owners, small shopkeepers and taxi-drivers. Small shopkeepers organized a *gremio* of some 160,000 members (claimed to be close to 90 per cent of the national total). Lorry owners, many of them running only one vehicle, could call on 25,000 members. The twenty or so professional associations, or *colegios,* including such large organizations as those of the 20,000 accountants or the 7,000 doctors, formed a confederation during the UP period. These groups were led by men associated with, or members of, right-wing parties or the PDC, and some of them, such as León Villarín of the truckers, became prominent opponents of the Allende government. These groups were not passive instruments of the dominant industrial and business circles. They enjoyed a robust independence and actively sought to further their members' interests by putting pressure on the government of the day. The Frente Nacional del Area Privada (FRENAP) became a major co-ordinating body of large and small businesses. Some anti-Marxist unions, like the Confederación Marítima backed the *gremialistas*. In 1973 a Comando Nacional de Defensa Gremial was formed to co-ordinate the activities of various groups. More than a thousand *gremios* were in active opposition to the UP in 1973, and some of them could count on generous funding from the United States.

The UP hoped to win at least some of these groups to its side. Allende himself, in speech after speech, emphasized that small and medium-sized entrepreneurs and farmers had nothing to fear from the UP. But these groups had never given much electoral support to the parties that made up the UP, apart from the declining Radical Party. Although many of them benefited materially during the first two years of the UP, the fear of loss of privileges, of worker lack of discipline, of a Communist take-over and a situation like that in Cuba (Castro's prolonged visit to Chile in 1971 did nothing to reassure them) was more real than any attractions the UP offered. And whatever Allende said, there was little reassurance from the speeches and writings of other UP politicians. UP rhetoric stressed its Socialist and popular character; little attempt was made to construct proposals in a way that would attract these sectors. The press and radio, controlled largely by the opposition, played an active, sometimes hysterical, role in spreading fear of the long-term aims of the UP.

The major confrontation with the government came in October 1972 after a proposal was made to increase state control over supplies to the trucking companies. The importance of this sector is obvious in a country with a geography like Chile's. The vital transport sector was virtually paralysed for a month, and there were powerful solidarity strikes by other professional and petty bourgeois sectors. More than one hundred *gremios* went on strike, in a movement that shook the government and that received the support of the PDC and National Party. As a result of the strike, the armed forces were incorporated into the cabinet, but it was too late to arrest the process of polarization.   .

With government and opposition now lined up against one another in bitter confrontation, with the economy out of control, with the commander-in-chief of the armed forces, General Carlos Prats, resigning his command in acceptance of his failure to mediate the crisis and control the officer corps, with the Church unable to bring the sides together and with growing violence and an increasing number of assassinations, there was little prospect of a peaceful solution. The end came with a violent military coup on 11 September 1973, in which La Moneda, the presidential palace, was bombed, President Allende was killed and thousands of Chileans were murdered.

Before 1973 the Chilean military had intervened only intermittently in the political process, and the political views of its officers corps were not generally made public. The military tended to be ignored by civilian politicians, though there were signs that this neglect could be dangerous, as in the minor uprising that occurred in 1969. But it was generally believed that the military would not depart dramatically from its accustomed political neutrality. General Prats, who had succeeded the assassinated General Schneider as commander-in-chief of the armed forces, adhered to the same strict constitutional interpretation of the role of the armed forces. Allende was consistent in his policy of not interfering in the institutional concerns of the military. Officers' salaries were improved. Spending on arms increased. Some officers were involved in the administration of public services, but they were very few, not in command of troops and obviously did not include those whose sympathies were alien to the UP. Allende abstained from interfering in the army hierarchy, and those few members of the UP who wished to appeal over the heads of the officers to the rank and file received no encouragement.

The military, however, could hardly have remained aloof from the intensifying polarization and violence that marred the last year of the Allende government. Politicians of the Right were calling for a coup and were constantly trying to instigate military plots.[22] Even the PDC, by its support for the strike of October 1972, by its backing of the congressional declaration of illegality in 1973 and through the increasing violence of its

---

[22] The direct involvement of the United States in the coup remains a matter of dispute. What is certain, however, is the long and close relationship between the United States and the Chilean military. Between 1950 and 1972 Chile received U.S. $43 million in U.S. arms and military supplies; between 1973 and 1976, it received $143 million. Allende's foreign minister, Clodomiro Almeyda, alleges that the U.S. armed forces, especially the Naval Intelligence Service, participated in the technical planning of the coup. Almeyda, 'The Foreign Policy of the UP government', in S. Sideri (ed.), *Chile. 1970–1973: Economic Development and Its International Setting* (The Hague, 1979), p. 116. This, however, is denied in the account of U.S. Ambassador Nathaniel Davis, *The Last Two Years of Salvador Allende* (Ithaca, 1985).

attacks on the government, seemed to point to a military coup as the only way to resolve the conflict.[23] Indeed, several prominent PDC leaders openly welcomed the coup, though many did not.

Various incidents contributed to the deterioration of relations between the government and the military. The military was notably unenthusiastic about Castro's long visit to Chile in 1971. The army and police resented the existence of Allende's personal bodyguard, the Grupo de Amigos del Presidente, which was drawn from the ranks of the extreme left wing of the UP. They grew uneasy at rumours of workers being armed and at the presence in Chile of many revolutionaries from other Latin American countries, especially Cuba. Resentment was publicly expressed at the proposal to set up an Escuela Nacional Unida (ENU). Although educational reform was overdue and the proposed reform itself progressive in many respects, the draft proposal employed a Marxist vocabulary that alarmed many sectors, and it was seen by the Church as a threat to its own private schools and to the teaching of religion in state schools. The Catholic Church as a whole had remained relatively neutral in the political battles of the period, though individual priests were active on both sides. But the ENU proposal was condemned by the bishops, and the army also made known its opposition.

It became impossible for the armed forces to maintain a united neutrality towards the political process once they entered the cabinet in November 1972 in an effort to restore some degree of political calm. But if their involvement in the cabinet produced temporary political solutions, it increased tensions within the army between those who supported Prats's constitutionalist stand and those who came to hate the UP and all it stood for. As the military officers in the cabinet refused to sign decrees of insistence that would have authorized more factory take-overs, they also increased the resentment of the left wing of the UP towards the military. The military became a direct participant in politics.

The military remained in the cabinet to oversee the March 1973 elections, but the inconclusive results convinced those military officers already plotting that a coup was the only solution. A premature coup attempt on 29 June, the so-called *tancazo*, had the support of an armoured regiment, but General Prats was able to contain the threat. Although the amount of overt support given to the rebels was limited, the *tancazo* had serious

---

[23] These points are made by Radomiro Tomic. Quoted from an article by Tomic in Gil et al. (eds.), *Chile at the Turning Point*, p. 273.

consequences. The government's call for workers to take over factories worsened relations with the military, which saw this as a prelude to worker resistance to the armed forces and even to the formation of workers' militias. When Allende met the army generals to seek their backing, only four of fourteen offered full support. For those military men concerned over the response of the workers, the lesson they drew was that the response was very limited: there was no march to the centre of Santiago. The military plotters concluded that a coup would meet only limited resistance.

The prelude to the coup itself was a confused period of increasing violence, rumours and counter-rumours. A final attempt by the cardinal-archbishop to bring together the PDC and the UP failed. Mutual suspicion was too great. When three armed forces chiefs were removed from their positions in the air force, army and navy, the plot could be consolidated. The most crucial removal was that of Prats. Although he had entered the cabinet again in August, he was increasingly isolated within the army. He resigned after a bizarre incident in which officers' wives staged a hostile demonstration outside his house.

By now the slide into anarchy was irreversible. The forcible searching of factories for arms by the military led to bitter clashes with the workers. Protests against alleged brutality by naval officers against conscripts who were resisting being used for anti-UP activities led to a call for an insurrection of naval conscripts against officers by the Socialist senator Carlos Altamirano and the MIR leader Miguel Enríquez. The officer corps was furious at such interference, and its resolve to go ahead with the coup and get rid of the naval chief, Admiral Montero, was stiffened. The last obstacle to the coup was dissolved with the removal of Admiral Montero on 7 September. The allegiance of General Augusto Pinochet to the plot came, it seems, very late but, once given, signalled the beginning of the final arrangements. On 11 September 1973, the armed forces rose and overthrew the government of Salvador Allende, the democratic system and the rule of law.

PINOCHET'S CHILE: LAISSEZ-FAIRE ECONOMY AND AUTHORITARIAN STATE

The unity of the Armed Forces is the unity of Chile. (Official statement, 11 September 1973)[24]

---

[24] Taken from the pamphlet issued by the Press Department of the Government entitled *September 11th, 1973: The Day of National Liberation*, p. 10. The propaganda agencies of the military

Although Chilean political life had seen outbreaks of violence, there had been nothing to compare with the intense repression that took place after the coup of September 1973. Thousands of Chileans were killed. The exact number will never be known, but estimates range between three thousand and thirty thousand. In the first six months after the coup, as many as eighty thousand political prisoners were taken. This scale of repression did not continue, but torture of political suspects, imprisonment, exile and even assassination continued to be part of the system of political control, centralized in the Dirección de Inteligencia Nacional (DINA).

Why was the coup so brutal? There was nothing in Chile to compare, for example, with the powerful urban guerrilla movements in Argentina or Uruguay. Talk of arming the workers was mostly talk, and whilst some political militants undoubtedly possessed weapons, the scale was tiny. However, the scale of social disintegration and polarization was very great. The feeling of civil war was in the air. In these circumstances, the members of the UP were defined as the enemy, not as mere political opponents.

The military in Chile had delayed intervention. A more interventionist military, as in Argentina or Brazil, would probably have taken action much earlier when the political temperature was lower. The brutality of the coup owes something to the feeling that army involvement in politics as had occurred with the UP government was a grave mistake. Solutions had to be, initially at least, military and not political; the coup was a move against all politicians and not just those of the Left. The aim of the plotters was to abolish political parties, not to make a deal with right-wing parties, however much those parties supported them. Finally, the intention of the military was to eliminate whole political and social movements from Chilean life. The military did not assume that the parties of the Left were creatures of a small political class.

Whatever explanations are offered for such terrible violence, it seems inconceivable that such barbarities could have been committed in a country like Chile. Yet very little is known about the way the military saw political life or why men who were not psychopaths acquiesed to the government's use of torture. Although many politicians foresaw the coup

government produced a flow of documents designed to prove the sinister intentions of the UP government, including a 'Plan Zeta' to assassinate leading political and military figures. This 'plan' and other imaginative inventions are contained in the *'White Book'* of the government published shortly after the coup. Other documents emphasize the national and patriotic character of the armed forces; see, e.g., the *Declaración de principios del gobierno de Chile* (Santiago, March 1974).

in 1973, only those of the extreme Right and Left expected such a high level of repression and such a prolonged period of military rule.

It is an error to attribute too uniform a degree of ideological conviction to the military or a very clear vision of its long-term aims once the initial destruction of the old regime had been accomplished, which was in itself seen as a long-term task. It was obvious that urgent measures of economic stabilization were necessary and that the coup could be legitimized only by the adoption of a dramatically new economic and political model. The lack of consensus on a basic programme helps to explain why power became so personalized. The cohesion of armed forces stemmed from the command structure rather than agreement on policy measures.

The doctrines with which the military were most familiar were those of 'national security'. These have been defined as a belief in the concept of the nation as an 'essence', 'tradition', or 'spirit' that has been ruined by political demagogy and menaced by antinational aggression, in the acceptance of social inequalities as the natural order, in the idea of government as authoritarian, and in the definition of Marxism as the principal enemy of society.[25] Vague as these authoritarian ideas are, they help to explain why the military accepted not simply the task of overthrowing Allende, but also the construction of a new society in which political divisions would be superseded by common action for national greatness. General Pinochet, fifty-eight at the time of the coup and with a record of forty years of service in the army, was a specialist in geo-politics.[26]

The Chilean military, having rejected its constitutional tradition, fell back on a direct transference to the political arena of military values – hierarchy, discipline and respect for order. This, like the lack of agreement on policy, helps to explain the personalization of authority of the regime under Pinochet – in contrast to the corporate rule of the Brazilian military after 1964, or the hostility towards personalism that developed in Argentina, Uruguay and Peru in the 1970s. Pinochet showed considerable political skill in outmanoeuvring his potential opponents in the officer corps (such as General Gustavo Leigh) and appointing loyal subordinates to all command posts in the armed forces. As head of state and commander-in-chief of the armed forces, Pinochet wielded immense

[25] Manuel Antonio Garretón, *El proceso político chileno* (Santiago, 1983).
[26] The other members of the ruling military junta were Admiral José Toribio Merino, aged 57, another specialist in geo-politics; General Gustavo Leigh, head of the air force, at first identified with the neo-fascist elements of the government but later dismissed by Pinochet for his criticisms on policy matters; and General César Mendoza, chief of the Carabineros.

power. After ratification of the new constitution, he appropriated much of the symbolic authority of the presidency.[27]

Belief in authoritarian doctrines such as national security is normally associated with an increase in the economic activities and role of the state, whereas Pinochet's Chile took the opposite course. However, conversion to the economic doctrines of the Chicago school of monetarism did not come immediately. Many officers were attracted initially to a kind of catholic integralism, or corporate state ideology. Their rejection of the values of socialism and their admiration for the role of the *gremios* led to a strong vein of nationalist corporatism, as expressed by the influence of reactionary theorists like Jaime Guzmán. Such ideas received political expression in institutions like the Council of State, which was set up in December 1975 on the pattern of a similar organization in Franco's Spain and included political notables and representatives of the *gremios*.

These ideas, however, were not an appropriate basis for legitimizing the regime. In the first place, the Church was not sympathetic to such reactionary doctrines (though it did not emerge as an outspoken opponent of the regime until 1975). Second, these ideas would not find favour with the external actors with which the regime wanted to ally itself, that is to say, the United States and the international banks. The regime wanted international approval, financial support and investment. Flirtation with fascist ideas – as distinct from militant anti-communism – was not likely to gain support. Third, corporatism might be used by the pre-existing political groups to manoeuvre their way back to power and dilute the military's monopoly on power. But most important of all, these doctrines offered little specific advice on how to deal with economic problems. The initial measures of the government – removal of price controls and subsidies, cutting of real wages, reduction of the fiscal deficit – had not convinced the country that inflation could be controlled. Inflation in 1974 was 376 per cent and in 1975 was 341 per cent.

A group of economists trained in the Catholic University and in Chicago, with considerable experience in the world of Chilean business, commerce and politics (several had been advisers to Alessandri in 1970), had been meeting since 1972 to prepare a policy for a new right-wing government. However, it was not until July 1974 that they started to

---

[27] The legislative function was exercised by the junta, serviced by a series of committees. These committees were staffed by civilians who played a crucial part in shaping and determining policy. But Pinochet maintained his own band of civilian advisers, conducting his affairs with great secrecy.

influence policy through the appointment as finance minister of Jorge Cauas, although he himself was a PDC adviser rather than a 'Chicago boy', as they were called. At the Economics Ministry Fernando Léniz (a business-man) was first advised and then, in April 1975, replaced by Sergio de Castro, a convinced monetarist. The dominance of the neo-liberal school of economists was complete.

The project that the Chicago economists offered the military involved a complete restructuring of the economy, society and the political system. The whole legacy of Chilean politics since the 1930s, and not just the UP period, would be changed. Such a transformation could be achieved only through strict authoritarian controls to eliminate the distortions brought about by populism and to create the right conditions in which market forces could operate. Reducing the size of the public sector would remove the basis for popular or sectoral pressures for concessions from the govern-ment; redirecting the surplus to the private capital market would strengthen those forces supportive of the military's policies and penalize those who were likely to be against them; opening the economy to free trade would provide the means for growth without having to give state support to uncompetitive sectors; allowing market forces to regulate wage rates would undermine the political bargaining strength of the labour movement. All of these would combine to eliminate that greatest propaga-tor of social unrest – inflation. And the beauty of the solution was that the regulatory mechanism would be that most liberal of concepts – the operation of free-market forces.[28] At the same time the old forms of political allegiance would be eroded, and new forms, classless and na-tional, would develop.

Monetarism offered a new utopia in contrast to the failures of the past, and the offer of a utopia could 'justify' the brutal suppression that followed the military coup. The new economic orthodoxy was attractive to the military because it offered coherence and discipline, and it was seen as technical and scientific and therefore ideologically neutral. Once under way, the process was to be irreversible and, as necessary means for national salvation, its premises were not to be questioned.

Many sectors were to find the new measures unpleasant. But entrepre-neurial groups accepted austerity and competition as the price to pay to

---

[28] The most sustained and informed critique of the government's economic policy comes from the economists at CIEPLAN. This section relies heavily on Ricardo Ffrench-Davis, 'El experimento monetarista en Chile', *Estudios CIEPLAN* no. 9 (1982); and Alejandro Foxley, *Latin American Experiments in Neo-Conservative Economics* (Berkeley, Calif., 1983).

avoid a repetition of the past. Many middle sectors welcomed any measures that would restore discipline and order. And the long-term promises of the Chicago boys were attractive. General Pinochet's rule was based not only on the army and repression, but also on support from influential groups in civil society.

The first economic decisions made by the government had already reversed the direction of economic policy of previous decades. Tariffs were reduced and prices were unfrozen. The process of 'privatization' of the state began. The exchange rate was devalued and unified. A new investment code was promulgated in an effort to attract foreign capital. But these measures did not halt the deterioration of the economy. Copper prices fell from 93.4 U.S. cents per pound in 1974 to 56.1 cents per pound in 1975, and export earnings fell by half. Moreover, the rise in oil prices was very detrimental to the economy. The deterioration in terms of trade was equal to a loss of 5.6 per cent of GDP in 1975.

One major problem for the policy-makers in Chile in this initial period was the difficulty of obtaining foreign funds to back a stabilization effort. Chile was to some extent an international pariah, although substantial help was given by the United States. In 1975, Chile received U.S. $93 million from AID and the Food for Peace programme, compared with $6.9 milion in 1973. In the first three years of the Pinochet government, Chile received loans of $141.8 million from the U.S. Export–Import Bank and other U.S. agencies (only $4.7 million went to Allende) and $304.3 million from the World Bank and the Inter-American Development Bank (compared with $11.6 million to Allende). But the volume of private bank lending fell sharply (it did not reach significant levels until 1976), and huge debt repayments had to be made.

It was in these circumstances that the doctrinaire monetarists took over and in April 1975, with Pinochet's full support, applied a 'shock' treatment. In effect this meant the president's long-term support for the Chicago boys; any retreat from the measures initiated in 1975 would have implied a confession that the severity of the measures then imposed was a mistake. And the measures taken were indeed severe. Real government expenditure was cut by 27 per cent in 1975, and the fiscal deficit from 8.9 per cent of GNP to 2.9 per cent. Tariffs on imports fell from an average of 70 per cent in mid-1974 to 33 per cent by mid-1976. Credit was severely restricted, and annual real interest rates rose from an already high 49.9 per cent to 178 per cent by the end of 1975. Public investment fell by half. The GDP fell by almost 15 per cent compared with the 1974 value. Industrial production fell by 25 per cent. Real wages fell yet again; by 1975 they reached their lowest point at 62.9 per cent of their 1970 value. Unemployment rose from 9.7 per cent of the labour force in December 1974 to 18.7 per cent in December 1975. Yet inflation was slow to respond and remained at 341 per cent in 1975. In spite of the worst recession in more than forty years, recovery was slow. The shock treatment needed more time to work and had to be applied with unbending rigour.

The Chicago boys completely dominated the scene until the exit of Sergio de Castro from the Finance Ministry in April 1982, and even then they continued to be influential and to occupy leading economic posts. The technocrats in charge of the economy were convinced that the state occupied far too important a role. Their intention was to reduce the state's involvement as much as possible by the sale of public enterprises. Apart from those companies in which the UP government had intervened, the state owned, through the Corporación de Fomento de la Producción (CORFO), some three hundred enterprises in 1973. By 1980 this number had declined to twenty-four, and half of those companies were in the process of being transferred. There were another dozen or so state enterprises that depended on governmental agencies other than CORFO – amongst them the state copper and petroleum corporations. The sale of assets took place in extremely favourable conditions for the new owners. Given the recession and the high domestic rates, those able to purchase state assets were the large conglomerates (*los grupos*) in the private sector with access to foreign funds at interest rates significantly lower than the domestic ones. In effect the state paid a substantial subsidy to the rich and the powerful to take over state assets – a subsidy that had been calculated as equivalent to up to 40 or 50 per cent of the purchase price. But the military resisted the sale of state assets it deemed to be strategic. Including the copper corporation CODELCO, the current revenue of state companies in 1982 still amounted to about 25 per cent of GDP. The Chicago boys were opposed by a sector of the military that still considered government control over certain vital services and sectors necessary for the maintenance of national security.

The adherents of free-market economies encouraged an intensification of economic concentration in Chile. A handful of multi-sectoral groups dominated the banking, financial, industrial and export-agriculture sectors. Two conglomerates, the Cruzat–Larrain and Javier Vial groups, were particularly important and dominated the private banking system until the economic collapse of 1982–3. Their access to international finance gave them immense advantages and benefits. The major groups made an estimated U.S. $800 million in profit between 1977 and 1980 simply by borrowing abroad and relending domestically at interest rates that varied from 100 per cent in 1976 to 30 per cent in 1978 above international rates. These profits were rather more than the cost of the state firms and banks sold back to the private sector between 1973 and 1978.

It has been calculated that by the end of 1978 five economic conglomerates controlled 53 per cent of the total assets of Chile's 250 largest private enterprises. These five, plus another four, controlled 82 per cent of the assets in the Chilean banking system, 60 per cent total bank credits and 64 per cent of loans made by financial institutions.[29] The conglomerates grew at dizzying pace and made windfall profits, as overseas banks attracted by high interest rates in Chile were prepared to make short-term loans, knowing that the government's economic fortunes were so bound up with the Chicago model that honouring international commitments would be top priority even if there was recession. Abolition of strict control over banking and over foreign exchange led to a process of concentration and of indebtedness that would destroy the foundations of the Chicago-inspired economic 'miracle'.

A similar process of privatization occurred in the agrarian sector. About a third of the land was returned to its former owners. Although something like 40 per cent of land was assigned to the peasants who worked it, lack of access to credit and technical assistance forced some 60 per cent to sell out. Unemployment in agriculture was significantly higher than it had been in previous decades, and by 1980 wage rates had declined to about their 1965 level. State support to agriculture was drastically reduced, apart from the profitable export sector.

The state retreated from many areas where previously it had played an important role. Fiscal expenditure as a percentage of GDP dropped from 29.1 per cent in 1972 to 19.7 per cent in 1978. There were significant reductions in social expenditure per capita in education, health, social security and housing. Government investment fell drastically, by almost one-half between 1970 and 1978. Pension funds were transferred to the private sector in a massive influx of liquidity to companies that were largely owned by the conglomerates. The political intention of this proposal, of course, was that the fortunes of workers would be tied to the

---

[29] Fernando Dahse, *El mapa de la extrema riqueza* (Santiago, 1979). The share of financial resources deposited in private institutions rose from 11% in 1970 to 64.7% in 1979.

fortunes of the private sector – 'socialism' would become a threat to pension rights. At the same time, labour legislation introduced in 1979 strictly limited the effectiveness of union collective bargaining. Unions lost much of their former power.

Government statistics tended to use the recession of 1975 as a base year and so give a somewhat distorted picture of the progress of the economy, following the 'shock' administered by the Chicago boys. But the government could point to a number of achievements. High growth rates were recorded in the period from 1977 to 1980, although the overall annual rate of growth of GNP between 1974 and 1980 was only 4 per cent; on a per capita basis, 2 per cent, lower than the rate of the 1960s.[30] The rate of inflation at last began to fall and in 1981 was 9.5 per cent. The fiscal deficit had been eliminated by 1979. Non-traditional exports tripled between 1974 and 1980. There was a balance-of-payments surplus in the period from 1978 to 1980 as a result of the accumulation of international reserves, based on a huge inflow of foreign capital that reached more than U.S. $16 billion annually in the 1978–80 period.

But there were negative features as well. The inflation rate was brought down by the application of a fixed exchange rate in 1979. This led to a severe balance-of-payments problem as cheap imports flooded the Chilean market and exports were made expensive. The trade gap was met by higher levels of foreign borrowing; but this borrowing was for short-term loans to the financial sector. The government was forced into a series of hasty, ill-timed devaluations of more than 70 per cent between June and October 1982. The rate of investment, whether private, state or foreign, remained well below past levels. Real interest rates at the high levels that prevailed in Pinochet's Chile discouraged investment and encouraged speculation. Even the vital copper sector was starved of new investment for expansion above existing levels of production. The lowering of tariffs hit national industry hard, and bankruptcies reached record heights. Most new imports were consumption goods of the luxury variety, and not the capital goods and machinery that were needed to maintain the level of industrial production. Although non-traditional exports grew, the rate was not fast enough to match the growth in imports.

The social costs of the experiment were also very high. Real wages in the 1974–81 period scarcely reached three-quarters of their 1970 level.

---

[30] These figures have been subject to careful revision which suggests that the growth rate was 20% *lower* for 1976–81 than claimed by the government. Patricio Meller et al., '¿Milagro económico o milagro estadístico?', *Mensaje* (May 1985), pp. 145–9.

Even by 1982 the level was lower than that in 1970. Unemployment rose to record heights: it was never lower than an annual rate of 16.5 per cent after the 1975 shock and rose to more than 30 per cent in 1982–3 (compared with 5.7 per cent in 1970). Income distribution worsened appreciably. The average monthly consumption of the poorest 20 per cent of households fell by 31.1 per cent between 1969 and 1978, while that of the highest 20 per cent rose by 15.6 per cent. The structure of employment also changed. The number of blue-collar workers fell by 22 per cent between 1970 and 1980 – a not unwelcome development to a government that opposed a strong union movement. The 'informal' sector of employment grew by 13.3 per cent in the same period.

Although the warning signs were there in 1980 for those who chose to read them, the regime remained confident and there was talk of an economic miracle. The international isolation of Chile was lessening as the memory of the coup faded. Moreover, the domestic political front was tranquil. A new constitution and a plebiscite in 1980 expressed the determination of the government to carry on as long as necessary to secure the success of its reforms.

A number of factors help to explain the consolidation of the Pinochet regime's power. First, there was support for the coup from wide sectors of society, and fear of a return to the disorder of the UP years kept many loyal to the new government even when promised benefits did not materialize. Second, the government was exceptionally ruthless. The development of a powerful secret police, DINA, made opposition to the government a crime, the consequences of which could easily be torture, exile or death. At least three prominent Chileans were victims of assassination attempts abroad by DINA agents. Two succeeded, those of General Prats in Buenos Aires in 1974 and Orlando Letelier, an effective and respected leader of the opposition in exile, in Washington in 1976; one failed, against the respected and moderate PDC leader Bernardo Leighton. Third, the process of economic concentration gave the government powerful backers. Fourth, although many foreign governments shunned Chile, international banks did not, and the external finance needed to run the economy was, after the mid-1970s, always available. Fifth, the way that Pinochet personalized power and concentrated authority in his own hands gave a dictatorial solidity to the regime. Pinochet's manipulation of the military and of civilian groups showed considerable political cunning. Potential military challengers did not last long. The military as such had no policy-making function, but it was well rewarded materially. Civilians were involved in government as individuals and not as representatives of powerful groups. Pinochet divided and ruled.

On the other side, the opposition was divided and hounded. Many of the prominent leaders of the UP parties and unions were killed or exiled after the coup. Although the PDC suffered less, it was soon suspended, and some of its leaders were forced into exile. Legislation made political actitivity virtually impossible. The opposition spent much time trying to analyse what went wrong in 1973, but the process of attributing blame did not help to unite it. Not until 1975 did the Church come out against the government. The press and the mass media were not only strictly controlled but also used to convey government propaganda. Universities were placed under military control, certain disciplines prohibited and many lecturers and students dismissed. Unions were similarly 'intervened', divided and controlled.

Two plebiscites were used to create the appearance of consultation. In 1978 Chileans were asked whether they supported General Pinochet in the face of international aggression. According to official sources, 75 per cent did. In 1980 the country was asked to approve a new constitution of markedly authoritarian form, with a transition period of eight years in which Pinochet was to exercise unconstrained executive power and with the possibility of his re-election for a further eight years after that. The 1980 constitution created a system of presidential rule with few limitations. A substantial part of the Senate was to be nominated rather than elected. The Chamber of Deputies lost any effective power of scrutiny over the executive. The constitution institutionalized the power of the armed forces in a Council of National Security, which was given a role in almost all important matters and a decisive role in constitutional affairs. The principle of civilian control over the military was effectively abolished. The government claimed that the results of the plebiscite on the constitution, in which 93.1 per cent of the total electorate participated, were 67 per cent in favour, 30 per cent against and the rest null or void. However, the absence of registers, complete government control over the electoral process, massive official propaganda, tiny opposition protests and, undoubtedly, fraud, intimidation and fear of expressing opposition in what might not be so secret a ballot cast considerable doubt on these figures.

General Pinochet's centralization of power owed a great deal to this control over the DINA (later renamed the Central Nacional de Informaciónes [CNI] in an attempt to introduce some cosmetic changes).

Pinochet had established a secret police system under his personal control, independent of any military structure. It became an instrument of surveillance not only over the civilian population but also over other intelligence agencies and the military itself. At the height of its power in 1977, the head of DINA, General Manuel Contreras, commanded a small army of more than nine thousand agents and a network of paid volunteer informants several times as large, pervading all aspects of life. The DINA obtained funds from illicit control over several firms nationalized under the UP government, and there was occasional evidence of corruption and extortion involving DINA officials. The DINA suffered a set-back as a result of the international scandal that followed the assassination of Letelier in Washington in 1976; Pinochet was eventually forced to dismiss Contreras and agree to the extradition of the U.S. citizen Michael Townley, who, while working for the DINA, had carried out the assassination. The newly named CNI essentially performed the same functions as the old DINA and was active in repressing the popular movements that broke out in opposition to the government in 1983.

Pinochet was politically astute in building on the strong tradition of loyalty and hierarchy in the Chilean armed forces. Neither the army as an institution nor individual officers had ever been the recipients of such lavish expenditure: the military budget almost doubled in real terms between 1973 and 1981. A disproportionate amount went to the army, police and security services – those sectors directly involved in internal repression. Chile was amongst the highest spenders on the armed forces in Latin America, with no less than 6 per cent of the GDP going to the military in 1980. The personnel of the armed forces had every material reason for identifying their futures with that of Pinochet. Yet Pinochet was careful to avoid giving the armed forces any institutional role in the political process. Generals who became cabinet ministers did so in a personal capacity and were strictly accountable to Pinochet. The number of generals increased from twenty-five in 1973 to forty-two in 1980 and to fifty-four in 1984; all were appointed by Pinochet and manipulated to remain loyal to him, not simply as president of the republic, but also as *capitán general* of the armed forces.

The most significant opposition to Pinochet came from the Catholic Church and its cardinal in Santiago. The Catholic Church and other denominations quickly became involved in relief agencies and in helping those who suffered from the massive repression of 1973. But the Church was slower to take a stand against the government's policies as opposed to its abuses. Indeed, the general tenor of ecclesiastical pronouncements was to praise the generals for having saved the country from Marxism. It took three and a half years before the hierarchy cast doubt on the legitimacy of the government. One of the reasons for this change in attitude was the suppression of the PDC and increasing repression directed at party members and at radical Catholics, both priests and laity. Once embarked on a process of criticizing the government, the Church became increasingly important. This was a grave source of embarrassment to a government that saw itself as the saviour of Christian civilization. The Church kept attention focussed on the continuing violation of human rights. It provided a forum within which trade unions and popular organizations could manage a precarious existence. And it provided shelter to those who would criticize the regime.

The development of unions in this period show how difficult it is, even for an authoritarian regime, to control trade unions if they are allowed even minimal rights. Class and political consciousness could not be abolished by decree. The copper workers, for example, rejected the leaders imposed by the government and played a crucial role in breaking the political deadlock in 1982–3. And there were many earlier examples of union members standing up against the regime, notably in the Coordinadora Nacional Sindical. But the trade union movement was seriously weakened by the years of military government. Union leaders considered threatening to the regime were persecuted, exiled and even killed. The murder of the prominent leader of Agrupación Nacional de Empleados Fiscales (ANEF), Tucapel Jiménez, a Radical and formerly a fierce opponent of the UP, showed that even politically moderate union leaders ran grave risks. Only 10 per cent of the labour force was unionized in 1983 compared with more than 30 per cent in the days of the Allende government. Union leaders, mostly unemployed themselves, realized how difficult it was to bring the employed out on strike, especially in the state sector, where the government's response was instant dismissal. Strikes were, in practice, demonstrations of the unemployed, who hoped to paralyse economic activity by impeding public transport and forcing shops to close. Although the Comando Nacional de Trabajadores, formed in June 1983, was the most representative national movement to emerge since the coup, it could only exhort and persuade. In view of the repression of the labour movement and the high level of unemployment, traditional industrial conflict had to give way to protest in the streets, to riots and demonstrations of the poor and unemployed.

The financial crisis that threatened Chile in 1981 broke with severity in 1982 and 1983. Chile was not alone in facing enormous problems of debt repayment; Argentina, Brazil, Mexico, Venezuela and even Cuba were facing similar problems. Indeed, the military's explanation of the crisis as the effect of the international recession was not without force. Copper prices were depressed, oil prices were still high and interest rates rose sharply on the international markets. Although other countries suffered from the recession, Chile was particularly hard hit.

The crisis developed rapidly. By 1981 the deficit on the current account of the balance of payments was 20 per cent larger than total exports and amounted to almost 15 per cent of GDP. International bankers became nervous, the enormous amounts of money that Chile needed were no longer so readily available and interest rates were higher. A squeeze on domestic credit and refusal to change the overvalued exchange rate led to a series of bankruptcies. Of the unprecedented 431 firms which went into liquidation in 1981, the most important was the sugar refinery Compañía Refinadora de Azúcar de Viña del Mar (CRAV), one of Chile's largest enterprises. In November 1981 the state was forced to intervene in four banks and four *financieras*. The government's failure to regulate the banking system was to have disastrous consequences, especially after it rescued the Banco Osorno from collapse in 1977, fearing that bankruptcy would damage internal and foreign confidence. As a consequence, depositors, domestic and foreign, felt that their loans to the private sector were effectively guaranteed by the state. This, as well as the failure to maintain a stable exchange rate and the international recession, led to huge increases in non-performing assets in the banking system: these rose from 11 per cent of the capital and reserves of the banking system in 1980 to 47 per cent in 1982 and to 113 per cent by mid-1983.

In 1982 GNP fell by 14.1 per cent and investment by nearly 40 per cent. The peso was devalued, contrary to government promises, and by the end of 1982 was down to 40 per cent of its previous parity; foreign exchange reserves fell by 40 per cent. The economic team began to change as rapidly as it had under any previous civilian government. In 1983 the government took over most of the private financial system and so acquired a large number of firms whose assets had passed to the banks. The fiscal deficit reappeared and the rate of inflation rose to 20 per cent in 1982. The major groups were broken up, and hostility between their former owners and the government replaced the formerly close working relationship. Monetarist policies of the kind applied in Chile were shown to be inapplicable in an economy with such a heterogeneous structure, segmented markets and sectoral and regional differences. The costs of economic adjustment were not only excessively high in social terms, but also extremely damaging to the very economy they were supposed to benefit. The heaviest cost fell to the poor. In mid-1983, 10.9 per cent of the economically active population (380,529 men and women) were working for the government Programa de Empleo Mínimo (PEM), receiving a monthly income of two thousand pesos, equivalent to the price of 1.3 kilograms of bread per day. The government also ended the linking of wage increases to the increase in the cost of living.

Opening the economy to international forces came to mean in practice the accumulation of an enormous short-term debt, mostly in private hands, as well as a process of de-industrialization. Between 1973 and 1979 the traditional foreign debt (public sector plus the private sector debt guaranteed by the government) fell by 35 per cent, but the private sector debt rose by 91.3 per cent. Even in 1978 Chile's debt service ratio was 45.3 per cent, one of the highest in the world, and it was to rise sharply. The debt constituted an immense burden on the Chilean economy.

After ten years of military rule, Chile was no advertisement for monetarism. Per capita income was 3.5 per cent lower than in 1970, and increasing inequality and unemployment meant that the poor were worse off than they had been twenty years ago. Industrial production was 25 per cent lower than in 1970. The foreign debt was equal to 80 per cent of GNP, compared with 8.2 per cent in 1970. And ironically in view of its aims, the state owned most of the financial sector and thereby much of national industry. International banks forced the government, against its will, to include private sector debt in its renegotiation.

Demonstrations organized on a monthly basis from May 1983 rocked the regime. It was in the shanty towns, above all in Santiago, that popular protest took its most potent form. At least a third of the population of the capital city lived in such areas, or urban slums, not notably better. Unemployment was rife – a level of 80 per cent was not uncommon – and many of the youth of the shanty towns never knew stable employment. Days of protest and struggles with the army and police in the shanty towns saw them converted into veritable battle-grounds. Not all shanty towns expressed their opposition in such militant fashion as La Victoria, where the French priest André Jarland was killed in early September 1984, but social deprivation and hostility to the regime were so widespread that they constituted the government's main political problem. As a result, the police and army staged a brutal repressive operation in the shanty towns in late October and in November 1984.

Opposition party activity was resumed in a more open form in 1983. The opposition parties of the Centre, led by the Christian Democrats and a faction of the Socialist Party, formed the Alianza Democrática (AD). They called for Pinochet's resignation, a properly elected constituent assembly and a broad social pact to oversee the return to democracy. But as it became clear that the government would make no more than token gestures and would not even discuss the question of Pinochet's resignation, the left-wing opposition parties, led by the Communist Party and another wing of the Socialists, formed the Movimiento Democrático Popular (MDP) and pressed for a policy of mass mobilization and confrontation. The Communist Party, much to the discomfort of the centrist AD, refused to renounce the right to use violence as a method of ridding the country of the dictatorship.

Given the unpopularity of the regime, it may seem paradoxical that the opposition was so divided, but it was extremely difficult to organize opposition in Chile. Opposition parties and movements had been denied means of communicating with their supporters for more than eleven years. They had no regular access to radio, television or the popular press, had not been able to organize internal elections and enjoyed only a brief period of relatively open activity after the protests began in May 1983. Politics was practised in a vacuum. No one really knew how much support any party, or internal faction of a party, enjoyed, and if there was no test of support, any group could claim to be representative. For the first decade of the dictatorship, parties had to concentrate on surviving and maintaining some degree of internal organization. This led, inevitably, to emphasis on immediate party tasks rather than initiatives to oppose the regime, but it also made the parties slow to recognize how many changes had taken place in Chile and how many ideas and policies had to be re-formulated.

A cycle of violence, protest and repression marked the years after 1983. The government's survival depended on the unity of the armed forces. The opposition's prospects depended on the extent to which it could create a broad agreement on the transition to democracy. At a time when most other military regimes – those in Argentina, Uruguay, Brazil, Peru and Ecuador – had returned power to civilians, General Pinochet demonstrated very effectively how dictatorial authority could be established in a society with even as long a tradition of democratic government as Chile. The key to Pinochet's power lay in his control over an army that was disciplined, loyal to its commander-in-chief and contemptuous of civilian politicians. Another element of his survival was the inability of the opposition to unite and offer a credible alternative. It seemed as if the opposition might do this with the Church-inspired Acuerdo Nacional para la Transición Hacia la Plena Democracia in 1985, but the exclusion of the Communist Party created one major problem outside the Acuerdo Nacional and party sectarianism created another within it.

If domestic politicians seemed unsure of how to confront their president, international politicians suffered the same fate. President Pinochet was unmoved, even defiant, in the face of international hostility. Although President Carter shunned the regime, Chile was a low priority for the United States, and unless the opposition could produce an effective alternative, there was always the fear that the Marxists might return if the general were overthrown. President Reagan was far more preoccupied with Central America than with Chile, and although the United States became noticeably cooler towards the Pinochet regime after 1985, it was no more effective in influencing the government, though it did help the opposition.

With economic recovery, the government was able to reward some of its followers and restore business confidence. At least some groups of the Right wanted to see Pinochet himself remain in power until 1997, and most supported a continuation of the authoritarian political system and free-market economy, even if not under the same leadership.

Recovery from the recession of 1982–3 was steady and sustained. Growth increased to about 5 per cent annually from 1986 to 1988, inflation remained contained, unemployment dropped to approximately 12 per cent and higher copper prices and good export earnings from non-traditional exports provided a favourable external financial position. Although political protests continued with the creation of the Asamblea de la Civilidad, the opposition did not seem to be making significant inroads into the government's authority. A failed assassination attempt against General Pinochet in September 1986 reinforced his prestige and lent credence to his claim that the opposition could not control those who were prepared to use violence. Although details of the assassination attempt are obscure, it seems almost certain that it was the work of the Frente Patriótico Manuel Rodríguez, a group created with the blessing and support of the Communist Party. The opposition had called 1986 the 'decisive year'; but if anything, it seemed to show that Pinochet could run rings around a still divided and relatively weak opposition.

Certainly, the president and his closest advisers assumed that they enjoyed the support of the majority of the population, and they looked forward with confidence to the outcome of a plebiscite that would be held no later than January 1989 to decide upon the first elected president to take power under the 1980 constitution. Pinochet himself would have preferred a sixteen-year presidency from 1980 but was persuaded that his rule would be more legitimate if he were to present himself to the electorate for a renewal of his mandate in 1988 or 1989. It was assumed that the military junta would in fact nominate Pinochet as the sole candidate of the plebiscite, and although air force, police and navy representatives made it clear on several occasions that they would have preferred a younger, civilian candidate, in the end they bowed to pressure from the army; Pinochet received their nomination in late August 1988. The immediate protests that greeted this decision should have been a warning that electoral victory was by no means a certainty, but the president's advisers, above all Minister of the Interior Sergio Fernández, the architect of the constitution, were confident of victory on 5 October 1988.

Such confidence in Pinochet's triumph was not unrealistic. Chile was at the time a highly efficient police state with the government exercising enormous power. A whole range of tactics from intimidation to persuasion could be used to secure votes for the '*sí*' option. Pinochet still enjoyed the undoubted support of the army, and the army governed Chile, especially at the regional level. Regional governors, provincial authorities and city mayors were expected to do their utmost to secure a majority for the government. Moreover, the government had virtually complete control of television, most radio stations and newspapers. The opposition was granted a fifteen-minute television 'spot' each day for three weeks before the vote, but that hardly offset fifteen years of sustained government propaganda. Chile was also enjoying an economic recovery, and pointed references were made to the political uncertainty and economic crises of neighbouring states.

Pinochet despised politicians and firmly believed that they were incapable of making a united and effective attack against his authority. There was evidence to the contrary, especially in February 1988, when the opposition signed a pact to organize the '*no*' vote in the plebiscite. But dictators tend to be told what it is expected they would like to hear, and Pinochet was no exception. The politicians of the Right were excluded from the campaign, which was firmly in the hands of a few top military advisers and Sergio Fernández. Even before the results were known, politicians of such parties as Renovación Nacional, the largest party of the

Right, were making it obvious that they felt the official campaign was poorly organized. The plebiscite was a fair and free choice, with massive participation. Of the potential electorate, some 93 per cent were registered to vote; and of the registered electorate of 7.4 million voters, 97 per cent voted. The result was 55 per cent for the '*no*' option and 43 per cent for the '*sí*', and 2 per cent null or void.

Many Chileans still felt excluded from the benefits of economic recovery. Income distribution remained grossly inequitable, and opposition claims that 5 million Chileans (40 per cent of the population) lived in poverty were not convincingly refuted by the government. Average wages in 1987 were 13 per cent less than in 1981 and still less than in 1970. Reduced expenditures on health and education were strong grievances amongst many Chileans. The privatized social security system provided excellent benefits for those who could afford to join. But more than 50 per cent of the population was excluded and had to endure an increasingly deficient state system. Such grievances help to explain support for the opposition. The government also suffered from its human rights record. Against expectations that this would be a minority preoccupation, the poll showed that a majority of the population was well aware of the widespread abuse of human rights and firmly condemned those abuses. Perhaps the strongest long-term factor working against the government, however, was the desire to resume democratic, competitive politics. This did not necessarily represent a rejection of the free-market economic model, or even of the main features of the 1980 constitution. It did, however, reflect popular support for a return to the predominant mode of political activity over the past hundred years in Chile. In the end, the plebiscite was not about the economy, but about politics – the freedom to choose and the right to vote. Even some admirers of General Pinochet felt that fifteen years had been enough and that it was time for him to step down.

The impact of the campaign itself was enormous, as was shown by the extraordinarily high level of participation. It was, after all, the first political campaign of this sort since 1973. There is little doubt that the government's negative and backward-looking campaign was inferior to that of the opposition. Pinochet was not a great success as a democratic politician seeking votes, and the efforts of his advisers to create such an image were often destroyed when Pinochet threw away his prepared speeches, recalled the crudest assaults on Communism and launched bitter attacks on former collaborators. Sweeping economic gestures to win support were ruled out by the very nature of the economic model he had constructed. An economy emphasizing fiscal restraint and sound management cannot suddenly make grand populist gestures without running the risk of undermining confidence.

By contrast, the opposition campaign was professional and forward looking, was aimed at youth and stressed reconciliation and political moderation. In February 1988, the opposition had at last reached an agreement to unite against the candidacy of Pinochet, and although the Communist Party was initially very hostile to playing the game by the general's rules and never officially formed part of the sixteen-party coalition, it lent important support. The opposition campaign would not have had the impact it had without months of careful political work persuading the electorate that the vote would be secret and that there would be no adverse consequences in voting '*no*'. The Church played an important role in this process with its Cruzada Cívica. Funding from the United States and Europe allowed the opposition parties to organize throughout the country and to count the vote with its own computer systems, thus minimizing the possibility of government fraud. A new 'instrumental' party created by Socialist leader Ricardo Lagos played an important role in bringing into political activity previously passive or independent citizens and focussed attention on the single issue of defeating the general. The presence of more than a thousand international observers was a support to the opposition and an indication to the government that the significance of the plebiscite was a matter of concern to the international community and not just to Chile.

Opposition politicians were surprised by the way in which powerful sectors of the Right immediately accepted the verdict. There was fear of a coup or some kind of interference with the voting or with the results. The Chilean armed forces, however, did not see the rejection of Pinochet as a rejection of the military as an institution, nor of the constitution of 1980, nor of the free-market economic model. Neither the armed forces nor the political Right, let alone the business sectors, would have welcomed the political violence that would inevitably have followed any attempt to interfere with the results of the plebiscite. Moreover, there remained more than a year before the presidential and congressional elections which had to be held following the rejection of Pinochet, and the Right expected in that period to build upon the 43 per cent vote gained by President Pinochet. For his part, Pinochet was determined to pass a series of laws that would make any future alteration of his constitution and economic model as difficult as possible.

From October 1988 until December 1989 Chile lived in a state of permanent electoral campaign. The opposition made few political errors. The man who had led the opposition in the plebiscite, former senator and PDC politician Patricio Aylwin, was chosen as its presidential candidate. Once chosen, Aylwin behaved with the confidence of a president-elect and assembled a political team of considerable experience and authority. Even the difficult task of selecting the candidates to represent the seventeen-party coalition, the Concertación de los Partidos por la Democracia, in the congressional electoral campaign was resolved without damaging public disputes. The Concertación was firm in its rejection of the Communist Party, which though it did present a few candidates in a separate coalition, in effect lent its support to Aylwin. The opposition also extracted two major concessions from Pinochet. In July 1990 a plebiscite approved major constitutional reforms which made further reform somewhat easier and also reduced the power of the military in the new post-Pinochet system. Just before the December elections, Pinochet accepted a formula which meant that the executive of the powerful Central Bank would be composed equally of representatives of the government and of the opposition, and not, as he originally wanted, members exclusively loyal to him.

By contrast, the campaign of the Right was disorganised and unimpressive. The chosen candidate, Hernan Buchi, who had been minister of finance since 1985, proved far less capable as a presidential candidate than as an economic technocrat. The two major parties of the Right, Renovación Nacional (RN), a moderate party which included politicians who had been active in right-wing politics before the coup, and the Unión Democrática Independiente (UDI), a combination of free-market technocrats and unconditional supporters of Pinochet, demonstrated much less unity than the opposition alliance, and it frequently appeared that they were more concerned with fighting each other than with opposing the coalition led by Aylwin.

President Pinochet kept aloof from the electoral campaign. Instead, his major concern was to press ahead with a series of measures that would reduce the power of the incoming government. The process of privatization of the economy, already well advanced, was accelerated. An electoral law was devised that at the congressional level would give substantial over-representation to the Right. An armed forces law was passed that would make presidential control over the military very difficult: the president, for example, would have no power to dismiss the commanders-in-chief of the various services. The composition of the Supreme Court was altered. A series of restrictions was imposed on the future Congress that would make it almost impossible to investigate the activities of the Pinochet government. The opposition protested against these measures, sometimes with success, as with the plebiscite on constitutional reform and with the composition of the executive of the Central Bank. But there was little doubt that the political agenda of the future government would be concerned largely with trying to amend the restrictions on its activities imposed by the government of Pinochet.

The results of the presidential election on 14 December 1989 resemble those of the October plebiscite. Aylwin won 55 per cent of the vote. The vote of the Right was divided between Buchi, who took 30 per cent, and a populist businessman, Francisco Javier Errázuriz, who gained 15 per cent. The results of the congressional elections gave a majority to the opposition alliance. However, although the Concertación won twenty-two seats in the Senate compared with sixteen for the Right, the presence of nine senators designated by the outgoing Pinochet government meant that the Aylwin government would lack the majority necessary for important measures of constitutional and political reform. In the election for the lower house the Concertación won seventy-two seats to the forty-eight of the Right. The most popular political party was clearly the PDC, which elected thirteen senators and thirty-eight deputies, followed within the opposition alliance by the PPD, which elected four senators and seventeen deputies. On the Right, RN did much better than the UDI, electing six senators to the two of the UDI; and most of the eight independent senators were close to RN.

The government of Patricio Aylwin, which took power in March 1990, faced a Chile that had changed in many respects since the 1973 coup. There was now much more agreement about economic policy: almost all parties accepted that the market and the private sector had a fundamental role in economic development. The former project of the Left to nationalize the commanding heights of the economy was now seen to be as irrelevant as the former PDC claim to establish a communitarian society. The Aylwin government promised to improve income distribution and to spend more on social services, but not at the expense of careful macroeconomic management. The ruthless policies of the Pinochet government had created a smaller and more efficient state apparatus, and there was little desire to inflate the role of the state to its previous dominant role in the economy. The incoming government wanted to maintain the successful export economy and welcomed the co-operation of foreign investment, even if it also intended to increase tax revenues.

This consensus in the field of economic policy was reflected more generally in attitudes towards the political system. There was widespread agreement about the need to make concessions in order to sustain a democratic system. On the Left, the popularity and influence of the Communist Party had been reduced by mistaken policies, by its toleration of political violence during the Pinochet years and by the crisis of international Communism. The Socialist Party, once more united, was more moderate than it had been in the past: the old sectarianism and admiration for the Cuban Revolution had disappeared. The PDC had abandoned its belief in the party as the natural governing party without allies and was more open to dialogue and negotiation than before. The political Right in Chile was not disturbed by the electoral results. It had the power to block reforms in Congress, and it had sufficient electoral backing to make it hopeful about future electoral victories. It was not alarmed by the government's economic policy.

The legacy of the Pinochet years had its harsh side as well. The problem of poverty was acute and challenging. Income distribution had worsened appreciably in Chile, and some 3 to 4 million Chileans were living in poverty. Moreover, many of the services that were necessary to alleviate poverty – health, education, social security – had been neglected by the Pinochet government and were badly underfunded. Sustaining economic growth and dealing with social inequality would be a challenge to governments for years to come.

One other legacy of the Pinochet government was the unresolved issue of justice for victims of human rights abuses. There is little doubt that human rights had been violated on a massive and unprecedented scale in Pinochet's Chile. Future governments would have to try to deal with those seeking redress and yet at the same time not provoke the military to withdraw its support from the democratic order. The fact that the commander-in-chief of the army under the Aylwin government remained General Pinochet indicated the nature of the problem the new government faced in trying to consolidate a fully democratic political system.

Yet the plebiscite of 1988 and the elections of 1989 were remarkable affirmations of popular desire to re-establish democracy in Chile. In both cases participation was massive, involving more than 90 percent of the registered electorate. Both elections were free and fair, neither produced significant political violence or conflict, and in the 1989 elections the vote for parties of the Left and Right that could be considered extreme or anti-democratic was insignificant. This popular affirmation of democracy gave a firm base for future governments to consolidate a stable constitutional order. The responsibility of the political parties was to design a democratic political system which did not repeat the errors that led to the overthrow of the constitutional order in 1973.

The process of democratic consolidation in Chile was greatly strengthened by the economic achievements of the Aylwin government in its first two years. The government managed to combine growth with stability. It pushed through a major tax reform, it implemented a fundamental reform of the labour code, and it retained the confidence of the union movement and gained the confidence of the entrepreneurial sector. The growth rate for 1990 was only just over 2 per cent as the government struggled to restrain the accelerating inflation created by the electorally motivated expansionist policies of the last two years of the Pinochet government. But in 1991 the growth rate was over 5 per cent, and exports rose by 10 per cent even though international economic conditions were not favourable. The inflation rate for 1991 met the government's target of 18 per cent. Moreover, a massive inflow of foreign investment indicated international confidence in the economy and created optimism about long-term prospects. Growth was expected to continue at levels of around 5 per cent annum and inflation to decline even further. But the accumulated social debt to the poor remained a heavy demand on an economy that despite its recent success still remained very vulnerable to international price movements.

On the political front the government proceeded with authority and determination. The parties of the Concertación remained loyal to the President, and the absence of any major cabinet change by midterm indicated a high degree of governmental unity. One of the major problems remained the presence of General Pinochet as head of the army. Pinochet's authority was shaken by the discoveries of mass graves of those who had 'disappeared' during his rule, of financial irregularities involving his son-in-law and leading officers, and of dubious arms deals. But the army continued to support him and, in a demonstration of solidarity with their chief, retreated to its barracks for a day in December 1990 in defiance of the government.

One of the central issues that clouded relations between the armed forces and the government was that of human rights. The committee set up by the government to examine human rights abuses, the Rettig Commission (*Comisión Nacional de Verdad y Reconciliación*), produced evidence of

2,279 cases of executions, disappearances and death by torture, and 641 more cases remained unconfirmed. At least one had international implications, for the United States continued to insist upon the extradition of Chilean military personnel involved in the assassination of Orlando Letelier in Washington in 1976.

The argument of the Rettig report was that truth is an absolute value and must be established. By and large that was done. But justice is more complicated. It was, of course, partly achieved through the vindication of those who were executed as alleged terrorists by the Pinochet government. It was also partly achieved through the compensation given to relatives of those executed or disappeared. But the perpetrators of acts of injustice have not been punished, and may never be. This may be deeply unsatisfactory, but was it politically necessary? In the words of José Zalaquett, a member of the Rettig Commission and a prominent member of Amnesty International, 'It can be argued that in a country that has been deeply divided, repentance and forgiveness could bring about unity, and that unity, in certain circumstances, would reinforce the foundations of democracy. I am talking in the abstract . . . but also thinking of Chile. Thus forgiveness could also be a means of prevention, if the truth has been revealed and there has been an admission of responsibilities'.[31]

The assassination of Senator Jaime Guzmán, the leader of the UDI, in April 1991 was a demonstration that the problem of political violence in Chile had not been solved. It was also a real setback to a party that he more than any one else had created, organized and controlled. The coincidence in timing between the assassination of Guzmán and the publication of the Rettig report on human rights diminished the likelihood that effective trials for those accused of human rights abuses would take place, and focused attention upon issues of law and order.

Although opinion polls continued to show majority support for the government, there were areas of considerable concern. In the first place, the relationship with the military was still too uneasy, too strained, too often a matter of scoring points in attempts to gain advantage. General Pinochet continued to make things difficult for the government. Secondly, the government was criticized for placing too much emphasis on macro-economic equilibrium and not on dealing with the social issues that demanded attention after years of neglect, although in fact government

---

[31] José Zalaquett, 'Human Rights: Truth and Responsibility in Chile', *The Ethics of Responsibility*. Paper 2, Washington Office on Latin America (Washington, D.C., 1991).

expenditures on health and education rose sharply. But the inequalities created by the Pinochet years were deep and would take years to correct. Not surprisingly, the government faced the accusations that it had gone too far in the direction of market liberalism and too far in abandoning the welfare role of the state.

Offsetting these criticisms was general recognition that there were also major and impressive achievements. The government had secured agreement for its policies from both Right and Left, and those policies were working well. The party sectarianism that had so scarred the past seemed to have been contained. Extra-parliamentary groups were few and insignificant even if capable of acts of individual terrorism. And although the army was far from fully under civilian control there was little fear that it constituted a serious threat to the political system. In its first two years, the government of President Aylwin had created a firm foundation for advancing to a more democratic system.

BIBLIOGRAPHICAL ESSAYS

1. FROM INDEPENDENCE TO THE
WAR OF THE PACIFIC

Invaluable work has been done since the late 1950s by the journal *Historia* (published from the Institute of History, Catholic University of Chile, Santiago) in keeping a detailed record of all materials published on Chilean history (in Chile and abroad) from year to year. These are listed in the journal's regular *Fichero bibliográfico*. The first such bibliographies were usefully collected in Horacio Aránguiz Donoso (ed.), *Bibliografía histórica, 1959–1967* (Santiago, 1970). Subsequent *ficheros* have been published in each issue of *Historia* except 21 (1986), the first of two special memorial issues for Mario Góngora, whose tragic death at the end of 1985 deprived Chile of one of its most respected twentieth-century scholars.

The publications appearing in Chile during the period from Independence to the War of the Pacific are listed (although not in accordance with modern bibliographical criteria) in Ramón Briseño (ed.), *Estadística bibliográfica de la literatura chilena,* 3 vols. (Santiago, 1965–6). Briseño's two original volumes were printed in 1862 and 1879. Vol. 3, produced under the auspices of the Biblioteca Nacional, Santiago, contains much-needed amendments and additions, compiled by Raúl Silva Castro. The Oficina Central de Estadística was founded in Chile in 1843, although it began work four years later; thereafter the government became reasonably assiduous in collecting statistical information, much of it subsequently published in the *Anuario estadístico* from 1861 onwards. Commerical statistics were published (after 1844), as were the censuses of 1854, 1865 and 1875. Statistical material from this period, however, must be used with critical awareness of its inadequacies. For a detailed list of Chilean government publications, including statistics, see Rosa Quintero Mesa (ed.),

Latin American Serial Documents, no. 7, Chile (New York, 1973). Markos Mamalakis (ed.), *Historical Statistics of Chile,* 6 vols. (Westport, Conn., 1979–89), provides much valuable material.

Traditional historical scholarship in Chile, which produced some memorable narratives between the mid-nineteenth century and the mid-twentieth, tended to focus less on the post-independence decades – 'the early republic' – than on the colonial era and the wars of independence. The great nineteenth-century historians played a part in the history of their own time, as is well illustrated in Allen Woll, *A Functional Past: The Uses of History in Nineteenth Century Chile* (Baton Rouge, La., 1982), but they did not usually write about it. This also tended to be true, with certain notorious exceptions, of their successors between 1900 and 1950. Recent work by scholars has begun to fill in some of the gaps in our knowledge of the period. Simon Collier, 'The historiography of the "Portalian" period in Chile, 1830–1891', *Hispanic American Historical Review* 57 (1977), pp. 660–90, reviews the literature as it existed in the mid-1970s. Some of the hopes for future research expressed in that article have now been fulfilled: since that time there have been very positive signs of a substantial new interest in the early republic.

The most extensive single description of the period as a whole is still the one to be found in Francisco Antonio Encina, *Historia de Chile desde la prehistoria hasta 1891,* 20 vols. (Santiago, 1942–52), vols. 9–17. This huge and idiosyncratically conservative work has not lacked critics, but it is instructive when used to consult the relevant passages of Ricardo Donoso's sustained attack, *Francisco A. Encina, simulador,* 2 vols. (Santiago, 1969–70). Amongst older works, the years from independence to 1833 are narrated in copious detail in Diego Barros Arana, *Historia general de Chile,* 16 vols. (Santiago, 1884–1902), vols. 11–16, while good narratives of specific presidencies include Ramón Sotomayor Valdés, 'Chile bajo el gobierno del general don Joaquín Prieto', in *Historia de Chile durante los cuarenta años transcurridos desde 1831 hasta 1871,* 2nd ed., 4 vols. (Santiago, 1905–6); Diego Barros Arana, *Un decenio de la historia de Chile, 1841–1851,* 2 vols. (Santiago, 1905–6), the greatest Chilean historian's serene swan-song; Alberto Edwards, *El gobierno de don Manuel Montt* (Santiago, 1932); and, on the four administrations between 1841 and 1876, Agustín Edwards, *Cuatro presidentes de Chile,* 2 vols. (Valparaíso, 1932). A very early political narrative that continues to repay close attention is Isidoro Errázuriz, *Historia de la administración Errázuriz, precedida de una introducción que contiene la reseña del movimiento y lucha de los partidos desde*

1823 hasta 1871 (Valparaíso, 1877). All the works mentioned show traditional Chilean historical writing at its best.

There are few extensive printed documentary collections for this period of the kind available for colonial times and the wars of independence. Congressional debates, however, were printed as *Sesiones del Congreso Nacional* from 1846 onwards, and congressional papers (and selected debates) from before that date may be found in Valentín Letelier (ed.), *Sesiones de los cuerpos legislativos de la República de Chile, 1811–1845,* 37 vols. (Santiago, 1887–1908). Complete lists of the names and dates of the presidents, cabinet ministers, senators and deputies for the years 1823–83 are printed in Luis Valencia Avaria (ed.), *Anales de la República,* 2nd ed., 2 vols. in 1 (Santiago, 1986), vol. 1, pp. 448–503, and vol. 2, pp. 22–281.

On the general political framework of the period, the stimulating essay (1928) of Alberto Edwards Vives, *La fronda aristocrática en Chile,* 10th ed. (Santiago, 1987), remains a classic source for its many asides and insights. Also still well worth consulting is the account of the ideological battles of the period provided by the doyen of mid-twentieth-century Chilean historians, Ricardo Donoso, in his *Las ideas políticas en Chile,* 3rd ed. (Buenos Aires, 1975). Valuable introductory texts by modern scholars, giving general coverage of the period, include Sergio Villalobos R., Fernando Silva V., Osvaldo Silva G. and Patricio Estellé M., *Historia de Chile,* 4 vols. (Santiago, 1974–6), vol. 3, pp. 404–578 and vol. 4, pp. 580–761; Gonzalo Izquierdo F., *Historia de Chile,* 3 vols. (Santiago, 1989–90), vol. 2, pp. 83–309; and Brian Loveman, *Chile: The Legacy of Hispanic Capitalism,* 2nd ed. (New York, 1988), chapters 4–5; this last is the best one-volume history of Chile in English to date. The older essay by Julio César Jobet, *Ensayo crítico del desarrollo económico-social de Chile* (Santiago, 1955), still merits a perusal. Luis Vitale, *Interpretación marxista de la historia de Chile* (Santiago, 1971), vol. 3, re-works the period up to 1859 from a further perspective. General ideas about the early republic along differing lines are offered in Sergio Villalobos R., 'Sugerencias para un enfoque del siglo XIX', *Estudios CIEPLAN,* no. 12 (Santiago, 1984), pp. 9–36; Mario Góngora, *Ensayo histórico sobre la noción de estado en Chile en los siglos XIX y XX* (Santiago, 1981), pp. 1–28; Simon Collier, 'Gobierno y sociedad en Chile durante la República Conservadora', *Boletín del Instituto de Historia Argentina y Americana 'Dr. Emilio Ravignani',* 3ª serie, 1 (Buenos Aries, 1989), pp. 115–26.

Political history in the traditional sense has attracted little attention since 1960; Chilean historians may still be unconsciously over-reacting to the giants of the past. A promising line of inquiry into the political elite of the period has been opened up in Gabriel Marcella, 'The Structure of Politics in Nineteenth-Century Spanish America: The Chilean Oligarchy, 1833–1891' (Ph.D. dissertation, Notre Dame University, 1973). The politics of the 1820s and early 1830s are analysed in Simon Collier, *Ideas and Politics of Chilean Independence, 1808–1833* (Cambridge, 1967), chapters 6–9, and Julio Heise González, *Años de formación y aprendizaje políticos, 1810–1833* (Santiago, 1978), part 4, chapters 1–6. The life and work of the supposed 'organizer of the republic', Diego Portales, have been re-evaluated, mildly in Jay Kinsbruner, *Diego Portales: Interpretative Essays on the Man and His Times* (The Hague, 1967), and more critically in Sergio Villalobos R., *Portales, una falsificación histórica* (Santiago, 1989). Whatever is said or written about him, the shade of the 'omnipotent minister' continues to haunt us: see the interesting collection of essays, Bernardino Bravo Lira (ed.), *Portales. El hombre y su obra: La consolidación del gobierno civil* (Santiago, 1989). Roberto Hernandez P., *Diego Portales, vida y tiempo* (Santiago, 1974), is a rare example of a modern 'straight' biography of any of the major politicians of the period: several others cry out for one. At the other end of the period, Aníbal Pinto's presidency (1876–81) receives a re-examination in Cristián Zegers A., *Aníbal Pinto, historia política de su gobierno* (Santiago, 1969). An important episode in the liberalization of the republic after 1861 is studied in Patricio Estellé M., 'El club de la reforma de 1868–71: Notas para el estudio de una combinación política del siglo XIX', *Historia* 9 (1970), pp. 111–35. Estellé's tragically premature death in 1975 cut short an especially promising scholarly career.

On the political ideas and attitudes of the Conservative party during its lengthy hegemony, see Simon Collier, 'Conservatismo chileno, 1830–1860. Temas e imágenes', *Nueva Historia* 7 (1983), pp. 143–63. An interesting new approach to liberalism in this period may be found in Alfredo Jocelyn-Holt L., 'Liberalismo y modernidad. Ideología y simbolismo en el Chile decimonónico: Un marco teórico', in Ricardo Krebs and Cristián Gazmuri (eds.), *La revolución francesa y Chile* (Santiago, 1990), pp. 303–3. For a study of the outstanding liberal of the time, see Bernardo Subercaseaux, *Cultura y sociedad liberal en el siglo XIX: Lastarria, ideología y literatura* (Santiago, 1981). The ideas of the two most prominent mid-century radicals are analysed in Alberto J. Varona, *Francisco Bilbao, revolucionario de América* (Panama City, 1973), and Cristián Gazmuri, 'El pensamiento político y social de Santiago Arcos', *Historia* 21 (1986), pp.

249–74. Gazmuri has also edited a valuable reprint of Arcos' best-known essay in *Carta a Francisco Bilbao y otros escritos* (Santiago, 1989).

Chile was at war three times during the early republic: against the Peru–Bolivian Confederation (1836–39), against Spain (1865–66), and once more against Peru and Bolivia in the War of the Pacific. These conflicts have not aroused very much scholarly interest in recent times. For the brief war with Spain, the older account by W. C. Davis, *The Last Conquistadores: The Spanish Intervention in Peru and Chile, 1863–1866* (Athens, Ga., 1950), is unlikely to be much improved on. The classic narrative of the War of the Pacific remains Gonzalo Bulnes, *La Guerra del Pacífico,* 3 vols. (Santiago, 1911–19). Numerous documents on the war were collected soon after it ended, as a gesture of national pride, in Pascual Ahumada Moreno (ed.), *Guerra del Pacífico: Recopilación completa de todos los documentos oficiales, correspondencias y demás publicaciones referentes a la guerra,* 9 vols. (Valparaíso, 1884–90), while more recently there has been a good facsimile edition of the official *Boletín de la Guerra del Pacífico* [1879–81] (Santiago, 1979). A solid technical description of the early land campaigns of the war may be found in Augusto Pinochet U., *La Guerra Del Pacífico: Campaña de Tarapacá,* 2nd ed. (Santiago, 1979). William F. Sater, *Chile and the War of the Pacific* (Lincoln, Nebr., 1986) is not a military history so much as an exhaustively detailed account of the impact of the war on different parts of the national life. Sater's earlier book, *The Heroic Image in Chile: Arturo Prat, Secular Saint* (Berkeley, Calif., 1973), analyses the treatment accorded by later generations to Chile's supreme hero of the war.

It must be noted here that there are few if any serious institutional studies of the nineteenth-century Chilean armed forces. Frederick M. Nunn, *The Military in Chilean History: Essays on Civil-Military Relations, 1810–1973* (Albuquerque, N.Mex., 1976), chapters 1–4, sketches relations over this period, but its main concern is with later times. Carlos López Urrutia, *Historia de la marina de Chile* (Santiago, 1969), chapters 1–14, offers a history of the navy – anecdotal rather than analytical – from its foundation to the War of the Pacific. The key institution of the national (or civic) guard is studied – such studies are long overdue – in Roberto Hernández P., 'La Guardia Nacional de Chile: Apuntes sobre su orígen y organizaciones, 1808–1848,' *Historia* 19 (1984), 53–113.

Some very interesting new work on nineteenth-century economic history has been done in recent times: a suitable synthesis must surely be within reach. For reviews of the available literature up to the 1970s, see Sergio Villalobos R., 'La historiografía económica de Chile: Sus comienzos', *Historia* 10 (1971), 7–56, and Carmen Cariola and Osvaldo Sunkel, 'Chile', in Roberto Cortés Conde and Stanley J. Stein (eds.), *Latin America: A Guide to Economic History, 1830–1930* (Berkeley, Calif., 1977), pp. 275–363. An excellent overview of the period is given in Luis Ortega, 'Economic Policy and Growth in Chile from Independence to the War of the Pacific', in Christopher Abel and Colin Lewis (eds.), Latin America: *Economic Imperialism and the State* (London, 1985), pp. 147–71. Markos Mamalakis, *The Growth and Structure of the Chilean Economy: From Independence to Allende.* (New Haven, Conn., 1976), pp. 3–85, deals with the period 1840–1930 in a single sweep. Also well worth consulting are the relevant sections of Marcello Carmagnani, *Sviluppo industriale e sottosviluppo economico: Il caso cileno, 1860–1920* (Turin, 1971) and José Gabriel Palma, 'Growth and Structure of Chilean Manufacturing Industry from 1830 to 1935' (D.Phil. thesis, Oxford University, 1979). The industrial growth of the later part of our period is well examined in a pioneering study by Luis Ortega, 'Acerca de los orígenes de la industrialización chilena, 1860–79', *Nueva Historia* 2 (1981), pp. 3–54.

Two valuable monographs from the 1980s that throw much-needed light on the mechanisms of external trade – the motor of Chilean economic change – and the all-important role of British trading houses are Eduardo Cavieres F., *Comercio chileno y comerciantes ingleses, 1820–1880: Un ciclo de historia económica* (Valparaíso, 1988), and John Mayo, *British Merchants and Chilean Development, 1851–1886* (Boulder, Colo., 1987). The theme of the economic consequences of independence is neatly explored by John L. Rector in two articles: 'El impacto económico de la independencia en América Latina: El caso de Chile', *Historia* 20 (1985), pp. 295–318, and 'Transformaciones comerciales producidas por la independencia de Chile', *Revista Chilena de Historia y Geografía* 143 (1975), pp. 107–27. John Mayo's article, 'Before the Nitrate Era: British Commission Houses and the Chilean Economy, 1851–1880', *Journal of Latin American Studies* 11 (1979), no. 2, pp. 263–303, is useful. The role of Valparaíso as an entrepôt is sketched in Jacqueline Garreaud, 'La formación de un mercado de tránsito, Valparaíso, 1817–1848', *Nueva Historia* 11 (1984), pp. 157–94. The operations of the commercial firms in the port itself are intelligently surveyed by Eduardo Cavieres F. in his 'Estructura y funcionamiento de las sociedades comerciales de Valparaíso durante el siglo XIX (1820–1880)', *Cuadernos de Historia* 4 (Santiago, 1984), pp. 61–86.

Thomas M. Bader, 'Before the Gold Fleets: Trade and Relations between Chile and Australia, 1830–1848', *Journal of Latin American Studies* 1 (1974), pp. 35–58, looks at early trans-Pacific links. A study is needed for the years after 1848. The French trading connection is well illustrated in M. Barbance, *Vie commerciale de la route du Cap Horn au XIXe siècle: L'Armement de A. D. Bordes et fils* (Paris, 1969). On foreign investment, in addition to the books by Cavieres and Mayo mentioned above, see Manuel A. Fernández, 'Merchants and Bankers: British direct and portfolio investment in Chile during the nineteenth century', *Ibero-Amerikanische Archiv* 9, no. 3–4 (1983), pp. 349–79.

The long-neglected theme of agriculture has been taken up in Arnold J. Bauer's first-class study, *Chilean Rural Society from the Spanish Conquest to 1930* (Cambridge, 1975), which, despite its title, largely focuses on or near our period. An interesting picture of one large hacienda and its subdivisions in the nineteenth century is Jorge Valladares, 'La hacienda Longaví, 1639–1959', *Historia* 14 (1979), pp. 117–93. Landowners' attitudes are examined in Gonzalo Izquierdo F., *Un estudio de las ideologías chilenas: La Sociedad de la Agricultura en el siglo XIX* (Santiago, 1968). Much more needs to be known about copper and silver mining, so immensely profitable in this period, but L. R. Pederson, *The Mining Industry of the Norte Chico, Chile* (Evanston, Ill., 1966), remains a good introduction, which can now be usefully complemented by Pierre Vayssière, *Un siècle de capitalisme minier au Chili, 1830–1930* (Paris, 1980), chapters 1–5. See also John Mayo, 'Commerce, Credit and Control in Chilean Copper Mining before 1880', in Thomas Greaves and William W. Culver (eds.), *Miners and Mining in the Americas* (Manchester, Eng., 1985), pp. 29–46, and William W. Culver and Cornel J. Reinhart, 'The Decline of a Mining Region and Mining Policy: Chilean Copper in the Nineteenth Century', in the same collection, pp. 68–81. Labour discipline in the northern mines is sketched in María Angélica Illanes, 'Disciplinamiento de la mano de obra minera en una formación social en transición. Chile, 1840–1850, *Nueva Historia* 11 (1984), 195–224. For coal-mining in the south, see the good, detailed study by Luis Ortega, 'The First Four Decades of the Chilean Coalmining Industry, 1840–1879', *Journal of Latin American Studies* 1 (1982), pp. 1–32. The story of nitrates to the end of the War of the Pacific can be followed in Oscar Bermúdez, *Historia del salitre desde sur orígenes hasta la Guerra del Pacífico* (Santiago, 1963), the classic work, and Thomas F. O'Brien, *The Nitrate Industry and Chile's Critical Transition, 1870–1891* (New York, 1982). See also O'Brien's article 'The Antofagasta

Company: A Case-Study in Peripheral Capitalism', *Hispanic American Historical Studies* 60 (1980), pp. 1–31.

The standard work on the ups and downs of Chile's merchant navy in this period remains Claudio Véliz, *Historia de la marina mercante de Chile* (Santiago, 1961). Railway-building and its economic context are intelligently covered in Robert B. Oppenheimer, 'Chilean Transportation Development: The Railroads and Socio-economic Change in the Central Valley' (Ph.D. dissertation, University of California at Los Angeles, 1976). See also the same author's articles: 'Chile's Central Valley Railroads and Economic Development in the Nineteenth Century', *Proceedings of the Pacific Coast Council on Latin American Studies* 6 (1977–9), pp. 73–86, and 'National Capital and National Development: Financing Chile's Railroads in the Nineteenth Century', *Business History Review* 56 (1982), pp. 54–75. Especially interesting on regional issues is John Whaley, 'Transportation in Chile's Bío-Bío Region, 1850–1915' (Ph.D. dissertation, Indiana University, 1974). A new and highly valuable source on the 'infrastructure' and technology in general is Sergio Villalobos R. and others, *Historia de la ingeniería en Chile* (Santiago, 1990), chapter 3.

Commercial policies in the early part of the period are discussed in John L. Rector, 'Merchants, Trade and Commercial Policy in Chile, 1810–1840' (Ph.D. dissertation, Indiana University, 1976), pp. 88–112, and in the later part by William F. Sater in his 'Economic nationalism and tax reform in late nineteenth-century Chile', *The Americas* 33 (1976), pp. 311–35. Sergio Villalobos R. and Rafael Sagredo B., *El proteccionismo económico en Chile, siglo XIX* (Santiago, 1987), looks at the tension between protectionism and free trade in economic legislation. The issues here are by no means wholly resolved. Perhaps the best recent summary of monetary problems in the period prior to the decree of 1878 is that of Pierre Vayssière, 'Au Chile: De l'économie coloniale à i'inflation', *Cahiers des Amériques Latines* 5 (1970), pp. 5–31. No close study of the recession at the end of the 1850s yet exists, but the altogether more severe crisis of the 1870s is covered in William F. Sater, 'Chile and the world depression of the 1870s', *Journal of Latin American Studies* 1 (1979), pp. 67–99, and also receives careful consideration in Luis Ortega, 'Change and Crisis in Chile's Economy and Society, 1865–1879" (Ph.D. dissertation, London University, 1979).

Social history, however broadly or narrowly we define the term, still needs an appreciable amount of research; there are some large gaps in our knowledge of particular social groups. Gabriel Salazar, *Labradores, peones y proletarios* (Santiago, 1985), gives a stimulating account of the 'popular classes' in this period (and in the decades to either side of it), with suggestive detail. Bauer, *Chilean Rural Society,* presents information about the rural labouring classes. Valuable findings about a traditional rural locality in the first part of our period (and the century preceding it) are offered in the highly rigorous study by Rolando Mellafe and René Salinas, *Sociedad y población rural en la formación de Chile actual: La Liga, 1700–1850* (Santiago, 1988): it would be splendid to have a dozen studies of this sort, focusing on different regions – the mining north, the forested south, Chiloé, etc.

Urban artisans and craftsmen up to the 1850s are studied in Luis Alberto Romero, *La Sociedad de la Igualdad: Los artesanos de Santiago de Chile y sus primeras experiencias políticas* (Buenos Aires, 1978); see also Romero's well-researched articles on the urban lower classes in general, mentioned below. Sergio Villalobos R. offers a sprightly portrait of the 'new rich' entering the upper class in his *Orígen y ascenso de la burguesía chilena* (Santiago, 1987). The importance of family links for the upper class is shown in Diana Balmori and Robert Oppenheimer, 'Family Clusters: Generational Nucleation in Nineteenth-Century Argentina and Chile', *Comparative Studies in Society and History* 21 (1979), pp. 231–61. More studies of family links are needed, in the manner of – although it touches only the edge of our period – Mary Lowenthal Felstiner, 'The Larraín family in the independence of Chile, 1789–1830' (Ph.D. dissertation, Stanford University, 1970).

Other distinctive groups in the nineteenth-century pattern have not been ignored in recent research. Jean-Pierre Blancpain, *Les allemands au Chili, 1816–1945* (Cologne, 1974), a magnificent piece of research in the modern French style, provides a fine picture of the German 'micro-society' in the south after 1850. Those who do not read French are directed to George Young, *The Germans in Chile: Immigration and Colonization, 1849–1914* (New York, 1974), not as detailed as Blancpain but a worthwhile account. For the British presence, not least in Valparaíso, see John Mayo, 'The British Community in Chile before the Nitrate Age;', *Historia* 22 (1987), pp. 135–50, as well as the monographs by Mayo and Cavieres mentioned above. The decline and fall of the Araucanian Indian enclave is summarized neatly in Jacques Rossignol, 'Chiliens et Indiens Araucans au milieu du XIXe siècle', *Cahiers du Monde Hispanique et Luso-Brésilien* 20 (1973), pp. 69–98, and thoroughly explored in José Bengoa, *Historia del pueblo mapuche* (Santiago, 1985), chapters 4–9, an account that uses oral histories and goes well beyond the older (but nonetheless useful) work of

Tomás Guevara, *Historia de la civilización de la Araucanía*, 3 vols. (Santiago, 1900–2), vol. 3. See also Leonardo León S., 'Alianzas militares entre los indios araucanos y los grupos indios de las pampas: La rebelión araucana de 1867–72 en Argentina y Chile', *Nueva Historia* 1 (1981), pp. 3–49. The first phase of the advance of the *huinca* (white man) south of the traditional frontier is well examined in Arturo Leiva, *El primer avance a la Araucanía: Angol 1862* (Temuco, 1984).

Urban histories are in general deficient in their coverage of the early republic. On Santiago, two works by René León Echaiz, *Historia de Santiago*, 2 vols. (Santiago, 1975) and *Nuñohue* (Buenos Aires, 1972), the latter dealing with the nowadays affluent eastern suburbs, can be seen as useful introductions but not much more. That research in this area is expanding can be seen in Armando de Ramón, 'Estudio de una periferia urbana: Santiago de Chile, 1850–1900', *Historia* 20 (1985), pp. 199–284, and Luis Alberto Romero, 'Condiciones de vida de los sectores populares en Santiago de Chile, 1840–1895: Vivienda y salud', *Nueva Historia* 9 (1984), pp. 3–86. The latter is a real contribution to social history, as is the same author's 'Rotos y gañanes: Trabajadores no calificados en Santiago, 1850–1895', *Cuadernos de Historia* 8 (1988), pp. 35–71.

Work on the demographic history of the period has made some good advances in recent times, though here, as with social history in general, the chronological boundaries have to be seen as very flexible. Robert McCaa, 'Chilean Social and Demographic History: Sources, Issues and Methods', *Latin American Research Review* 2 (1978), pp. 104–26, and Eduardo Cavieres F., 'Población y sociedad: Avance de la demografía histórica de Chile', *Cuadernos de Historia* 5 (Santiago, 1985), pp. 105–20, both give intelligent surveys of the issues. Good case-studies may be found in McCaa's book *Marriage and Fertility in Chile: Demographic Turning Points in the Petorca Valley, 1840–1976* (Boulder, Colo., 1983), and in Ann Hagerman Johnson, 'The impact of market agriculture on family and household structure in nineteenth-century Chile', *Hispanic American Historical Review* 58 (1978), 625–48, as well as in the relevant sections of Mellafe and Salinas, *Sociedad y población rural*, mentioned above.

The progress of education in the early republic, such as it was, is briefly summarized in Fernando Campos Harriet, *Desarrollo educacional, 1810–1960* (Santiago, 1960), though the larger and older work by Amanda Labarca, *Historia de la enseñanza en Chile* (Santiago, 1939), remains a basic source. The role of the University of Chile, a key institution, has been re-examined by Iván Jaksic and Sol Serrano in their 'In the Service of the

Nation: The Establishment and Consolidation of the University of Chile, 1842–1879', *Hispanic American Historical Review* 70 (1990), pp. 139–71. See also Sol Serrano's essays, 'Los desafíos de la Universidad de Chile en la consolidación del Estado, 1842–1879', in Juan Ricardo Couyoumdjian et al., *Reflexiones sobre historia, política y religión: Homenaje a Mario Góngora* (Santiago, 1988), pp. 111–29, and 'De la Academia a la especialización: La Universidad de Chile en el siglo XIX', *Opciones* 13 (Santiago, 1988), pp. 9–34. For the 'uses of history' in education, see Woll, *A Functional Past*, chapter 8. The role of philosophy and philosophers is sketched in Iván Jaksic, *Academic Rebels in Chile: The Role of Philosophy in Higher Education and Politics* (Albany, N.Y., 1989), chapter 1, though the book's main emphasis is on later periods. On the influence of Andrés Bello, see the essays collected in La Casa de Bello, *Bello y Chile: Tercer congreso del bicentenario*, 2 vols. (Caracas, 1981).

Ecclesiastical history has long been cultivated in Chile as a fairly specialized sub-discipline, but there have been no major recent investigations into the institutional history of the Catholic Church in the early republic or into church–state relations: for some useful suggestions, see Sergio Vergara Quiroz, 'Iglesia y Estado en Chile, 1750–1850', *Historia* 20 (1985), pp. 319–62. The study of freemasonry has not advanced since the standard account was published: Benjamín Oviedo, *La masonería en Chile* (Santiago, 1929), written from a rather starry-eyed masonic standpoint.

Chile's international relations and the development of its diplomacy can best be followed in Robert N. Burr, *By Reason or Force: Chile and the Balancing of Power in South America, 1830–1905* (Berkeley, Calif., 1965), and in Mario Barros' compendious account, *Historia diplomática de Chile, 1541–1938* (Barcelona, 1970), pp. 63–440. The vexed question of the northern frontier is covered in Eduardo Tellez L., *Historia general de la frontera de Chile con Perú y Bolivia, 1825–1929* (Santiago, 1989). The diplomacy of the first Chilean cabinet minister to hold the separate foreign affairs portfolio is analysed in Ximena Rojas V., *Don Adolfo Ibáñez: Su gestión con el Perú y Bolivia, 1870–1879* (Santiago, 1970). For a recent general view of early Chile–U.S. relations, see William F. Sater, *Chile and the United States: Empires in Conflict* (Athens, Ga., 1990), 9–50.

2. FROM THE WAR OF THE PACIFIC TO 1930

Among general works covering this period, the best to date are (in English) Brian Loverman, *Chile: The Legacy of Hispanic Capitalism*, 2nd ed.

(New York, 1988), chapters 6–7, and Frederick B. Pike, *Chile and the United States, 1880–1962* (South Bend, Ind., 1963) – much more comprehensive than its title suggests – and (in Spanish) Leopoldo Castedo, *Resumen de la historia de Chile, 1891–1925* (Santiago, 1982), a brilliantly illustrated book, and the voluminous work by Gonzalo Vial, *Historia de Chile, 1891–1973* (Santiago, vol. 1, in two parts, 1981; vol. 2, 1983; vol. 3, 1987), the first four books in an ambitious modern history; those published so far cover the period 1891–1925 in great detail.

The diplomatic history of the period is treated in Mario Barros, *Historia diplomática de Chile, 1541–1938* (Barcelona, 1970); see also William F. Sater, *Chile and the United States: Empires in Conflict* (Athens, Ga., 1990), especially chapters 3–5. Joyce Goldberg, *The "Baltimore" Affair* (Lincoln, Nebr., 1986) capably dissects a briefly tense moment in Chile–U.S. relations at perhaps greater length than the "affair" itself might seem to warrant.

Constitutional and political history of these years is stimulatingly covered in Julio Heise González, *Historia de Chile: El período parlamentario, 1861–1925,* 2 vols. (Santiago 1974–82). Published during the Pinochet dictatorship, these two volumes underscored the increasingly democratic content of Chile's history in the period concerned. General works dealing with the social and economic dimensions include Arnold Bauer, *Chilean Rural Society from the Spanish Conquest to 1930* (Cambridge, 1975), especially the later chapters; Brian Loveman, *Struggle in the Countryside: Politics and Rural Labor in Chile, 1919–1973* (Bloomington, Ind., 1976), whose early chapters are particularly useful; Henry Kirsch, *Industrial Development in a Traditional Society: The conflict of Entrepreneurship and Modernization in Chile* (Gainesville, Fla., 1977); Alan Angell, *Politics and the Labour Movement in Chile* (Oxford, 1972); Jorge Barría, *El movimiento obrero en Chile* (Santiago, 1971); and Peter DeShazo, *Urban Workers and Labor Unions in Chile, 1902–1927* (Madison, Wis., 1983), a significant 'revisionist' study which seriously challenges the role of Recabarren and the nitrate workers as the 'onlie begetters' of class consciousness and the left-wing parties. See also Charles Bergquist, *Labor in Latin America* (Stanford 1986), chapter 2, for an interesting new interpretation of Chilean labor history, focusing largely on this period. The quickest way into economic history is through the bibliography contained in Carmen Cariola and Osvaldo Sunkel, 'Chile', in Roberto Cortés Conde and Stanley J. Stein (eds.), *Latin America: A Guide to Economic History, 1830–1930* (Berkeley, Calif., 1977) pp. 275–363; this is accompanied by an interpretative essay. Literary history is surveyed in Raúl Silva Castro *Historia crítica de la novela chilena, 1843–1956* (Madrid, 1960), and also by Castedo, *Resumen de la historia de Chile,* which admirably covers cultural matters more generally.

The presidency of Balmaceda and the civil war of 1891 dominate the first part of the period. Harold Blakemore, 'The Chilean revolution of 1891 and its historiography', *Hispanic American Historical Review* 3 (1965), pp. 393–421, remains a valuable discussion of the issues. Also indispensable is the same author's *British Nitrates and Chilean Politics, 1886–1896: Balmaceda and North* (London, 1974). Of several notable contemporary accounts, J. Bañados Espinosa, *Balmaceda, su gobierno y la revolución de 1891,* 2 vols. (Paris, 1894), remains the best and most detailed. Hernán Ramírez Necochea, *Balmaceda y la contrarrevolución de 1891,* 2nd ed. (Santiago, 1969), is a suggestive Marxist interpretation. Much recondite material and contrasting interpretations may be found in Oscar Bermúdez, *Historia del salitre desde le Guerra del Pacífico hasta la revolución de 1891* (Santiago, 1984), the sequel to Bermúdez' earlier volume, *Historia del salitre desde sus orígenes hasta la Guerra del Pacífico* (Santiago, 1963); Thomas F. O'Brien, *The Nitrate Industry and Chile's Critical Transition, 1870–1891* (New York, 1982); Michael Monteón, *Chile in the Nitrate Era: The Evolution of Economic Dependence, 1880–1930* (Madison, Wis., 1982). Students of the nitrate issue cannot afford to ignore Robert Greenhill, 'The Nitrate and Iodine Trades, 1880–1914', in D. C. M. Platt (ed.), *Business Imperialism, 1840–1930* (Oxford, 1977), pp. 231–83.

The so-called Parliamentary Republic (1891–1920) has finally begun to command the attention of historians that it deserves, as is witnessed by the works of Castedo, Vial and Heise González mentioned above. For general thoughts on the period, see Harold Blakemore, 'El período parlamentario en la historia chilena: algunos enfoques y reflexiones', in *Dos estudios sobre salitre y política en Chile* (Santiago, 1991). Paul Reinsch, 'Parliamentary Government in Chile', *American Political Science Review* 3 (1908–9), is not only a brilliant portrait but also an outstanding example of the writing of 'contemporary history'. Two studies of particular presidencies merit citation here: Jaime Eyzaguirre, *Chile durante el gobierno de Errázuriz Echaurren, 1896–1901* (Santiago, 1957), and Germán Riesco, *Presidencia de Riesco, 1901–1906* (Santiago, 1950). For a straightforward narrative of the years 1900–38, see Fernando Pinto Lagarrigue, *Crónica política del siglo XX* (Santiago, 1970). Among older works, the highly polemical study of Ricardo Donoso, *Alessandri, agitador y demoledor,* 2 vols. (Mexico, 1952–4), gives a detailed chronicle of the whole period, including the Ibáñez administration and the 1930s: it remains indispensable. Equally fundamental, though less well organized, is the compilation of writings by Manuel Rivas Vicuña, a key figure of the epoch, *Historia política y parlamentaria de Chile* (3 vols., Santiago, 1964), prepared by Guillermo Feliú Cruz. It is a mine of information, but the historian has to dig for the ore. Interesting insight into the politics and legislation of 'parliamentary' times is to be found in Karen L. Remmer, *Party Competition in Argentina and Chile: Political Recruitment and Public Policy, 1890–1930* (Lincoln, Nebr., 1984).

The social history of the parliamentary decades can be approached in a handful of useful articles: Ricardo Krebs W., 'Apuntes sobre la mentalidad de la aristocracia chilena en los comienzos del siglo XX', *Mentalidades* (Santiago, 1986), pp. 27–55; Eduardo Cavieres F., 'Grupos intermedios e integración social: La sociedad de artesanos de Valparaíso a comienzos del siglo XX', *Cuadernos de Historia* 6 (1986), pp. 33–47; Isabel Torres Dujusin, 'Los conventillos en Santiago (1900–30)', *Cuadernos de Historia* 6 (1986), pp. 67–85. On German immigration (and influence), see Jean-Pierre Blancpain, *Les allemands au Chili, 1816–1945* (Cologne, 1974), especially book 2, chapters 5–6, and book 3, chapters 1–4; this masterly study is unlikely ever to be surpassed. Aspects of labour history are addressed in two French contributions: Pierre Vayssière, 'Militantisme et messianisme ouvriers au Chile à travers la presse de la pampa nitrière', *Caravelle* 46 (1986), pp. 93–108, and Maurice Fraysse, 'Aspects de la violence dans la presse anarchiste du Chili, 1898–1914', *Caravelle* 46 (1986), pp. 79–92. Luis Emilio Recabarren, *Escritos de prensa*, 4 vols. (Santiago, 1987), is a useful compilation of writings by Chile's early labour hero.

As with Balmaceda, there is a massive literature (both panegyric and polemical) on Alessandri and Ibáñez, the figures who overshadow the later part of our period. The vital presidential election of 1920 is carefully analysed in René Millar C., *La elección presidencial de 1920* (Santiago, 1981). A cool 'revisionist' approach to the supposed 'electoral revolt' of the period may be found in Wolfgang Hirsch-Weber, 'Aufstandt der Massen? Wahlkampf und Stimmenhaltung in Chile 1915–21', *Ibero-Amerikanische Archiv* 8 no. 1–2 (1982), pp. 5–83. Apart from Donoso, *Alessandri,* key works on Alessandri himself are his own (by no means self-critical) *Recuerdos de gobierno*, 3 vols. (Santiago, 1967); Augusto Iglesias, *Alessandri, una etapa de la democracia en América* (Santiago, 1960); and Luis Durand, *Don Arturo* (Santiago, 1952). Ibáñez, who wrote no memoirs, is well covered in René Montero, *La verdad sobre Ibáñez* (Santiago, 1953);

Víctor Contreras Guzmán, *Bitácora de la dictadura* (Santiago, 1942); Ernesto Würth Rojas, *Ibáñez, caudillo enigmático* (Santiago, 1958); Aquiles Vergara Vicuña, *Ibáñez, césar criollo* (Santiago, 1931), a strong critique; and Luis Correa Prieto, *El presidente Ibáñez* (Santiago, 1962), based on personal interviews. The most sustained philippic is Carlos Vicuña, *La tiranía en Chile*, 2 vols. (Santiago, 1939); this was usefully reprinted in 1987.

The best book in English on the whole period from 1920 to 1931 – and the most comprehensive source for further bibliography on military matters – is Frederick Nunn, *Chilean Politics, 1920–1931: The Honorable Mission of the Armed Forces* (Albuquerque, N.Mex., 1970). Arturo Olavarría Bravo, *Chile entre dos Alessandri*, 4 vols. (Santiago, 1962–5), vol. 1, is full of information from a figure close to the heart of Chilean politics for forty years, but the richer veins take some finding. A valuable documentary compilation on the military interventions of 1924–5 is General E. Monreal, *Historia documentada del período revolucionario 1924–1925* (Santiago, 1926), to which Raúl Aldunate Phillips, *Ruido de sables* (Santiago, n.d.), with its fascinating photo reproductions, provides an excellent pendant. Some new insight (and evidence) regarding the state of mind of the officer corps prior to the interventions may be found in Wolfgang Ettmüller, 'Germanisierte Politik, 1920–1932', *Ibero-Amerikanische Archiv* 8 no. 1–2 (1982), pp. 83–160. The role of the Navy is analysed in Philip Somervell, 'Naval affairs in Chilean politics, 1910–32', *Journal of Latin American Studies* 16/2 (1984), pp. 381–402.

Economic issues of the 1920s and the 'great crash' are well discussed in Santiago Macchiavello Varas, *Política económica nacional*, 2 vols. (Santiago, 1931), and in P. T. Ellsworth, *Chile, an Economy in Transition* (New York, 1945), chapter 1. Albert O. Hirschman's 'Inflation in Chile', in his *Journeys toward progress* (New York, N.Y., 1963), is a brilliant and provocative discussion of that perennial problem in modern Chilean history. The nearest thing to an overall economic history is Markos Mamalakis, *The Growth and Structure of the Chilean Economy: From Independence to Allende* (New Haven, Conn., 1976). See also the valuable article by José Gabriel Palma, 'Chile, 1914–1935: De economía exportadora a sustitutiva de importaciones', *Estudios CIEPLAN*, no. 12 (Santiago, 1984), pp. 61–88. The earlier perturbations caused by World War I (and changes in the longrunning Chile–Great Britain connection) are admirably dealt with in Juan Ricardo Couyoumdjian, *Chile y Gran Bretaña durante la primera guerra mundial y la postguerra, 1914–1921* (Santiago, 1986). This theme is also taken up in Bill Albert, *South America and the First World War* (Cambridge, 1988), which covers Chile along with Argentina, Brazil and Peru.

Two other sources for the period, often neglected, should be mentioned: travel accounts and unpublished theses. The most informative and perceptive travel accounts are C. Wiener, *Chili et Chiliens* (Paris, 1888); Eduardo Poirier, *Chile en 1908* (Santiago, 1908), a massive compilation; Frank G. Carpenter, *South America: Social, Industrial and Political* (New York, 1900); Francis J. G. Maitland, *Chile: Its Land and People* (London, 1914); G. F. Scott Elliott, *Chile* (London, 1907); and Earl Chapin May, *2000 Miles through Chile* (New York, 1924). Good unpublished theses include Andrew Barnard, 'The Chilean Communist Party, 1922–1947' (Ph.D. dissertation, University of London, 1977); Peter Conoboy, 'Money and Politics in Chile, 1878–1925' (Ph.D. dissertation, University of Southampton, 1977); and José Gabriel Palma, 'Growth and Structure of Chilean manufacturing industry from 1830 to 1935' (D.Phil. thesis, Oxford University, 1979).

3. CHILE, 1930–1958

Most important among the primary sources for this period are newspapers, especially *El Mercurio* and *El Diario Ilustrado* from the Right, *La Nación* from the government, and *La Opinión* and *El Siglo* from the Left. Periodicals, notably *Ercilla* and *Zig-Zag,* are also useful; see in particular a series of candid retrospectives with past political actors arranged by Wilfredo Mayorga in *Ercilla* during 1965–8. The tables compiled by Markos Mamalakis, *Historical Statistics of Chile,* 6 vols. (Westport, Conn., 1979–89), are an indispensable source of information.

The most valuable memoirs come from President Arturo Alessandri Palma, *Recuerdos de gobierno,* 3 vols. (Santiago, 1967); U.S. Ambassador Claude G. Bowers, *Chile through Embassy Windows* (New York, 1958); President Gabriel González Videla, *Memorias,* 2 vols. (Santiago, 1975); Communist Elías Lafertte, *Vida de un comunista* (Santiago, 1961); professional politician Arturo Olavarría Bravo *Chile entre dos Alessandri,* 4 vols. (Santiago, 1962–1965); disillusioned Comintern agent Eudocio Ravines, *La gran estafa* (Santiago, 1954); and Army General Carlos Sáez Morales, *Recuerdos de un soldado,* 3 vols. (Santiago, 1934).

The best general history of Chile is Brian Loveman, *Chile: The Legacy of Hispanic Capitalism,* 2nd ed. (New York, 1988). A comprehensive contribution on the period from the 1930s to the 1950s is Paul W. Drake,

Socialism and Populism in Chile, 1932–1952 (Urbana, 1978). Other basic works include the collection of articles in Universidad de Chile, *Desarrollo de Chile en la primera mitad del siglo XX*, 2 vols. (Santiago, 1953); Julio César Jobet's revisionist *Ensayo crítico del desarrollo económico-social de Chile* (Santiago, 1955); and Frederick B. Pike's landmark *Chile and the United States, 1880–1962* (South Bend, Ind., 1963). Also see Mariana Aylwin et al., *Chile en el siglo XX* (Santiago, 1983).

For political history of the period, the following works by Chileans are especially recommended: Ricardo Boizard, *Historia de una derrota* (Santiago, 1941); Fernando Casanueva Valencia and Manuel Fernández Canque, *El Partido Socialista y la lucha de clases en Chile* (Santiago, 1973); César Caviedes, *The Politics of Chile: A Sociogeographical Assessment* (Boulder, Colo., 1979); Carlos Charlín O., *Del avión rojo a la república socialista* (Santiago, 1972); Luis Correa, *El presidente Ibáñez* (Santiago, 1962); Ricardo Cruz-Coke, *Geografía electoral de Chile* (Santiago, 1952) and *Historia electoral de Chile, 1925–1973* (Santiago, 1984); Luis Cruz Salas, 'Historia social de Chile, 1931–1945' (Ph.D. dissertation, Universidad de Chile, 1969); Ricardo Donoso, *Alessandri, agitador y demoledor*, 2 vols. (Mexico City, 1952, 1954); Florencio Durán, *El Partido Radical* (Santiago, 1958); Alberto Edwards Vives and Eduardo Frei Montalva, *Historia de los partidos políticos chilenos* (Santiago, 1949); Julio Faúndez, *Marxism and Democracy in Chile: From 1932 to the Fall of Allende* (New Haven, Conn., 1988); Juan F. Fernández C., *Pedro Aguire Cerda y el Frente Popular chileno* (Santiago, 1938); Marta Infante Barros, *Testigos del treinta y ocho* (Santiago, 1972); Julio César Jobet, *El partido socialista de Chile*, 2 vols. (Santiago, 1971); Norbert Lechner, *La democracia en Chile* (Buenos Aires, 1970); Tomás Moulián and Isabel Torres Dujisin, *Discusiones entre honorables: Las candidaturas presidenciales de la derecha, 1938–1946* (Santiago, 1988); Alfonso Stephens Freire, *El irracionalismo político en Chile* (Santiago, 1957); Germán Urzúa Valenzuela, *Historia política electoral de Chile, 1931–1973* (Santiago, 1986); Carlos Vicuña Fuentes, *La tiranía en Chile*, 2 vols. (Santiago, 1939); and Ignacio Walker, *Socialismo y democracia: Chile y Europa en perspectiva comparada* (Santiago, 1990). For encyclopaedic citations, scholars can refer to Jordi Fuentes and Lia Cortés, *Diccionario político de Chile* (Santiago, 1967).

The most useful political accounts by non-Chileans are Robert J. Alexander's political biography, *Arturo Alessandri*, 2 vols. (Ann Arbor, 1977); Frank Bonilla and Myron Glazer, *Student Politics in Chile* (New York, 1970); Donald W. Bray, 'Chilean Politics during the Second Ibáñez Gov-

220 *Bibliographical essays*

ernment, 1952–58' (Ph.D. dissertation, Stanford University, 1961); Michael J. Francis' treatment of a neglected topic, *The Limits of Hegemony: United States Relations with Argentina and Chile during World War II* (Notre Dame, Ind., 1977); Carmelo Furci, *The Chilean Communist Party and the Road to Socialism* (London, 1984); Federico G. Gil's standard, *The Political System of Chile* (Boston, 1966); George Grayson, *El Partido Democrata Cristiano chileno* (Buenos Aires, 1968); Ernst Halperin's ideological analysis, *Nationalism and Communism in Chile* (Cambridge, Mass., 1965); Kalman Silvert's insightful *The Conflict Society* (New Orleans, 1961); Brian Smith, *The Church and Politics in Chile: Challenges to Modern Catholicism* (Princeton, 1982); and John Reese Stevenson's narrative, *The Chilean Popular Front* (Philadelphia, 1942).

On the economic history of the period, the place to begin is Markos Mamalakis, *The Growth and Structure of the Chilean Economy: From Independence to Allende* (New Haven, Conn., 1976). Other vital works include Jorge Ahumada, *En vez de la miseria* (Santiago, 1965); Oscar Alvarez Andrews, *Historia del desarrollo industrial de Chile* (Santiago, 1936); P. T. Ellsworth, *Chile, an Economy in Transition* (New York, 1945); Ricardo Ffrench-Davis, *Políticas económicas en Chile, 1952–1970* (Santiago, 1973); Albert O. Hirschman, *Journeys toward Progress* (New York, N.Y., 1963); Francisco Illanes Benítez, *La economía chilena y el comercio exterior* (Santiago, 1944); Ricardo Lagos Escobar, *La concentración del poder económico* (Santiago, 1961); Rolf Luders, 'A Monetary History of Chile, 1925–1958' (Ph.D. dissertation, University of Chicago, 1968); Markos Mamalakis and Clark Reynolds, *Essays on the Chilean Economy* (New York, 1965); Oscar Muñoz, *Crecimiento industrial de Chile, 1914–65* (Santiago, 1968); Luis Ortega Martínez et al., *Corporación de fomento de la producción: 50 años de realizaciones, 1939–1989* (Santiago, 1989); Aníbal Pinto Santa Cruz, *Antecedentes sobre el desarrollo de la economía chilena, 1925–52* (Santiago, 1954) and *Chile, un caso de desarrollo frustrado* (Santiago, 1962); Enrique Sierra, *Tres ensayos de estabilización en Chile* (Santiago, 1970); United Nations, Economic Commission for Latin America, *Antecedentes sobre el desarrollo de la economía chilena, 1925–1952* (Santiago, 1954); Universidad de Chile, Instituto de Economía, *Desarrollo económico de Chile, 1940–1956* (Santiago, 1956); and Enrique Zañartu Prieto, *Hambre, miseria e ignorancia* (Santiago, 1938).

Agricultural and labor issues are considered in a number of monographs. On the rural sector, George M. McBride, *Chile: Land and Society* (New York, 1936); Gene Ellis Martin, *La división de la tierra en Chile central* (Santiago, 1960); Brian Loveman, *Struggle in the Countryside: Politics and Rural Labor in Chile, 1919–1973* (Bloomington, Ind., 1976); Enrico Hott Kinderman, 'Las sociedades agrícolas nacionales y su influencia en la agricultura de Chile' (Ph.D. dissertation, Universidad de Chile, 1944); Jean Carriere, *Landowners and Politics in Chile* (Amsterdam, 1981); and Thomas C. Wright, *Landowners and Reform in Chile: The Sociedad Nacional de Agricultura, 1919–40* (Urbana, 1982), stand out. On trade unions, see Jorge Barría, *El movimiento obrero en Chile* (Santiago, 1971); Alan Angell, *Politics and the Labour Movement in Chile* (Oxford, 1972); J. Samuel Valenzuela, 'Labor Movement Formation and Politics: The Chilean and French Cases in Comparative Perspective, 1850–1950' (Ph.D. dissertation, Columbia University, 1979); and Crisóstomo Pizarro, *La huelga obrera en Chile* (Santiago, 1986).

The social and cultural-intellectual history of the middle decades of the twentieth century have been virtually neglected. One exception is Felícitas Klimpel, *La mujer chilena: el aporte femenino al progreso de Chile, 1910–1960* (Santiago, 1962). A valuable recent addition is Iván Jaksic, *Academic Rebels in Chile: The Role of Philosophy in Higher Education and Politics* (Albany, N.Y., 1989). Some older works remain valuable, especially Arturo Torres Ríoseco, *Breve historia de la literatura chilena* (Mexico, 1956); Fernando Alegría, *Literatura chilena del siglo XX,* 2nd ed. (Santiago, 1962); Julio Durán Cerda, *Panorama del teatro chileno, 1842–1959* (Santiago, 1959); and Raúl Silva Castro, *Historia crítica de la novela chilena, 1843–1956* (Madrid, 1960). Also see David Foster, *Chilean Literature: A Working Bibliography of Secondary Sources* (Boston, 1978).

4. CHILE SINCE 1958

An important source for this period are reviews and magazines. The invaluable *Mensaje* provides a monthly mixture of political, economic and religious analysis. *Panorama Económico* is very useful on the economy. *¿Qué Pasa?* is important for the politics of the Right. *Ercilla* is an essential weekly news magazine for much of the period. The *Ercilla* journalists formed *Hoy,* after one of the many takeover deals of the Pinochet era brought *Ercilla* closer to the politics of the Pinochet government. *Hoy* is close to the PDC There are numerous other weekly magazines, intermittently affected by the capricious censorship of Pinochet's Chile; two of the best are *APSI* and *Análisis.*

Amongst the academic publications, *Estudios CIEPLAN* provides excellent critical analysis of the economy, and *Estudios Públicos* a mixture of economic, political and philosophical analysis from the neo-classical Right. The exile journal *Chile–América* published in Rome is indispensable for the decade following the coup of 1973. Of the many publications that appeared during the Allende government, the *Cuadernos de la Realidad Nacional, Chile Hoy* and *Revista EURE* are important.

There are several useful bibliographical studies, including Arturo Valenzuela and J. Samuel Valenzuela, 'Visions of Chile', *Latin American Research Review* 10, no. 3 (Fall 1975); William Sater, 'A Survey of Recent Chilean Historiography, 1965–1976', *Latin American Research Review* 14, no. 2 (1979); Paul Drake, 'El Impacto académico de los terremotos políticos: Investigaciones de la historia chilena en inglés, 1977–1983' *Alternativas* (January–April, 1984); Benny Pollack and Jean Grugel, 'Chile before and after Monetarism', *Bulletin of Latin American Research* 3, no. 2 (1984); Lois Hecht Oppenheim, 'The Chilean Road to Socialism Revisited', *Latin American Research Review* 24, no. 1 (1989).

There are few good general accounts of the whole period, but for the period up to 1970 see Mariana Aylwin et al., *Chile en el siglo XX* (Santiago, 1983). For electoral data, see Germán Urzua, *Historia política electoral de Chile, 1931–1973* (Santiago, 1986). A useful guide to parties and movements is Reinhard Friedman, *1964–1988: La política chilena de la A a la Z* (Santiago, 1988). An excellent interpretation of the politics of the Left is Julio Faúndez, *Marxism and Democracy in Chile: From 1932 to the Fall of Allende* (New Haven and London, 1988). Social change is examined in Javier Martínez and Eugenio Tironi, *Las clases sociales en Chile: Cambio y estratificación, 1970–1980* (Santiago, 1986). An excellent study of the origins of the urban poor is Vicente Espinoza, *Para una historia de los pobres de la ciudad* (Santiago, 1988).

Most writing on the politics of this period tends to concentrate on one administration. Although it was written in 1966, Federico Gil, *The Political System of Chile* (Boston, 1966) has stood the test of time as an invaluable reference work. Rather over-rated is James Petras, *Politics and Social Forces in Chilean Development* (Berkeley, Calif., 1969). Paul Sigmund, *The Overthrow of Allende and the Politics of Chile, 1964–1976* (Pittsburgh, 1978) is good on the Christian Democrats, but tends to be polemical thereafter. Although it focuses on the Allende government, Arturo Valenzuela, *The Breakdown of Democratic Regimes: Chile* (Baltimore, 1978), is full of insights for the structure of Chilean politics, and is an indispensable source. Another book by Valenzuela is of more general interest than its title might suggest: *Political Brokers in Chile: Local Government in a Centralized Polity* (Chapel Hill, N.C., 1977).

Political parties have attracted far less attention than their central political role merits. An excellent set of essays, however, is Adolfo Aldunate et al., *Estudios sobre el sistema de partidos en Chile* (Santiago, 1985). A conservative historian gives his account in Bernadino Bravo Lira, *Régimen de gobierno y partidos políticos en Chile, 1924–1973* (Santiago, 1978). A set of comparative essays which includes articles on Chile, notably one by Tomás Moulián and Isabel Torres on the Chilean Right, is Marcelo Cavarozzi and Manuel Antonio Garretón, *Muerte y resurrección: Los partidos políticos en el autoritarismo y las transiciones del cono sur* (Santiago, 1989).

On the PDC, see George Grayson, *El Partido Demócrata Cristiano chileno* (Buenos Aires, 1968), and Michael Fleet, *The Rise and Fall of Chilean Christian Democracy* (Princeton, N.J., 1985). On the Socialists, see Fernando Casanueva and Manuel Fernández, *El Partido Socialista y la lucha de clases en Chile* (Santiago, 1973); and Benny Pollack et al., *Mobilization and Socialism in Chile* (Liverpool, 1981). Ernst Halperin, *Nationalism and Communism in Chile* (Cambridge, Mass., 1965) is still useful. More recent is Benny Pollack and Hernán Rosenkranz, *Revolutionary Social Democracy: The Chilean Socialist Party* (London, 1986). See also Ignacio Walker, *Socialismo y democracia: Chile y Europa en perspectiva comparada* (Santiago, 1990). Three books develop Socialist rethinking: Jorge Arrate, *La fuerza democrática de la idea socialista* (Santiago, 1985) and *La renovación socialista* (Santiago, 1987), and Ricardo Lagos, *Democracia para Chile: Proposiciones de un socialista* (Santiago, 1986). On the Communists, see Carmelo Furci, *The Chilean Communist Party and the Road to Socialism* (London, 1984); Eduardo Godard Labarca, *Corvalán, 27 horas* (Santiago, 1973), and Augusto Varas (ed.), *El partido comunista en Chile* (Santiago, 1988).

The eruption of the military into political life took academics as well as politicians by surprise. There were very few useful accounts of the military, apart from Alain Joxe, *Las fuerzas armadas en el sistema político de Chile* (Santiago, 1970), and Frederick Nunn, *The Military in Chilean History: Essays on Civil–Military Relations, 1810–1973* (Albuquerque, N. Mex., 1976). A more recent study is Hugo Fruling et al., *Estado y fuerzas armadas* (Santiago, 1982). An early military plotter tells his story in Florencia Varas, *Conversaciones con Viaux* (Santiago, 1972). Carlos Prats tells his own story in *Memorias: Testimonio de un soldado* (Santiago, 1985). A prominent military supporter of Pinochet has written his memoirs: Ismael Huerta Díaz, *Volvería a ser marinero,* 2 vols. (Santiago, 1988).

A pioneering study of foreign policy, partly dealing with this period, is Frederick Pike, *Chile and the United States, 1880–1962* (South Bend, Ind., 1963). A Chilean study covering a long period is Walter Sánchez and Teresa Pereira, *Ciento cincuenta años de política exterior chilena* (Santiago, 1979). A useful account is Francisco Orrego Vicuña, *La participación de Chile en el sistema internacional* (Santiago, 1974). The journal *Estudios Internacionales* (Santiago) carries interesting and well-documented articles on Chilean foreign policy – for example, Manfred Wilhelmy, 'Hacia un análisis de la política exterior chilena contemporánea', *Estudios Internacionales* (October–December, 1979). A detailed and well-argued account of the foreign policy of the Allende government is Joaquín Fermandois, *Chile y el mundo: 1970–1973* (Santiago, 1985). The most comprehensive treatment of recent foreign policy is Heraldo Muñóz, *Las relaciones exteriores del gobierno militar chileno* (Santiago, 1986). On relations with the United States, see Heraldo Muñóz and Carlos Portales, *Una amistad esquiva: Las relaciones de EE. UU. y Chile* (Santiago, 1987); and William F. Sater, *Chile and the United States: Empires in Conflict* (Athens, Ga., 1990).

A useful summary of the major issues in Chilean economic development is Robert Zahler et al., *Chile 1940/1975: Treinta y cinco años de discontinuidad económica* (Santiago 1985). The economic policies of the Alessandri and Frei administrations are dealt with in Enrique Sierra, *Tres ensayos de estabilización en Chile* (Santiago, 1970). A very useful collection in the area of political economy is Aníbal Pinto et al., *Chile, hoy* (Mexico City, 1970). An excellent technical account is Ricardo Ffrench-Davis, *Políticas económicas en Chile, 1952–1970* (Santiago, 1973). A controversial and stimulating work is Markos Mamalakis, *The Growth and Structure of the Chilean Economy: From Independence to Allende* (Washington, D.C., 1976). A great deal of useful data is available in the World Bank Report, *Chile: An Economy in Transition* (Washington, D.C., 1980). Markos Mamalakis has published six volumes of the indispensable *Historical Statistics of Chile* (Westport, Conn., 1979–89). An interesting comparative study of the three civilian administrations is Barbara Stallings, *Class Conflict and Economic Development in Chile* (Stanford, 1978). Markos Mamalakis and Clark Reynolds, *Essays on the Chilean Economy* (New York, 1965), are excellent on copper and public policy. A useful collection of data appears in ODEPLAN, *Antecedentes del desarrollo económico, 1960–1970* (Santiago, 1971). Oscar Landerretche, 'Inflation and Socio-Political Conflicts in Chile, 1955–1970 (D.Phil. thesis, Oxford, 1983) is extremely perceptive. Industrialization is examined in Oscar Muñóz, *Chile y su industrialización: Pasado, crisis y opiniones* (Santiago, 1986).

Social policy is examined in José Pablo Arellano, *Políticas sociales y desarrollo: Chile 1924–1984* (Santiago, 1985). The copper sector is covered in two excellent studies, Theodore Moran, *Multinational Corporations and the Politics of Dependence: Copper in Chile* (Princeton, 1974); and Ricardo Ffrench-Davis and Ernesto Tironi (eds.), *El cobre en el desarrollo nacional* (Santiago, 1974). See also earlier but still useful studies by Mario Vera, *La política económica del cobre* (Santiago, 1961), and *Una política definitiva para nuestras riquezas básicas* (Santiago, 1969).

A scholarly and impressive account of rural labour, which perhaps over-emphasizes the extent of conflict, is in Brian Loveman, *Struggle in the Countryside: Politics and Rural Labour in Chile, 1919–1973* (Bloomington, Ind., 1976). The basic source of data is the CIDA report, *Chile: Tenencia de la tierra y desarrollo socio-económico del sector agrícola* (Washington, D.C., 1966). See also Luz Eugenia Cereceda and Fernando Dahse, *Dos décadas de cambios en el agro chileno* (Santiago, 1980). For the PDC and UP reforms, see Solon Barraclough and Juan Fernández, *Diagnóstico de la reforma agraria chilena* (Buenos Aires, 1974); Kyle Steenland, *Agrarian Reform under Allende: Peasant Revolt in the South* (Albuquerque, N. Mex., 1978); and Robert Kaufman, *The Politics of Land Reform in Chile, 1950–1970* (Harvard, 1973). For more recent developments, see Sergio Gómez, *Instituciones y procesos agrarios en Chile* (Santiago, 1982). Jacques Chonchol's work is important: see, for example, the chapter in A. Pinto (ed.), *Chile, hoy*, and 'La Reforma agraria en Chile, 1970–1973' in *El Trimestre Económico* 53 (1976). Post-coup policies are examined in Lovell S. Jarvis, *Chilean Agriculture under Military Rule* (Berkeley, Calif., 1985), and in Patricio Silva, *Estado, neoliberalismo y política agraria en Chile, 1973–1981* (Amsterdam, 1987), and José Garrido (ed.), *Historia de la reforma agraria en Chile* (Santiago, 1988). An excellent recent set of essays is David Hojman (ed.), *Neo-Liberal Agriculture in Rural Chile* (London, 1990).

The pioneer of labour studies in Chile, Jorge Barría, wrote extensively on the subject: see especially *Trayectoria y estructura del movimiento sindical chileno* (Santiago, 1963) and *Historia de la CUT* (Santiago, 1971). Urban and mining labour is examined in Alan Angell, *Politics and the Labour Movement in Chile* (Oxford, 1972), for the period up to 1970. Indispensable for the rural union movement up to 1970 is Almino Affonso, Sergio Gómez and Emilio Klein, *Movimiento campesino chileno*, 2 vols. (ICIRA, Santiago, 1970). An excellent study of labour under Pinochet is Guillermo Campero and José Valenzuela, *El movimiento sindical chileno en el capitalismo autoritario* (Santiago, 1981). A fascinating study at the local level – an altogether too rare example – is Penelope Pollitt, 'Religion and Politics in a Coal Mining Community in Southern Chile' (Ph.D. dissertation, Cambridge, 1981). Another rare example of detailed empirical work is Manuel Barrera et al., *El cambio social en una empresa del APS* (Santiago, 1973). An earlier study of worker attitudes is Torcuato di Tella et al., *Huachipato et Lota: Etude sur la conscience ouvrière dans deux entreprises chiliennes* (Paris, 1966).

The role of workers under the U.P. is examined in Juan Espinosa and Andy Zimbalist, *Economic Democracy: Workers' Participation in Chilean Industry, 1970–1973* (New York, 1978); and in two short monographs by Francisco Zapata, *Los mineros de Chuquicamata: Productores o proletarios?* (Mexico City, 1975) and *Las relaciones entre el movimiento obrero y el gobierno de Allende* (Mexico City, 1974). A brilliant account of a worker takeover is Peter Winn, *Weavers of Revolution: The Yarur Workers and Chile's Road to Socialism* (New York, 1986). Useful accounts of labour under Pinochet are Gonzalo Falabella, *Labour in Chile under the Junta* (Working Papers no. 4, Institute of Latin American Studies, University of London, 1981); the collective publication of Vector, *El movimiento sindical* (*Revista de Talleres* no. 2, Santiago, 1981); J. Roddick and N. Haworth, 'Labour and Monetarism in Chile', *Bulletin of Latin American Research* 1, no. 1 (1981); and Manuel Barrera et al., *Sindicatos y estado en el Chile actual* (Geneva, 1985).

On the entrepreneurial sector, there is a detailed analysis of the structure of organizations in Genaro Arriagada, *La oligarquía patronal chilena* (Santiago, 1970). Marcelo Cavarozzi, 'The Government and the Industrial Bourgeoisie in Chile, 1938–1964' (Ph.D. dissertation, Berkeley, 1975) contains a great deal of useful information. An excellent study of recent entrepreneurial behaviour is by Guillermo Campero, *Los gremios empresariales en el período 1970–1983* (Santiago, 1984). The ideology of an important voice of the entrepreneurial sector is examined in Guillermo Sunkel, *El Mercurio: Diez años de educación política ideológica, 1969/1979* (Santiago, 1983).

Three books begin the task of writing the history of womens' involvement in political life: Julietta Kirkwood, *Ser política en Chile: Las feministas y los partidos* (Santiago, 1985); María Angélica Maza, *La otra mitad de Chile* (Santiago, 1986); and María Elena Valenzuela, *La mujer en el Chile militar* (Santiago, 1987). See also Patricia M. Chuchryk, 'Feminist Anti-American Politics: The Role of Women's Organizations in the Chilean Transition to Democracy', in Jane Jaquette (ed.), *The Women's Movement in Latin America* (London 1989), pp. 149–84.

An impressive study of the Church in the last few decades in Chile is Brian Smith, *The Church and Politics in Chile: Challenges To Modern Catholicism* (Princeton, 1982). On the role of the Church in the Pinochet years see, Enrique Correa and José Antonio Viera Gallo, *Iglesia y dictadura* (Santiago, 1986); and Patricio Dooner (ed.), *La iglesia católica y el futuro político de Chile* (Santiago, 1988). On protestantism, see Humberto Lagos, *Los Evangélicos en Chile: Una lectura sociológica* (Santiago, 1988). See also Maria Antonieta Huerta and Luis Pacheco Pastene, *La Iglesia chilena y los cambios sociopolíticos* (Santiago, 1988).

Education is examined in Kathleen Fischer, *Political Ideology and Educational Reform in Chile, 1964–1976* (Los Angeles, 1979), and in Guillermo Labarca, *Educación y sociedad: Chile, 1969–1984* (Amsterdam, 1985). An interesting account of the development of philosophy in Chile, including the Pinochet period, is Iván Jaksic, *Academic Rebels in Chile: The Role of Philosophy in Higher Education and Politics* (Albany, N.Y., 1989).

An excellent study of policy-making during the Frei government is Peter Cleaves, *Bureaucratic Politics and Administration in Chile* (Berkeley, Calif., 1974). An insider's account is Sergio Molina, *El proceso de cambio en Chile* (Santiago, 1977). Arturo Olavarría Bravo has written several volumes of opinionated narrative under the title *Chile bajo la Democracia Cristiana* (Santiago, 1966, 1967, 1968, 1969). The best overall account is Ricardo Yocelevsky, *La Democracia Cristiana chilena y el gobierno de Eduardo Frei* (Mexico, 1987). See also Patricio Dooner, *Cambios sociales y conflicto político: El conflicto político nacional durante el gobierno de Eduardo Frei* (Santiago, 1984).

There is a huge literature on the Popular Unity period. For a fascinating account of the origins of the UP government, see Eduardo Labarca, *Chile al rojo* (Santiago, 1971). A great deal of sociological data for the period is contained in Manuel Castells, *La lucha de clases en Chile* (Buenos Aires, 1974). Excellent collection of essays are S. Sideri (ed.), *Chile, 1970–1973: Economic Development and Its International Setting* (The Hague, 1979); Arturo Valenzuela and Samuel Valenzuela (eds.), *Chile: Politics and Society* (New Brunswick, N.J., 1976); and Federico Gil et al. (eds.), *Chile at the Turning Point: Lessons of the Socialist Years, 1970–1973* (Philadelphia, 1979). A valuable account, compiled during the UP period, is Ann Zammit (ed.), *The Chilean Way to Socialism* (Sussex, 1973), and, after the coup, Philip O'Brien (ed.), *Allende's Chile* (New York, 1976). The collection edited by Ken Medhurst, *Allende's Chile* (London, 1972), has some interesting essays. A useful recent account of the period is Edy Kaufman, *Crisis in Chile:*

New Perspectives (New York, 1988). An intelligent critique from a conservative standpoint is Mark Falcoff, *Modern Chile, 1970–1988: A Critical History* (New Brunswick, N.J., 1989).

A collection of Allende's speeches gives some idea of his policy and aims: Salvador Allende, *Chile's Road to Socialism* (London, 1973). Allende's aims are more interestingly explored in Regis Debray, *Conversations with Allende* (London, 1971). At times rather pretentious, but at other times an indispensable source, is the account by Allende's aide, Joan Garces, *Allende y la experiencia chilena* (Barcelona, 1976). Widely used, though written rather too close to the event, is Ian Roxborough et al., *Chile: The State and Revolution* (London, 1977). Perceptive reflections of a journalist-politician are contained in Luis Maira, *Dos años de Unidad Popular* (Santiago, 1973). Two leading Chilean sociologists provide an interpretation in Manuel A. Garretón and Tomás Moulián, *Análisis coyuntural y proceso político* (San José, Costa Rica, 1978). See also Eduardo Novoa, *¿Vía legal hacia el socialismo? El caso de Chile, 1970–1973* (Caracas, 1978). Few leading politicians of the period have written their memoirs, but in Patricia Politzer, *Altamirano* (Buenos Aires, 1989), a leading Socialist radical justifies his role.

On the economic policy of the UP, the best argued and most informative work is that of a former minister of the government, Sergio Bitar, *Chile: Experiment in Democracy* (Philadelphia, 1986). Another leading economist gives his account in Gonzalo Martner, *El gobierno de Salvador Allende, 1970–1973: Una evaluación* (Santiago, 1988). An influential early post mortem is Stefan de Vylder, *Allende's Chile: The Political Economy of the Rise and Fall of the Popular Unity* (Cambridge, 1976). Not very accessible, but of importance, is José Serra and Arturo León, *La redistribución del ingreso en Chile durante el gobierno de la Unidad Popular,* Documento de Trabajo no. 70, FLASCO (Santiago, 1978). See also Edward Boorstein, *Allende's Chile: An Inside View* (New York, 1977). Two reports of the Instituto de Economía of the University of Chile are worth consulting, *La economía chilena en 1971,* and *La Economía chilena en 1972.*

An interesting case study of the State sector of the economy is Samuel Cogan, 'The Nationalization of Manufacturing Firms in Chile, 1970–1973: A Case Study of the Building Materials Sector' (D.Phil. thesis, Oxford, 1981). A rather optimistic account of the UP's economic strategy written before the coup in Sergio Ramos, *Chile: Una economía de transición* (Havana, 1972). A work that stresses the neglect of short-term financial management is Stephany Griffith-Jones, *The Role of Finance in the Transition to Socialism* (London, 1981).

The frantic politics of the period are not treated so well as the economy. A detailed article is by Atilio Borón, 'La Movilización política en Chile', *Foro Internacional* (July–September, 1975). See also Alan Angell, *Political Mobilization and Class Alliances in Chile, 1970–1973* (Rotterdam, 1978), which contains extensive references to discussions on *poder popular*. A case study of an important strike is Sergio Bitar and Crisóstomo Pizarro, *La caída de Allende y la huelga de El Teniente* (Santiago, 1987). The left-wing Socialist, Carlos Altamirano, offers his explanation of what went wrong in *Dialéctica de una derrota* (Mexico City, 1977). Very moving is the work of French sociologist Alain Touraine, *Vida y muerte del gobierno popular* (Buenos Aires, 1974). Problems of ideology and cultural politics are discussed in Manuel Antonio Garretón et al., *Cultura y comunicaciones de masas* (Barcelona, 1975). Relations with the Soviet Union are the theme of Isabel Turrent, *La Unión Soviética en América Latina: El caso de la Unidad Popular chilena* (México, 1984). The important episode of the educational reform proposal is well treated in Joseph Farrell, *The National Unified School in Allende's Chile* (Vancouver, 1986), and judicial changes are discussed in Jack Spence, *Search for Justice: Neighborhood Courts in Allende's Chile* (Boulder, Colo., 1979).

The question of U.S. involvement in the coup first surfaced in the U.S. Senate Staff Report of the Select Committee to Study Governmental Intelligence Activities, *Covert Action in Chile, 1963–1973* (Washington, D.C., 1975), though a Chilean Ambassador had already documented some covert interference in Armando Uribe, *Le livre noir de l'intervention américaine au Chile* (Paris, 1974). See also James Petras and Morris Morley, *The United States and Chile: Imperialism and the Allende Government* (New York, 1975). There is a fascinating account by U.S. Ambassador Nathaniel Davis, *The Last Two Years of Allende* (Ithaca, N.Y., 1985). A savage attack by a leading journalist on U.S. policy is contained in Seymour Hersh, *The Price of Power: Kissinger in the White House Years* (Boston, 1980).

There is relatively little on the opposition to Allende. Some suggestive ideas are contained in Paul Drake, 'Corporatism and Functionalism in Modern Chilean Politics', *Journal of Latin American Studies* (May, 1978), and also in the last chapter of the same author's *Socialism and Populism in Chile, 1932–1952* (Urbana, 1978), which is a valuable political commentary on events leading to the coup. Pablo Baraona et al., *Chile: A Critical*

Survey (Santiago, 1972), contains some interesting essays from the Right. The events of the coup itself are brilliantly narrated in Ignacio González Camús, *El día en que murió Allende* (Santiago, 1988).

On the Pinochet period, there are several excellent studies of the economy. See in particular Alejandro Foxley, *Latin American Experiments in Neo-Conservative Economics* (Berkeley, Calif., 1983); the collective work by the economists at CIEPLAN, *Modelo económico chileno: Trayectoria de una crítica* (Santiago, 1982); Ricardo Ffrench-Davis, 'The Monetarist Experiment in Chile', *World Development* (November 1983); and Christian Anglade and Carlos Fortin, *The State and Capital Accumulation in Latin America* (London, 1985). Plans for escaping from the collapse of the boom of the 'Chicago boys' are contained in CIEPLAN, *Reconstrucción económica para la democracia* (Santiago, 1983).

Laurence Whitehead's chapter in Rosemary Thorp and Laurence Whitehead (eds.), *Inflation and Stabilisation in Latin America* (London, 1979) is a perceptive account of the problems of economic stabilization in this period. See also Whitehead's account in Rosemary Thorp and Laurence Whitehead (eds.), *Latin American Debt and the Adjustment Crisis* (London, 1987). A study of the process of economic concentration which caused a minor political storm is Fernando Dahse, *El mapa de la extrema riqueza* (Santiago, 1979). An excellent criticism of free-market policies, and alternative recommendations, is Alejandro Foxley, *Para una democracia estable* (Santiago, 1985). A defence of free-market policies is Alvaro Bardon et al., *Una década de cambios económicos: La experiencia chilena, 1973–1983* (Santiago, 1985). See also Sebastián Edwards and A. C. Edwards, *Monetarism and Liberalism: The Chilean Experiment* (Cambridge, Mass., 1986).

An insider account of the role of the 'Chicago Boys' is given in Arturo Fontaine, *Los economistas y el Presidente Pinochet* (Santiago, 1988). The origins of the free-market school in Chile are thoroughly analysed in Juan Gabriel Valdes, *La escuela de Chicago: Operación Chile* (Buenos Aires, 1989). A highly publicised eulogy of the free-market experiment is Joaquín Lavin, *La revolución silenciosa* (Santiago, 1987). A damaging critique stressing the social costs of the experiment is presented in Eugenio Tironi, *Los silencios de la revolución* (Santiago, 1988). The extent of poverty is documented in Eugenio Ortega and Ernesto Tironi, *Pobreza en Chile* (Santiago, 1988). Two journalists provide an up-to-date account of the whole Pinochet period: M. Delano and H. Traslavina, *La herencia de los Chicago Boys* (Santiago, 1989).

The politics of the Pinochet era is discussed in the brief but useful P.

O'Brien and J. Roddick, *Chile: The Pinochet Decade* (London, 1983). A massively detailed and indispensable book by three journalists that covers the whole period is Ascanio Cavallo, Manuel Salazar and Oscar Sepulveda, *La historia oculta del régimen militar* (Santiago, 1988). An overall interpretation of the political economy of the Pinochet period is found in Karen Remmer, *Military Rule in Latin America* (London, 1989). The constitution of 1980 is examined in detail in Luz Bulnes Aldunate, *Constitución política de la República de Chile* (Santiago, 1981). A set of essays covering events up to 1980 is J. Samuel Valenzuela and Arturo Valenzuela (eds.), *Military Rule in Chile: Dictatorship and Oppositions* (Baltimore, 1986). Covering the 1980s is the excellent collection of essays in Paul Drake and Iván Jaksic (eds.), *The Struggle for Democracy in Chile, 1982–1990* (Lincoln, Nebr., and London, 1992).

The role of the press is explored in Fernando Reyes Matta et al., *Investigaciones sobre la prensa en Chile (1974–1984)* (Santiago, 1986). Cultural policy is analysed in José Joaquín Brunner, *La Cultura autoritaria en Chile* (Santiago, 1981). An excellent study of public opinion is Carlos Huneeus, *Los chilenos y la política: Cambio y continuidad en el autoritarismo* (Santiago, 1987).

Pinochet's own account of his involvement in the coup is contained in Augusto Pinochet, *El día decisivo* (Santiago, 1977). Rather more revealing of the man and his ideas is Raquel Correa and Elizabeth Subercaseaux, *Ego sum Pinochet* (Santiago, 1989). Another military man – now disillusioned – gives his views in Florencia Varas, *Gustavo Leigh: El general disidente* (Santiago, 1979). The best accounts are Genaro Arriagada, *La política militar de Pinochet* (Santiago, 1985), and Augusto Varas, *Los militares en el poder: régimen y gobierno militar en Chile, 1973–1986* (Santiago, 1987).

An impressive attempt to evaluate the politics of Chile since 1970 is found in Manuel Antonio Garretón, *El proceso político chileno,* (Santiago, 1983), of which a welcome English translation is *The Chilean Political Process* (London, 1989). The numerous FLACSO documents by Garretón and Tomás Moulián constitute a running commentary on politics and society since 1973. Moulián's constantly stimulating ideas are brought together in his *Democracia y socialismo en Chile* (Santiago, 1983). A useful collection of writings of FLACSO researchers is contained in Manuel Antonio Garretón et al., *Chile, 1973–198 ?* (Santiago, 1983). A leading political figure collects his articles together in Genaro Arriagada, *10 años: Visión crítica* (Santiago, 1983). On the first phase of military rule, see

Tomás Moulián and Pilar Vergara, 'Estado, ideología y política económica en Chile, 1973–1978', in *Estudios CIEPLAN, no.* 3 (1980). A comprehensive account of the ideology of the regime is given in Pilar Vergara, *Auge y caída del neoliberalismo en Chile* (Santiago, 1985). Two lucid and informative articles are Carlos Huneeus, 'La política de la apertura y sus implicancias para la inauguración de la democracia en Chile', and 'Inauguración de la democracia en Chile', in *Revista de Ciencia Política* 7, no. 1 (1985), and 8, nos. 1–2 (1986).

An impressive study of the shanty towns in the Pinochet years is Rodrigo Baño, *Lo social y lo político* (Santiago, 1985); another is Guillermo Campero, *Entre la sobrevivencia y la acción política* (Santiago, 1987). A series of interviews explains the desperation of the youth of the shanty towns in Patricia Politzer, *La ira de Pedro y los otros* (Santiago, 1988). The research institute PREALC has documented the work and lives of the poor in Chile in a series of scholarly works. Amongst them are PREALC, *Sobrevivir en la calle: el comercio ambulante en Santiago* (Santiago 1988); David Benavente, *A medio morir cantando: 13 testimonios de cesantes* (Santiago 1985); and Jorge Alvarez, *Los hijos de la erradicación* (Santiago 1988). There are numerous studies of the social conditions of the pobladores. Amongst them are Clarisa Hardy, *Organizarse para vivir: Pobreza urbana y organización popular* (Santiago 1987), and Dagmar Raczynski and Claudia Serrano, *Vivir la pobreza: Testimonios de mujeres* (Santiago, 1985).

The murky world of state terrorism is, by definition, difficult to examine, but the book by Thomas Hauser, *Missing* (London, 1982), asks some awkward questions – later given wide publicity in a film of the same name. On the hideous assassination of Orlando Letelier, see John Dinges and Saul Landau, *Assassination on Embassy Row* (New York, 1980), and Taylor Branch and Eugene Propper, *Labyrinth* (New York, 1982). An account of domestic brutality is contained in Máximo Pachecho, *Lonquén* (Santiago, 1980). The issue of exile is examined by Alan Angell and Susan Carstairs in 'The Exile Question in Chilean Politics', *Third World Quarterly* (January 1987). Three leading politicians write movingly of their experience of exile, of imprisonment, and of their beliefs in Erich Shnacke, *De improviso la nada* (Santiago, 1988), Clodomiro Almeyda, *Reencuentro con mi vida* (Santiago, 1988), and Jorge Arrate, *Exilio: Textos de denuncia y esperanza* (Santiago, 1987).

The violation of human rights by the Pinochet government has been extensively documented. See for example the report of Amnesty International, *Chile* (London 1974), and those of the Inter-American Commission on Human Rights of the Organization of American States, *Report on the Status of Human Rights in Chile* (Washington, 1974), and subsequent reports of the same organization issued in 1976, 1977 and 1985. A three-volume work by members of the *Vicaria de la Solidarida* provides a graphic account of human rights violations: Eugenio Ahumada et al., *Chile: La memoria prohibida* (Santiago, 1989). See also Hugo Fruhling (ed.), *Represión política y defensa de los derechos humanos* (Santiago, 1986). A moving account of massacres in the north of Chile following the coup is found in Patricia Verdugo, *Caso Arellano: Los zarpazos del puma* (Santiago, 1989). The Truth and Reconciliation Commission set up by the Aylwin government published its findings in *Informe de la Comisión Nacional de Verdad y Reconciliación*, 3 vols. (Santiago, 1991). Of the many books that have recounted the long years of suffering under the Pinochet dictatorship, two are quite outstanding. Sergio Bitar describes his fate in the concentration camps created by the regime for leading members of the UP government in *Isla 10* (Santiago, 1988). An account of the fate of various individuals – some of whom did very well, some of whom suffered appallingly – is Patricia Politzer, *Miedo en Chile* (Santiago, 1985).

The theme of the transition to democracy is explored with great insight in Manuel Antonio Garretón, *Reconstruír la política: Transición y consolidación democrática en Chile* (Santiago, 1987). The plebiscite of October 1988 is examined in the 'Report by the International Commission of the Latin American Studies Association to Observe the Chilean Plebiscite', *Bulletin of Latin American Research* 8, no. 2 (1989), and in the report of the National Democratic Institute for International Affairs, *Chile's Transition to Democracy: The 1988 Presidential Plebiscite* (Washington, 1988). An examination of the role of international support for the opposition to Pinochet both before and during the plebiscite is Alan Angell, 'La cooperación internacional en el apoyo de la democracia en America Latina: El caso de Chile', *Foro Internacional* (Mexico), no. 118 (October 1989). A graphic account of the whole year is presented in Esteban Tomic, *1988 y el general bajó al llano* (Santiago, 1989). The elections of December 1989 are analysed in Alan Angell and Benny Pollack, 'The Chilean Elections of December 1989 and the Politics of the Transition to Democracy', *Bulletin of Latin American Research* 9, no. 1, 1990. See also César Caviedes, *Elections in Chile: The Road toward Redemocratization* (Boulder, Colo., and London, 1991).

INDEX

Chileanization, of copper, 135, 149–51
chilenidad. 26–7
Christian Democrats, 95, 100, 124–9, 143,
 144, 148, 155, 170, 192; *see also* Partido
 Demócrata Cristiano
church, *see* Roman Catholic Church
church and state, separation of, 78–9
CIA, *see* Central Intelligence Agency
civil war: of 1851, 8; of 1859, 8–9; of 1891,
 53–5; threat of, during Alessandri presidency, 73–5
class, 21–2, 33–4, 57–9, 61–2, 65, 89–91,
 95, 105–6, 111–13; elite/upper, 3, 21, 90,
 112, 158; harmony, 129; middle, relatively
 large size, 132; and party, 140–1; working,
 22, 52–3, 64
Coalición, 66, 70; *see also* National Union
Cold War, 117
colegios. 173–4
colonialism, internal, 89
colonization, 43–4, 46; of independent Indian
 lands, 43
Communal Autonomy law, 57
communications, 18–19, 59; *see also* press
Communist party, 66, 80, 95, 102–5, 108,
 110–17, 120, 121, 127, 129, 143–4, 160,
 170, 172–4, 192, 197, 199
Compañía de Salitre y Ferrocarril de
 Antofagasta, 29
Concepción, 25, 45; power, in the 1820s, 2
Confederación General de Trabajadores (CGT),
 101
Conservative party, 2–4, 58, 66, 90, 91, 95,
 118, 127; national party conference, 10; reformers within, 100
constitution, 3, 4, 6, 35, 50–1; Balmaceda,
 50; crisis, of 1890s, 46–58; interpretations
 of, 10; of 1925, 78–81; parliamentary system, 50–1; reform of, 34, 51, 76
constitutionalism, 158–9, 167–9; crisis of,
 139–42; stable, tradition of, 1–2, 9, 11, 33
convencionalistas. 49, 51
convivencia chilena. 57–8
co-optation, 90, 109
copper, 13–15, 18, 31, 33, 34, 82, 116, 119,
 124, 167; chileanization of, 135, 149–51;
 effects of Depression of 1929 on, 83–4;
 1930–1958, 81
corruption, 57
de la Cruz, José María, 8
Cuba, 92–3, 141, 145, 155, 174, 176, 190

Darwin, Charles, 15
Dávila Espinoza, Carlos, 96
De Rerum Novarum. of 1891, 64
debt, foreign, payment of, 98, 130; after 1958,

144–5, 162; international crisis (1982–3),
 190–1; prompt, 34, 61, 84;
Democratic party, 52, 58–9, 63, 66, 115, 116
depressions, world: in 1873, 27–30, 34–5, 39;
 after WWI, 69, 71–3, 92; of 1929, 83–4,
 87, 88, 93–7
desert, southward advance, 14
development: frustrated, 133; underdevelopment, 88
DINA, *see* Dirección de Inteligencia Nacional
Dirección de Inteligencia Nacional (DINA),
 178, 186–9

earthquake: of 1906, 67; of 1939, 109
ecology, desert's advance, 14
economy, 124–6: between 1820s and 1870s,
 11–21; exports, 14–20, 25, 27–8, 33, 34,
 45, 83–4, 93, 130; government stimulation,
 in parliamentary period, 61; great depression, of 1873, 27–9, 30, 34–5, 39; growth
 of nitrate industry (in 1880s), 36, 39–42;
 inflation, 28, 62, 109, 111, 125, 132–8;
 international, 27–30, 34–5, 39, 69, 71–3,
 82–4, 87, 88, 93–7; modernization of, 129;
 monetarism, 130, 132–8, 142, 180–5; national (rather than international), 66–7; onset of WWII, 108, 114–16; postwar (WWI)
 depression, 69, 71, 73, 82; prosperity, under
 Ibáñez, 82; social services, 61–2; stabilization of, 179; unstable, 131–8
education, 25–6, 33, 58, 61, 62, 127; public
 spending on, 46–7; reforms, 81
Edwards Ossandón, Agustín, 14–15
Egaña, Juan, 3
El Mercurio. 25, 97
El Trabajo. 64–6
elections, 139; changes in procedure, 10; electoral intervention, 6–7, 9, 36, 38, 47–8,
 50, 51, 56–8; separating dates of, 79
elite, 2, 33, 89–90, 112, 158
empleados. 132
Errázuriz, Crescente, 79
Errázuriz, Francisco Javier, 198
Errázuriz, Ladislao, 72, 77
Errázuriz Zañartu, Federico, 9–10, 19
estanqueros. 3
exile, 6, 76, 78–9
exploitation: of indigenous peoples, 24–5, 43–
 4; of labour, 52, 63; of outlying regions, 89
exports, 14–20, 25, 27–8, 33, 34, 45, 83–4,
 93, 130; effects of 1929 depression on, 83–4

factionalism, 56
Falange, 91, 95, 100, 105, 107, 110, 112–13,
 115, 118, 127